'Uncertainty will always exist, but what matters is how leaders prepare for it, who they include in navigating it, and how they sustain the people who carry it forward. *The Protector's Edge* offers a practical, human-centered framework for enterprise security leadership rooted in stewardship rather than spectacle. Drawing on real-world experience across intelligence, technology, GSOCs, and executive protection, Randolph, Wackrow, and Burton show how protection enables trust, continuity, and sound decision-making. Grounded in ethics, inclusion, and a culture of care, this book meets leaders where they are and helps them grow into the kind of protectors their people and their organizations need for what comes next.'

Arian Avila, *Corporate Safety & Security Executive; co-editor of Vocal Lanterns*

'*The Protector's Edge* is a timely and important blueprint identifying the steps an effective protection professional team must undertake in order to succeed in today's ever changing threat environment. A wide range of risk exposures must be anticipated, prepared for, and mitigated in a purposeful and strategic manner. Limiting preparations to reacting to visible threats alone is no longer enough. Careful assessment of threats and vulnerabilities, preparing for "what if" scenarios, and ensuring robust and coordinated preventative action are among the capabilities today's protection professionals must embrace.'

Gary W. Noesner, *Chief, FBI Crisis Negotiation Unit (retired) and author of "Stalling For Time, My Life as an FBI Hostage Negotiator"*

'Whether it is the assassination of a major corporate executive in Midtown Manhattan on the way to an investors conference, a ransomware, kidnap, or an AI-generated video that can cause viral reputational damage, one thing is clear: This is not your father's security business. In The Protector's Edge: Leadership Through Strategy and Action, Burton, Randolph, and Wackrow take us into the currents of the threat-stream rapids. They give us a roadmap to intelligence to see problems on the horizon, tactics to confront them, and leadership to develop a team that is ready for all threats. These are "right now problems" which makes this a "right now read".'

John Miller, *CNN Chief Law Enforcement and Intelligence Analyst; Former Deputy Commissioner of Intelligence & Counterterrorism of the New York Police Department*

'With a radically changing threat landscape, including the continuously evolving effect of the ubiquitous technical surveillance environment on the protection industry, this is a must read, an indispensable roadmap for leaders who understand that change is upon us, and we either adapt or fail.'

Marc Polymeropoulos, *CIA Senior Intelligence Service (retired) and current MSNow national security contributor*

‘*The Protector’s Edge* is a masterclass in leading under pressure from three exceptional security professionals who have actually lived it; blending real-world insights with timeless principles of trust, foresight, and resilience. It’s an essential read for anyone seeking to navigate high-stakes geopolitical environments with clarity, courage, and strategic influence.’

Michael T. Evanoff, *Former Assistant Secretary of State for Diplomatic Security and author of “High Value Target$”*

‘Today’s threat environment is unlike any previous time. Attacks on a Presidential candidate, influential figures, political protests, and threats of violence have become commonplace. Security professionals will have to be at the top of their profession, every time, adversaries only have to be on target once. This book will become the protection professional’s bible and will help to save and protect lives.’

Robert J. Bodisch, Sr., *Deputy Director/Chief of Staff (Retired), Texas Dept. of Public Safety, Texas Homeland Security*

The Protector's Edge

The protection profession has evolved dramatically over the past two decades and is no longer confined to the shadows as bodyguards or operational security managers: today's protectors are trusted advisors, strategic risk leaders, and organizational influencers. *The Protector's Edge: Leadership Through Strategy and Action* examines how leadership in protection has evolved in an era of converged risk, where physical, digital, reputational, and narrative threats intersect. Drawing on decades of experience across intelligence, executive protection, government service, and enterprise security, the authors present a practical framework for moving from reactive protection to intelligence-led leadership.

This book translates protective tradecraft into strategic decision-making, showing how intelligence, technology, and human judgment combine to anticipate risk, enable continuity, and build trust before crises emerge. Through real-world case studies, leadership insights, and operational lessons, the authors outline how protection professionals must move beyond daily operations and think like business leaders—integrating risk intelligence, influencing cross-functional teams, and aligning protective strategies with organizational goals. The twelve chapters provide concrete frameworks that show how protectors can lead themselves, their teams, and their principals through crises ranging from active shooter incidents to reputational attacks.

Written by three recognized leaders in the protection profession, this book combines decades of experience to deliver practical insights and strategic vision. It challenges experienced protectors, security leaders, intelligence professionals, and risk managers to think beyond the current mission and invest in developing the next generation of protective leaders. *The Protector's Edge* reframes protection as a strategic capability, one that strengthens leadership, continuity, and resilience rather than serving as a reactive safeguard.

The Protector's Edge
Leadership Through Strategy and Action

Chuck Randolph, Jonathan Wackrow, and Fred Burton

CRC Press
Taylor & Francis Group
Boca Raton London New York

CRC Press is an imprint of the
Taylor & Francis Group, an **informa** business

Front cover image: Sharomka/Shutterstock

First edition published 2027
by CRC Press
2385 NW Executive Center Drive, Suite 320, Boca Raton FL 33431

and by CRC Press
4 Park Square, Milton Park, Abingdon, Oxon, OX14 4RN

CRC Press is an imprint of Taylor & Francis Group, LLC

ISBN: 978-1-041-13623-1 (hbk)
ISBN: 978-1-041-13624-8 (pbk)
ISBN: 978-1-003-67070-4 (ebk)

DOI: 10.4324/9781003670704

Typeset in Sabon
by codeMantra

Printed in Great Britain
by TJ Books, Padstow, Cornwall

FSC
www.fsc.org
MIX
Paper | Supporting responsible forestry
FSC® C013056

Contents

Figure

About the Authors

Charles "Chuck" Randolph is a recognized leader in protective intelligence, executive protection, and enterprise risk leadership, with more than 30 years of experience spanning military, government, and the private sector. He has led global security, intelligence, and executive protection programs at Microsoft, Ontic, and AT-RISK International and currently serves as Chief Strategy Officer at 360 Privacy.

A retired U.S. Army Lieutenant Colonel, Randolph was recognized for valor during combat operations in Afghanistan and spent his military career leading pioneering Information Operations initiatives. He is a co-founder of the International Protective Security Board (IPSB) and the Pathfinder Collective and is a frequent speaker and published author on protective intelligence, resilience, and security leadership.

Jonathan Wackrow is a CNN Law Enforcement Analyst and former U.S. Secret Service Special Agent with more than 25 years of experience in national security, executive protection, and crisis response. He served on the Presidential Protective Division, serving on the President's and First Lady's details. He developed and led security operations worldwide, working with law enforcement, intelligence agencies, and the military to protect senior government officials and visiting foreign dignitaries. He also played key roles in securing National Special Security Events, including the Presidential Inauguration and the United Nations General Assembly.

In the private sector, Wackrow has provided exclusive on-air analysis for CNN on law enforcement and national security issues, as well as coverage of critical incidents, for over ten years. Wackrow is Managing Director of Sentinel Resource Group, advising Fortune 500 companies, boards, and ultra-high-net-worth individuals on enterprise risk, executive protection, and organizational resilience.

Fred Burton is a former police officer, special agent, and *New York Times* best-selling author, recognized in 2021 by *Security Magazine* as one of the Most Influential People in Security. As an author and terrorism and protective intelligence expert, Burton has appeared on The Daily Show with Jon Stewart, Fox Nation, CNN, Morning Joe, Good Morning America, Drug Wars, SNIPER film, and many others. He is an advisor to several companies, to include Ontic, 360 Privacy, Altr, and Centerseat.ai.

Foreword

By Lt. Gen. (Ret.) Giles Hill

Leadership in the modern security environment demands more than experience or technical proficiency. It requires judgment under pressure, moral courage in uncertainty, and the discipline to make decisions that safeguard not only people but also the trust placed in an organization. As threats evolve through geopolitical instability, rapid technological change, and the convergence of cyber and physical domains, the leaders responsible for navigating this landscape must evolve with them.

Throughout my military career and later in global security, I have witnessed how quickly stability can erode and how essential it is to develop leaders who think critically, act decisively, and hold themselves to enduring principles. Those who succeed do so by understanding their environment and by anticipating what may come next. They prepare their teams with clarity and purpose. The most effective leaders make decisions informed by intelligence, shaped by experience, and grounded in character.

The Protector's Edge speaks directly to this need. It offers a thoughtful and timely exploration of leadership within the protection and security professions, roles that increasingly influence the resilience and continuity of organizations around the world. What sets this work apart is the authors' insistence that leadership is the decisive factor in navigating complexity. Tools will change and technologies will advance, but leadership remains the foundation of good judgment and effective action.

Fred Burton, Chuck Randolph, and Jonathan Wackrow are long-respected voices in this field. Across government service, corporate leadership, intelligence roles, and global risk programs, they have earned reputations for expertise and for elevating the standards of their profession. They recognize that protection is not simply the prevention of harm. It is the stewardship of people, ideas, and institutions that allow organizations and societies to function. Their collective experience allows them to articulate what modern protective leadership requires with clarity and depth.

Importantly, this book does not portray leadership as a position or an accolade. It presents leadership as a discipline shaped by habits, values, and decisions made well before any crisis appears. It challenges practitioners to think beyond tactical response and to adopt the strategic mindset required in a world where threats cross borders and domains with increasing speed. It reinforces that intelligence is more than information; *it is insight.* Vigilance is more than caution; *it is preparation.* Courage is not the absence of fear, but *the willingness to act responsibly despite it.*

For the next generation of protectors, security leaders, and risk professionals, this book offers a clear and compelling guide. For the experienced practitioner, it provides reflection, refinement, and a reminder of why the work matters. For organizations operating in an uncertain world, it offers a vision of the leadership necessary to build resilience and uphold trust.

Risk will continue to evolve, yet the principles of clarity, character, and courageous decision-making remain constant. I commend the authors for contributing meaningfully to the profession and for helping shape leaders who can stand at the edge with confidence, humility, and purpose.

This is a book not only to be read *but also to be applied.*

—Lt. Gen. (Ret.) Giles Hill
Global Head of Security
International SOS

Acknowledgments

This book reflects decades spent confronting uncertainty, responsibility, and consequence. It is informed by many people and institutions whose influence shaped our understanding of protection long before these ideas were committed to the page. While we cannot name them all, their imprint is unmistakable throughout this work.

We begin with those who formed us professionally. Mentors, commanders, senior leaders, and executives who demonstrated that protection is not a matter of proximity or presence, but of judgment, discipline, and foresight. They taught us that leadership is revealed not in moments of calm, but in periods of ambiguity, pressure, and imperfect information. Their example established the standards against which we continue to measure ourselves.

We are deeply indebted to the teams and professional communities with whom we served across military, intelligence, law enforcement, and corporate environments. These teams reinforced a central truth of the profession: protection is inherently collective. Success is rarely visible, failure is often shared, and leadership is exercised through trust built long before a crisis emerges. The lessons learned in those settings, often through friction and challenge, remain foundational to our thinking.

Several peers and colleagues served as thought partners throughout the development of this book. They questioned assumptions, challenged frameworks, and forced us to refine our language and logic. Their willingness to engage critically strengthened this work and ensured it reflects debate rather than doctrine. Any errors or omissions remain our responsibility alone.

We are grateful to our editors and the team at Taylor & Francis for their guidance and professionalism. Their commitment to rigor, clarity, and relevance helped keep this project grounded in contribution rather than commentary. The discipline of the editorial process sharpened both structure and intent.

We also acknowledge our families for their support of this effort. The demands of writing extend well beyond the regular boundaries, and their patience and understanding provided the steadiness required to complete this work.

This book is written for leaders. It is offered not as a definitive answer, but as a contribution to an evolving profession. While written from within the protection profession, its intent is broader, addressing the leadership demands faced by anyone who must make decisions at the edge of risk, where uncertainty, consequence, and accountability converge.

Periods of volatility have always forced moments of reassessment. The late 1960s and early 1970s reshaped how protection was conceived and practiced. Today presents a similar inflection point. If history teaches anything, it is that what lies ahead is rarely entirely new. It is shaped by patterns, pressures, and choices made before us. In that sense, what is past is indeed prologue. Our hope is that this book helps today's leaders read that prologue more clearly and act with greater foresight as they shape what comes next.

Preface—At the Edge of Leadership

Fred Burton, Chuck Randolph, and Jonathan Wackrow

Every generation of protectors stands at a threshold where vigilance meets vision and where leadership begins. From Dealey Plaza to digital doxing, from political violence to privacy exposure, each era has forced our profession to evolve. The modern protector now operates in an environment where the physical and digital are inseparable, where risk is amplified by speed and perception, and where leadership, not merely proximity or procedure, defines success.

We live and lead in an age of convergence. Threats no longer respect boundaries; *they migrate across systems, identities, and narratives*. The same forces that manipulate information online can inspire violence offline. The same data that empowers an organization can endanger its people. In this new landscape, protection is no longer just about preventing harm; it is about enabling trust, continuity, and confidence in a world that tests all three daily.

We wrote *The Protector's Edge* because we believe our profession stands on the cusp of transformation. The future will not reward those who react the fastest, but those who think the farthest. Protection must become intelligence-led, data-informed, and purpose-driven. Leadership is what turns that intelligence into judgment, that data into decision, and that purpose into action. This book explores that transformation: how protectors evolve into strategists, how teams mature into systems, and how leadership sustains it all.

Between the three of us, we have stood on many edges: crises, command posts, and boardrooms alike. We've each led operations in moments of uncertainty, briefed decision-makers under pressure, and built programs meant to endure when the unexpected becomes reality.

Our careers span investigations, national security, corporate leadership, intelligence, and strategy; disciplines that often intersect more than they diverge. Together, they have taught us one enduring truth: *leadership is the ultimate form of protection.*

Throughout this book, we explore that leadership across the full spectrum of practice:how to build character and resilience; how to make decisions under pressure; how to guide teams through fatigue and uncertainty; how to influence executives and boards; and how to align intelligence and technology to protect both people and reputation. These lessons are not theoretical; they come from lived experience, from moments when insight mattered more than instinct, and when calm became the decisive skill.

Leadership in the protective profession has always been adaptive, but today it must also be anticipatory. The threats are faster, but so are the tools. Artificial intelligence, analytics, and automation are reshaping awareness; yet they do not replace judgment. Foresight remains a human endeavor. Technology extends our reach, but only leadership sharpens our focus. At the edge of leadership, wisdom is not measured by what we know, but by how we choose to act amid uncertainty.

This book is for those who have answered the call to stand watch: for protectors, intelligence professionals, executives, and anyone entrusted with the safety and stability of others. The principles we discuss apply far beyond our field. They are lessons in trust, humility, and courage, qualities that sustain leadership in any discipline.

We invite you to join us at the edge – not the edge of danger, but of discovery. The place where leadership demands reflection as much as action, where vigilance meets purpose, and where service becomes legacy.

This is the perimeter we stand on together. **This is** *The Protector's Edge.*

For those who stand the watch,

—The Authors

SECTION 1

Introduction: The Landscape of Leadership

We are living through a new era of volatility, one where grievance, digital radicalization, and narrative warfare collide in ways that challenge the traditional protective model. Executives, public figures, and organizational leaders no longer face threats defined solely by physical proximity; they are targeted through ideology, online exposure, and the accelerating contagion of "assassination culture." Recent high-profile acts of targeted violence have shaken boards and C-suites, prompting a familiar response: deploying resources quickly, without fully understanding the underlying shifts driving this new threat environment.

Yet we have been here before. As Shakespeare reminds us, "what's past is prologue." The late 1960s and early 1970s saw political assassinations, mass unrest, hijackings, and more than 2,500 domestic bombings in an 18-month span. Those first "Days of Rage" reshaped the protection industry and gave rise to modern executive protection.

Today marks another inflection point, one where the pace, complexity, and convergence of threats demand far more than reactive security measures. What's required now is a shift in mindset: from guarding to anticipating, from responding to interpreting, from protection as a function to protection as leadership. This is the defining challenge of our time, and the defining opportunity for those who choose to lead.

DOI: 10.4324/9781003670704-1

CHAPTER 1

Leading in the New Risk Landscape

The global security and executive protection (EP) landscape has undergone profound and irreversible changes over the past two decades. The role of EP professionals, or protectors, has expanded beyond ensuring physical safety to navigating a highly interconnected, multi-domain risk environment. No longer confined to the tactical realm, today's protectors are evaluated on their ability to anticipate threats, interpret intelligence, influence organizational decision-making, and safeguard not only their principal's safety but also their brand, reputation, and data.

Modern protectors are no longer defined solely by their physical presence or tactical skillset. They are expected to navigate a landscape shaped by hybrid threats, information warfare, and reputational risk, often stepping into roles that demand operational agility, strategic foresight, and the ability to advise and influence at the highest levels of an organization. As the threat environment grows more dynamic and multifaceted, the most effective protectors emerge not just as security professionals but as leaders who bridge the gap between risk, business, and trust. This shift in the protector's role is driven by an equally dramatic evolution in the threats they face.

THE EVOLUTION OF THREATS

The early days of corporate security and EP focused heavily on direct, observable threats, stalkers, disgruntled employees, assassins, or opportunistic criminals. This traditional reliance on physical deterrence and static defenses is no longer sufficient—the stakes have changed dramatically. Traditional physical security measures alone prove insufficient in an era of asymmetric and hybrid dangers. As one security advisor noted, simply relying on *"guns, guards, and gates" isn't enough anymore.*[1] Modern threats move too quickly and cross into cyberspace and

DOI: 10.4324/9781003670704-2

public perception, forming a complex web of risks that demand new approaches. Security industry analyses reinforce that threats are now multifaceted, combining cyberattacks, industrial espionage, and geopolitical unrest into challenges no single barrier can stop.[2] In short, corporate protectors have had to evolve from static defense toward proactive risk intelligence, also called protective intelligence.

Today, the threat spectrum is broader, more sophisticated, and far less predictable. The rise of digital activism, doxxing, disinformation campaigns, and reputational warfare has added complexity, requiring protectors to monitor not only the immediate physical environment but also the online and informational space where threats often originate. For example, a CEO might face not only a physical stalker but also a social media smear campaign that inspires such behavior. The convergence of physical and digital threats means protective-leaders must be intelligence-driven and tech-savvy. They scan for data breaches and viral rumors with the same vigilance used for suspicious people on a perimeter. As the global security firm Securitas observed in 2023, businesses now navigate an environment where *cyber threats, insider risks, and global tensions intersect*, and only a proactive, intelligence-led security strategy can allow organizations to survive and thrive.[3] In practical terms, this has shifted protectors' mindsets from just standing posts to also focusing on protecting information and reputation. Corporate security teams increasingly include analysts watching the dark web for leaked personal data, communications specialists ready to counteract false narratives, and liaisons to law enforcement cyber units. The evolution of threats has blurred the line between traditional security and broader risk management, forcing protectors to become adept in domains their predecessors never imagined.

CASE STUDY: THE ELON MUSK DOXXING INCIDENT (2022)—A MODERN HYBRID THREAT

In late 2022, shortly after Elon Musk's acquisition of Twitter, activists publicly posted his home address, details about family members, and real-time travel routes across multiple platforms. This act of doxxing, the malicious release of personal information, illustrated how a modern threat can unfold simultaneously in the cyber and physical realms. It was not only a direct threat to Musk's personal safety but also a reputational and business crisis, as news of the doxxing spooked some investors and briefly impacted the public perception of Twitter and Tesla. Musk himself tweeted in frustration that criticizing him was fair game but "doxxing my real-time location and endangering my family is not," underscoring the gravity of the incident.[4]

In situations such as this, protective intelligence teams must respond at speed and in coordination with multiple departments. Legal teams must be engaged to pursue takedowns of the sensitive information and potentially identify and manage the perpetrators under anti-harassment or cyberstalking laws, while cybersecurity analysts work to determine how the information had leaked—for instance, whether insiders, hacking, or scraping of flight data was involved—and to secure any vulnerable accounts or systems.

Meanwhile, communications and public relations (PR) personnel drive a narrative, reassuring employees, investors, and the public that the principal was protected and that steps were being taken to address the breach, while also preparing for potential stock volatility or media scrutiny stemming from the incident. On the ground, physical security around Musk and his family were likely ramped up, with residential security teams deploying counter-surveillance, local police being alerted to provide extra patrols, and travel plans were adjusted to be less predictable. This rapid, cross-functional mobilization demonstrated the convergence of physical security, cybersecurity, and corporate reputation management—usually coordinated at the protective leader's level.

Notably, in situations such as this, teams also leverage intelligence from law enforcement and private threat monitoring firms. In this case, it was discovered that online extremists were sharing the doxed information and encouraging harassment. Federal agencies were contacted in case of credible plots, reflecting how an EP detail now must liaise with government cyber units as much as with local police. Security experts later commented that the Musk incident highlighted a new "doxxing dynamic" facing executives: those who are doxed face heightened risks of stalking, harassment, and even physical attack, often requiring round-the-clock monitoring of online threats.[5] In Musk's case, just a day after the doxxing, a self-described stalker in Los Angeles aggressively approached a car he believed Elon was in—a stark reminder of how quickly online information can translate into offline danger. This incident illustrated that modern EP teams must operate like an incident response task force, uniting legal action, cyber defense, intelligence gathering, PR, and physical protection. The incident sparked broader conversations across the corporate world about executive privacy, leading to heightened scrutiny of flight tracking data, personal address exposure, and how companies manage the digital footprint of high-profile individuals. It demonstrated how a single security event, especially one amplified by public platforms, can trigger reevaluation of privacy protocols and risk tolerance at the organizational level. In today's threat environment, the role of the protector-leader is not confined to physical safety; it involves anticipating and countering multi-domain threats that target reputation, digital exposure, and personal security simultaneously.

Addressing hybrid threats like Musk's doxxing requires protectors to move beyond tactical roles and become strategic business advisors.

THE PROTECTOR AS A BUSINESS ASSET AND STRATEGIC ADVISOR

The protector's evolution into a strategic advisor is among the most important shifts of the past decade. In the past, corporate security functions were often perceived as cost centers, necessary but peripheral to core business strategy. Security leaders typically operated in the background, tasked with keeping threats at bay but seldom contributing to executive discussions. Today, leading organizations increasingly recognize protective intelligence and corporate security as essential elements of business resilience, risk management, and reputation protection. In an age when a single security incident can shut down operations or destroy customer trust, the security leader has become a key stakeholder in enabling enterprise risk decisions. Forward-thinking CEOs now invite their chief security officer (CSO) or security directors into strategic planning sessions. A recent industry commentary put it bluntly: if there isn't an informed CSO/chief information security officer (CISO) "sitting at the table" with the C-suite when major decisions are made, the CEO risks flying blind to threats that could derail the business. In other words, positioning security leaders as more than just risk managers turns them into *business enablers and trusted advisers* who are integral to the C-suite.[6]

Real-world events have driven this change. In 2008, the kidnapping of a senior oil executive in Nigeria illustrated the shifting role of the protector. Following the executive's safe recovery, the corporation's protective intelligence and security leadership teams used the incident as leverage to reshape corporate travel policies, contractor vetting procedures, and executive risk tolerance frameworks across the region. This marked the transition of the security leader from a reactive, operational enforcer to a proactive strategic advisor. The security team in that case didn't simply return to the status quo after resolving the crisis—they presented data on how a lack of preparation and intelligence had exposed a strategic business leader to harm, and they advocated for changes (like stricter travel protocols and armored vehicles) that directly aligned with business continuity. The company's executives took notice that security insight could prevent costly disruptions, and from that point the CSO had a *standing voice in regional strategy discussions*. This trend has only accelerated in today's threat environment.

Additional examples abound of the protector becoming a true business asset. At many technology firms, for instance, the security and safety team now collaborates with product development to anticipate how launching a controversial feature might provoke user backlash or regulatory inquiries that endanger executives. Meta (Facebook), as one example, created an "Executive Risk" team that works alongside policy and communications units, advising on how changes in content moderation might ignite public anger toward leadership or trigger threats. This underscores protector-leaders moving beyond "guarding the boss" to shaping decisions about *where the boss goes, what the boss says, and even how the company positions itself*, all through the lens of risk mitigation.

This shift is reinforced by thought leadership in corporate governance. Consultancies like Deloitte and McKinsey have emphasized that organizations with strong risk cultures include security voices in top-level decisions. Modern CEOs have come to value their security chiefs similar to legal counsel—as advisors who highlight hidden pitfalls, such as regulatory fines or reputational damage, and protect the company's ability to execute its strategy safely. A Forbes Technology Council piece noted that CEOs must get to know their security leaders and bring them into planning, because a savvy CSO can "ensure the biggest decisions are made with full awareness of risks and threats."[7] In many corporations, the protector-leader now contributes to discussions on expansions into volatile regions, M&A due diligence (flagging security vulnerabilities in target companies), and brand initiatives (planning executive engagements with an eye on protest risks).

All of this represents a maturation of the protective function. No longer relegated to the basement office, the head of EP or corporate security is increasingly seen as a business asset—someone who safeguards not only people but the enterprise's ability to pursue its goals confidently. Protectors who embrace this strategic role have learned to translate security threats into the language of business. They frame a threat in terms of potential revenue loss, regulatory scrutiny, or reputational impact, which earns them credibility in boardrooms. By doing so, the protector becomes a bridge between security and strategy, ensuring that risk considerations are baked into business decisions from the start, not afterthoughts. This evolution sets the stage for protective leaders to be viewed as indispensable strategic advisors in the modern C-suite.

THE RISE OF HYBRID THREATS AND REPUTATIONAL WARFARE

Modern protective leaders must operate in a world where threats are no longer confined to physical attacks. Reputation management and narrative manipulation campaigns increasingly intersect with personal safety, blurring the once-neat boundaries between security domains. In security parlance, we now talk about "hybrid threats," a term originally used for nation-state tactics, but equally apt for the corporate context. *Hybrid threats* refer to coordinated attacks that combine multiple tactics—cyber intrusions, misinformation, legal pressure, and physical intimidation—to achieve their aims while staying below the threshold of outright conflict.[8] State or non-state actors exploit vulnerabilities across various arenas simultaneously. In the corporate world, this might look like a threat actor launching a hacking attempt to steal confidential data while also seeding false stories in social media to damage an executive's reputation. The result is a multifaceted assault on an organization and its leaders, requiring an equally multifaceted defense. An executive protector must understand that a defamatory viral video or artificial intelligence (AI)-generated "deepfake" can be as dangerous as an angry person with a weapon. Indeed, *fake imagery and fabricated media are now being used to cause reputational harm and even financial fraud*, with the tools for creating deepfakes widely accessible.[9] In this hybrid threat environment, information warfare—like disinformation and doxxing—often precedes or accompanies physical danger.

Activist campaigns against high-profile executives, particularly in technology, energy, and finance, regularly combine multiple threat vectors to achieve their aims. For example, a campaign might start by doxxing an executive (releasing their home address and family information) on extremist forums, then escalate to coordinated targeted harassment both online (threatening messages, swarms of negative social posts) and offline (protests at the office or home). Simultaneously, the campaigners might attempt to influence shareholders or regulators by leaking damaging internal emails or launching petitions, creating pressure on the company's governance. Increasingly, sophisticated adversaries even leverage AI-generated images or fake audio recordings to lend credence to false narratives—for instance, generating a bogus video of a CEO appearing to make insensitive remarks, which then spreads outrage among the public or employees. Each of these tactics alone is a challenge; together, they form a hybrid onslaught that is difficult to predict and counter.

A stark example of this convergence occurred in December 2024, when Brian Thompson, CEO of UnitedHealth Group, was fatally shot in New York City, allegedly by 26-year-old Luigi Mangione. In the days following the attack, authorities discovered a handwritten manifesto in Mangione's apartment expressing (amongst other things) anger at the high cost of healthcare in the United States and citing the country's poor life expectancy ranking. His writings revealed a deeply personal grievance with the healthcare system and referenced anti-establishment literature, including a review of Ted Kaczynski's Industrial Society and Its Future.

While not directly linked to a disinformation campaign, Mangione's radicalization underscores how individual grievance, amplified by ideological exposure, can escalate into targeted violence. This case illustrates the evolving challenge for protective intelligence teams: to identify not only externally coordinated threats but also lone actors driven by personal ideology and perceived injustice.[10] Security experts point out that this case followed a chilling pattern or continuum: *grievance leads to public denouncement, which leads to doxxing, harassment, and ultimately attack*.[11] The narrative in cyberspace blurred into a real-world threat to life. In the aftermath, corporate security professionals widely discussed how better narrative monitoring and early intervention might have made a difference. Scott Stewart, a veteran intelligence expert, noted that the incident "sparked an outpouring of anti-corporate vitriol" and even inspired copycats, warning of a *contagion effect* if such extremist sentiments are lionized. Indeed, within weeks, there were reports of other threats against executives accompanied by "wanted" posters and menacing memes circulating online.

Cases like these underscore how false narratives, when amplified widely, can blur the line between reputational risk and personal safety. Modern protectors must not only monitor these influence campaigns but also understand how a digital smear can quickly morph into a physical threat. This requires protective intelligence teams to fuse narrative monitoring with threat management strategies. In practice, that means keeping an ear to the ground on social media, extremist platforms, and dark web forums for early signs of targeting or incitement against their principals. It means collaborating closely with corporate communications and PR teams—an unusual pairing in decades past—to counteract dangerous misinformation before it metastasizes. Some companies now employ "reputation intelligence" analysts whose job is to detect hostile narratives and help craft responses (be it factual rebuttals, legal actions, or quiet personal security adjustments for the executive). Protectors also coordinate with IT and cybersecurity to lock down personal data that adversaries might exploit. In the Thompson case, analysts later suggested that the removal of personal info online (home addresses, etc.) and early warning to law enforcement of escalating online threats would support mitigating targeted violence.[12]

The modern protector must understand this hybrid threat landscape, where physical, cyber, reputational, and even regulatory risks converge into a single operating picture. Protective leaders must strive to be invited to sit in on enterprise risk committee meetings that discuss everything from data breaches to activist shareholder motions, because all these issues intertwine. They must also collaborate seamlessly with corporate communications, legal, and IT teams to mitigate these multi-domain threats. For instance, if a tech CEO is targeted by an online harassment campaign, the protector-leader might work with IT to harden the executive's online accounts, with legal to pursue restraining orders against particularly aggressive harassers, and with communications to support a strategy that de-escalates tensions publicly. This cross-silo collaboration marks a new era of integrated risk management. In essence, the protector-leader in 2025 is part bodyguard, part intelligence analyst, and part reputation manager. By embracing that expanded role, they act as guardians of not just the principal's physical well-being, but their digital footprint and public persona as well. The rise of hybrid threats has made protective leadership an exercise in holistic risk management, demanding agility and unity across what were once disparate security functions.

CORE LEADERSHIP TRAITS IN MODERN PROTECTIVE LEADERSHIP

The best protective leaders exhibit traits that combine traditional leadership competencies with attributes specifically adapted for the protective intelligence and EP field. These traits enable them to navigate fast-moving crises and win the trust of those they protect and advise. Key core traits include:

Strategic Foresight

Defines anticipating and preparing for emerging threats, often in ambiguous situations. Modern protectors must be adept at seeing around corners. They analyze trends in technology, geopolitics, and social behavior to predict what new risks might be on the horizon. For instance, effective protector-leaders began preparing for the risks of pandemic disease or civil unrest *before* they hit, ensuring their organizations were a step ahead. As one famous sports metaphor from hockey legend Wayne Gretzky goes, great players (and by extension, great leaders) "skate to where the puck is going to be, not where it has been." Protective leaders embody this idea—they position their security strategies not for the threats that were, but for those that will be. A real-world example of strategic foresight was when several global companies quietly started bolstering executive travel security in late 2019 after noticing unusual disease outbreak reports—a prescient move that paid off when COVID-19 struck months later. By cultivating strategic foresight, protector-leaders help their organizations avoid or mitigate threats that others might never see coming.

Operational Agility

Describes maintaining flexibility to pivot between evolving crises, from reputational incidents to cyber intrusions and physical security breaches. In the heat of an incident, protective leaders cannot afford paralysis or rigidity. They must rapidly assess the situation, prioritize actions, and execute decisively. Navy SEAL veteran Jocko Willink describes this approach as "Relax, look around, make a call"—a mantra for keeping calm and making quick decisions amid chaos.[13] For protective leaders, operational agility might mean quickly redeploying a security team from a low-risk event to an emerging hotspot, or simultaneously managing a data breach response while handling a VIP's emergency evacuation. A classic illustration came during the 2015 Paris terror attacks: multiple U.S.-based corporate security heads had to *change plans on the fly* to account for unfolding dangers—diverting executives from affected areas, reinforcing facilities worldwide in case of copycat attacks, and communicating continuously with travelers. The agile protector triages threats, adapts contingency plans in real time, and communicates clearly to stakeholders throughout. This trait goes hand-in-hand with training and experience; protector-leaders often drill crisis scenarios so that when the real thing hits, they can pivot smoothly rather than freeze. Their teams know the directive: prioritize the most critical threat and tackle it first, then move down the list (the "Prioritize and Execute" principle).[14] Such agility in operations ensures that even if a protector faces two or three different crises in a day, they can handle each effectively without dropping the ball.

Influence Without Authority

Leading cross-functional teams and advising executives, even when the protector lacks formal hierarchical authority. Protectors often find themselves in situations where they must persuade others—including those above them in rank—to take actions for safety's sake. A protective leader might have no direct authority over a marketing team's plans, yet may need to convince the Chief Marketing Officer (CMO) to cancel a high-profile event due to credible threats. The ability to influence without direct power relies on credibility, communication, and trust. Effective protective leaders build strong relationships across the organization so that in a crisis, people listen to their guidance. They hone skills in presenting risk information in compelling business terms. For example, instead of saying "This threat is scary," they will quantify the risk ("there's a 40% chance of a significant protest at our product launch, which could lead to injuries or bad press, costing us millions"). This trait is akin to what leadership experts call "leading up and down the chain of command"—communicating effectively to both superiors and subordinates.[15] An illustrative case: a regional security director at a multinational learned of a potential coup in a country where their CEO planned to visit. Lacking direct authority to change the CEO's schedule, the director quickly gathered intelligence and convinced the CEO's chief of staff to reroute the trip by emphasizing not just the physical danger but the potential business fallout of being in-country during unrest. By exercising influence through fact-based advice and clear concern for the business's welfare, the protector-leader averted a potentially disastrous situation. In summary, protectors succeed through influence by earning respect and articulating their vision, rather than by formal power.

Resilience under Pressure

Functioning effectively in high-stakes, high-visibility environments with little margin for error. EP scenarios are often intense: one moment you're managing a routine meeting, the next you're dealing with a medical emergency or a security breach in front of the whole company. Protective leaders must remain composed and clear-headed, projecting calm confidence to their teams and principals. This psychological stamina means they can absorb the shocks of crises, adapt, and keep leading without succumbing to panic or fatigue. A notable example of this resilience under pressure was demonstrated on March 30, 1981, outside the Washington Hilton Hotel, when John Hinckley Jr. opened fire on President Reagan as he was leaving an event. Special Agent in Charge (SAIC) Jerry Parr, leading President Reagan's detail, reacted instantly to gunfire, pushing Reagan into the limousine within seconds and shielding him from further harm. Inside the vehicle, Parr noticed President Reagan was injured and, despite the shock of the moment, made the critical decision to divert to George Washington University Hospital, ultimately saving the President's life. Throughout the ordeal, Parr maintained steady communication to calm Reagan and, upon arrival at the hospital, coordinated security operations and emergency protocols.[16] In doing so, SAIC Parr embodied the very psychological resilience that separates exceptional protectors, those who adapt, lead, and safeguard lives even in the face of acute shock. Such steady leadership under duress reassures everyone around and often prevents a bad situation from spiraling. Protective leaders often cultivate this resilience through rigorous training (e.g., simulated crises), experience in military or law enforcement, and mindset techniques. They also know how to take care of their teams' morale in protracted crises, providing rest and rotation to avoid burnout. The mantra could be "stay cool, stay effective." A resilient protector doesn't just survive pressure—they thrive in it, turning chaos into controlled action.

Ethical Integrity

Making principled decisions even under intense political or financial pressure. Protective leaders are frequently the guardians of an organization's ethical line when it comes to safety and security. They may face pressure to downplay a risk to avoid bad publicity or to cut corners to save money, but the best leaders hold firm to what is right and safe. Integrity means prioritizing human life and ethical conduct over other considerations. A famous case in point is the Tylenol cyanide poisoning crisis of 1982. Johnson & Johnson's CEO James Burke ordered a nationwide recall of Tylenol, pulling the product off shelves at immense cost, because it was the only acceptable way to protect consumers. Burke's guidance to his team was, "How do we protect the people? Then, how do we save the product?"—in that order.[17] That decision is now heralded as a gold standard of corporate integrity in crisis. Protective leaders often channel similar principles. If an executive's data is compromised, an integrity-driven protector will insist on notifying affected parties and fixing the issue properly, even if others suggest quietly handling it to avoid embarrassment. If a principal asks for an unsafe exception ("I want to ignore the security protocol this time"), the protector-leader with integrity will respectfully refuse and explain why adherence matters. This trait also encompasses confidentiality, honesty, and fairness. Protectors are privy to the most sensitive information about their principals and companies; ethical leaders handle that trust with utmost care, refusing to misuse or disclose it inappropriately. They also ensure that their security measures respect the rights and dignity of others (e.g., not abusing surveillance tools or engaging in unlawful activity even if provoked by adversaries). By demonstrating unwavering integrity, protective leaders not only prevent legal and moral pitfalls but also build the trust that is essential for their advisory role. Principals know that a protector who always tells the truth and stands for what's right is an invaluable confidant. In sum, integrity is the compass that keeps protective leadership on course, even when navigating the fog of crises and pressure from all sides.

CASE STUDY: COVID-19 AND THE PROTECTOR-LEADER'S ROLE

The COVID-19 pandemic tested protective leaders' agility and foresight, redefining their strategic role and was a defining moment on a global scale. Practically overnight, travel bans, quarantine mandates, and worldwide supply chain disruptions forced security leaders to redefine "duty of care" across the enterprise. Protectors who had long managed travel security and crisis evacuations suddenly found themselves at the forefront of an unprecedented public health emergency. At many multinational corporations, protective intelligence teams rapidly developed global risk dashboards to track infection rates, local lockdown policies, and employee evacuation needs, ensuring executives had real-time risk intelligence to inform operational decisions. Corporate security departments morphed into 24/7 war rooms, digesting health data and government edicts from every country where their company operated. This was far beyond the traditional remit of physical security—it required understanding epidemiological reports and coordinating with HR and health and safety units constantly.

Early in the pandemic, evacuation and relocation were urgent challenges. In January 2020, as the coronavirus outbreak escalated in Wuhan, China, numerous companies took the extraordinary step of evacuating their expatriate staff and families from the region. Automakers like Honda and Nissan, for example, relied on protective leaders to coordinate logistics for repatriating employees from Wuhan via government-chartered flights, rightly judging that the situation would deteriorate.[18] At the same time, U.S. tech firms like Facebook swiftly suspended all non-essential travel to China and instructed staff who had recently returned from affected areas to self-isolate and work from home.[19] These measures, initiated or advised by protective leadership, were critical in safeguarding personnel before formal government actions took place. Protective leaders had to persuade business executives to halt travel or shut down offices in high-risk locations at a time when such moves seemed drastic. Those who succeeded often did so by presenting clear risk assessments—essentially becoming internal crisis diplomats, balancing safety with business continuity.

As the pandemic spread, protective leaders shifted focus to maintaining operations under new constraints. They coordinated site closures and reopenings, implemented health screenings and access controls, and enforced quarantine and testing protocols—all the while navigating a patchwork of local regulations. Many companies formed COVID-19 task forces or committees, and it was common to find the head of security co-chairing these groups alongside HR or medical officers. The U.S. CDC issued detailed *Guidance for Businesses and Employers* on pandemic response, which security leaders helped translate into action plans.[20] This included steps like reducing office occupancy, enhancing cleaning, and planning for significant absenteeism. Protective leaders played a key role in scenario planning: "What do we do if 30% of our workforce is out sick? How do we evacuate an executive from Country X if borders close?" Their expertise in crisis logistics was invaluable. Companies with strong protective intelligence functions even leveraged their geopolitical analysts to forecast which regions might impose lockdowns next, giving their business a head start in planning.

One noteworthy aspect was how some corporate security teams expanded their remit to employee health and well-being. For instance, a few large corporations enlisted their security departments to help stand up on-site COVID testing centers and vaccination clinics for employees once vaccines became available. In one example, Amazon's security and operations leaders famously helped build an in-house COVID-19 testing lab to serve the company's workforce.[21] Such initiatives went beyond traditional security, demonstrating protective leadership's adaptability—the goal was to reduce risk to employees and thus keep the business running. Protective leaders also had to remain vigilant that the chaos of the pandemic didn't create openings for other threats. They monitored for cyberattacks (which spiked as hackers exploited the situation), social unrest, or any individuals who might blame or target company leaders for pandemic-related issues. It was truly a juggling act: protect the people, protect the facilities, protect the data, and do it all under never-before-seen conditions.

The pandemic ultimately highlighted the expanded strategic importance of protective leadership. Those protective leaders who were able to translate public health intelligence into actionable business guidance earned significant credibility in the C-suite. For example, if a protector advised postponing a major product launch event due to virus concerns and suggested a virtual format instead—and that decision later proved wise—their stature grew. Executives realized that the protector's insight helped *save the company from a blunder.* These contributions did not go unnoticed. Many CEOs openly praised their security teams in 2020 and 2021 for keeping the company resilient. In some firms, the CSO became seen as the chief crisis officer, coordinating across departments and guiding the company through a maze of risks.

In hindsight, COVID-19 proved that effective protective leadership can directly correlate with an organization's ability to weather disruptions. Companies that fared better often had protective leaders who acted early and decisively. A McKinsey study of corporate COVID responses found that resilient organizations, those that thrived, were often those that empowered agile, cross-functional crisis teams (which included security leaders) to make quick decisions and adaptations. This newfound recognition has had a lasting impact: security leaders now often have a permanent seat on enterprise risk committees, and their purview has expanded to include *health security and business continuity planning.* In essence, the pandemic broke any remaining stereotype of the protector as merely a "guarding" function; they proved to be strategic executives capable of steering the organization through one of the most complex challenges in modern history.

BUILDING HIGH-TRUST LEADERSHIP IN THE C-SUITE

For protective leaders to succeed in influencing executive decisions, they must cultivate trust and credibility over time. A protector-leader's effectiveness is heavily dependent on the principal (and other top executives) trusting their judgment. To build this high-trust relationship, effective protector-leaders do several things consistently:

Understand the Principal's Worldview

They invest time in truly knowing their principal's concerns, priorities, and blind spots. By understanding what keeps the CEO awake at night—be it family safety, brand legacy, or specific threat anxieties—the protector can tailor their advice to align with those priorities. This might involve informal conversations to learn the principal's values and risk tolerance. When a protector shows they *"get" the principal's perspective*, their warnings carry more weight. For example, if a principal is very concerned about privacy, a protector who proactively addresses online personal data exposures will earn trust.

Frame Risk in Business Terms

Rather than using only security jargon, skilled protector-leaders translate threats into tangible impacts on revenue, reputation, or regulatory exposure. They might explain that a protest isn't just a security issue but could disrupt operations for days (affecting sales), or that lax executive cybersecurity could lead to a data breach (triggering regulatory fines). By linking security recommendations to business outcomes, they speak the language of fellow executives. This framing reassures decision-makers that the protector understands the business and is weighing security in balance with other objectives. It elevates the protector from a "security guard" mindset to that of a strategic advisor safeguarding the enterprise's interests.

Demonstrate Discretion and Judgment

High-trust protectors avoid unnecessary alarms but are candid when real risks emerge. Nothing erodes an executive's confidence more than a protector who cries wolf at every shadow. Conversely, failing to speak up about a serious threat is equally damaging. Striking the right balance is key. The protector-leader must exercise excellent judgment about when to escalate an issue. If they inform the CEO about threats only when truly warranted, their warnings will be taken seriously. Moreover, in a sensitive situation (say, an executive's family member facing a threat), a trusted protector handles it quietly and effectively, not drawing unwanted attention. Over time, principals appreciate a protector who is *low-drama, solutions-focused,* and reliable in a crisis.

Operate with Absolute Confidentiality

Protecting both corporate and personal privacy is sacrosanct. Because protector-leaders are privy to executives' itineraries,

> private communications, and sometimes intimate family details, they must be fortresses of confidentiality. Executives quickly learn whom they can confide in. Breaching confidentiality destroys trust; discreet protectors become valued confidants. On the other hand, a protector who consistently maintains secrecy and discretion becomes a true confidant to the principal. For example, if a CEO is quietly considering stepping down for health reasons and informs the security chief to prepare contingency plans, the security chief's ability to keep that information sealed is a litmus test of trust. High-trust protectors treat sensitive information on a strict need-to-know basis and often formalize this by implementing rigorous data security for executive info. They understand that loyalty and confidentiality are the foundation of trust in their relationship with the principal.

In building this trust, emotional intelligence is as important as technical skill. The protective leader's relationship with the principal is an asset in itself. Great protector-leaders often act almost like a consigliere, a counselor who the leader knows always has their back. They attend key meetings not just for security, but also to understand the context and provide better advice. They might gently remind a principal of their own values when making a tough call (e.g., "I recall you said employee safety is paramount, so canceling this trip fits that value"). Over time, such a relationship can become one where the principal doesn't want to make a major move without checking with their protector, not out of fear, but because the protector's perspective adds so much value.

Establishing that level of rapport doesn't happen overnight. It requires consistency, empathy, and performance. Every successfully managed situation, every piece of sage advice that prevents trouble, every confidence kept, these build the principal's belief that "my protector is not only my shield but also my trusted advisor." When that high trust is achieved, the protector-leader can operate at the highest levels of influence, truly integrating security into the fabric of executive decision-making. And, from the principal's viewpoint, they have gained something priceless: peace of mind that someone is relentlessly looking out for their safety and the company's well-being, with complete trust and discretion.

DEFINING THE PROTECTOR-LEADER OF THE FUTURE

With trust established, protectors are poised to shape the future of risk leadership. They transcend beyond being simply a security technician; they become a strategic risk advisor, a crisis leader, and a guardian of organizational reputation and continuity. Looking ahead, the role will only continue to expand in scope and importance. The future of protective leadership will be defined by a few key attributes and capabilities:

Cross-Domain Competence

The future protector-leader must be fluent across physical security, cybersecurity, information warfare, and operational risk. Demarcation between "security disciplines" will disappear. This means a CSO will be as comfortable discussing firewall vulnerabilities or deepfake threats as they are discussing executive travel protocols. Future protectors will lead interdisciplinary teams, blending security, data science, and intelligence expertise. This breadth is necessary because threats are interconnected; a protector might start the day addressing a network intrusion and end it managing a protective detail for a public event, with both situations potentially linked (e.g., a hacker threatening an executive's physical safety). Multi-domain fluency will be a hallmark of effective future protectors.

Influence Across Corporate Silos and External Stakeholders

Protectors will need the ability to influence not just within the security realm, but across all parts of the organization and even outside of it. Internally, they must work with boards, legal, HR, IT, facilities, and more, championing a culture of security and resilience. Externally, they will engage with law enforcement, government agencies, international bodies, and industry peers as part of a wider risk ecosystem. By 2030, we can expect protector-leaders to be active in networks like Information Sharing and Analysis Centers for threat intelligence, public-private cybersecurity partnerships, and global security forums. They might liaise with the company's investors or insurers to communicate how the firm is managing executive risks. This requires strong communication skills and credibility well beyond the traditional security function. Essentially, tomorrow's protective leader might also be a diplomat and advocate, influencing policy and public perception about security issues that affect their organization.

Insight into Global Trends and Emerging Risks

A deep understanding of how global, social, and technological trends affect personal and organizational risk will be imperative. The world in which 2030s protector operates will likely feature accelerated technological change (AI, quantum computing), evolving geopolitical tensions, climate-related disruptions, and shifting social attitudes. Protective leaders will rely on forward-looking risk assessments, for example, anticipating how AI-driven disinformation could spark violent activism, or how climate change could intensify resource conflicts that endanger executives in certain

> regions. The World Economic Forum's Global Risks Report for 2025 already highlights issues like state conflict, misinformation, and environmental crises dominating the risk landscape.[22] By the end of this decade, protector-leaders will be expected to know the implications of such macro risks on their micro security plans. They will use advanced tools, from predictive analytics to scenario simulation, to prepare their organizations. For instance, they might conduct "future threat" drills: *What if* an executive is targeted by a synthetic video scandal? *What if* an economic war between major powers triggers local unrest near our headquarters? From this, then devise strategies accordingly. Embracing continuous learning and curiosity will be key; many protector-leaders will pursue education in fields like data science or psychology to broaden their horizon on risk.

Another aspect of the future protector-leader is the concept of the "risk immune system" for organizations. Borrowing from General Stanley McChrystal's leadership philosophy, companies must develop an integrated risk immune system with unified controls, communication, technology, and culture, working as one. The protector-leader of the future will often be the *orchestrator* of this immune system. They will ensure that all the different risk controls, from IT security to crisis communications to physical safeguards, function as a unified whole. This holistic, systems-thinking approach means the protector will intervene not just when threats emerge, but in shaping the organization's structure and culture to be inherently more resilient. For example, they might advocate for decentralized decision-making in crises (to react faster) or push for a strong corporate narrative to preempt misinformation (strengthening what McChrystal calls the "narrative" and "communication" elements of the risk immune system). By being intentional and consistent in reinforcing these factors,[23] the protector-leader helps build an organization that can absorb shocks and bounce back—a trait which will be invaluable amid the uncertainties of the coming decade.

Looking to 2030 and beyond, we see the protector-leader as a figure at the crossroads of security, technology, and strategy. They will leverage AI for threat detection, perhaps using AI to scan open sources for early warning signs—but they will also guard against AI's misuse (like deepfakes targeting their principals). They will champion privacy and ethics, recognizing that how they protect is as important as what they protect. They will also likely deal with climate-related security issues: as extreme weather events increase, ensuring executive safety and continuity during natural disasters will become a bigger part of the role.

Finally, protector-leaders in the future will play a part in shaping corporate culture around risk. By consistently advocating preparedness and responsible risk-taking, they help leaders make bolder yet smarter decisions. Thought leaders in risk management often say the greatest risk is not understanding your risks; protector-leaders will embody this by educating and advising their companies continuously.

The challenge is clear: embrace these leadership skills to safeguard organizations across physical, digital, and reputational domains, paving the way for a resilient and fearless future. The new risk landscape has permanently expanded the protector's mandate, no longer just a guardian of physical safety, today's leader must safeguard reputation, data, and the very mission of the enterprise. Understanding the "why" behind this evolution is only the beginning. The next chapter turns to the deeply personal question every protector must answer: how do you make the internal transition from tactical operator to strategic leader, and earn a permanent seat at the decision-making table?

NOTES

1 Kritika, "Beyond Guns, Gates, Guards: Why Intelligence is the New Shield in Executive Protection," *Medium,* March 27, 2025, https://medium.com/@raokritika864/beyond-guns-gates-guards-why-intelligence-is-the-new-shield-in-executive-protection-f6cebfe82aff.

2 Securitas USA, "The Intelligent Security Era Is Here," *Securitas Blog* 2023. https://www.securitasinc.com/united-states-old/news-and-resources/blog/the-intelligent-security-era-is-here/.

3 Securitas USA, "The Intelligent Security Era Is Here," *Securitas Blog* 2023. https://www.securitasinc.com/united-states-old/news-and-resources/blog/the-intelligent-security-era-is-here/.

4 Bobby Allyn, "Twitter Suspends Several Journalists Who Shared Information about Musk's Jet," *NPR,* December 15, 2022. Musk quote on doxxing. https://www.npr.org/2022/12/15/1143291081/twitter-suspends-journalists-elon-musk-jet.

5 Insikt Group (Recorded Future), "Violent Extremists Dox Executives, Enabling Physical Threats," *Recorded Future,* March 27, 2024, Research report https://www.recordedfuture.com/research/violent-extremists-dox-executives-enabling-physical-threats.

6 Endre J. Walls, "Chief Security Officers Must Have A Seat At The Table," *Forbes*, March 18, 2022, https://www.forbes.com/sites/forbestechcouncil/2022/03/18/chief-security-officers-must-have-a-seat-at-the-table/.

7 Endre J. Walls, "Chief Security Officers Must Have A Seat At The Table." *Forbes*, March 18, 2022, https://www.forbes.com/sites/forbestechcouncil/2022/03/18/chief-security-officers-must-have-a-seat-at-the-table/.

8 European Commission, "What are Hybrid Threats?" *EU Defence – Hybrid Threats* 2023. Definition of hybrid threats. https://defence-industry-space.ec.europa.eu/eu-defence-industry/hybrid-threats_en

9 Booz Allen Hamilton, "Deepfakes Pose Business Risks, Here's What to Know," BoozAllen.com 2021. Note on fake imagery causing reputational harm. https://www.boozallen.com/insights/ai-research/deepfakes-pose-businesses-risks-heres-what-to-know.html.

10 Chris Rhatigan, "A Man Radicalized by Statistics," *Minnesota Reformer*, December 12, 2024, https://minnesotareformer.com/2024/12/12/a-man-radicalized-by-statistics/

11 Claire Meyer, "EP Trends: ... Shifting Tactics," *Security Management (ASIS),* February 2025, https://www.asisonline.org/security-management-magazine/.../executive-protection-trends/.

12 Claire Meyer, "EP Trends: ... Shifting Tactics," *Security Management (ASIS),* February 2025, https://www.asisonline.org/security-management-magazine/.../executive-protection-trends

13 Jocko Willink and Leif Babin, *Extreme Ownership: How U.S. Navy SEALs Lead and Win* (New York: St. Martin's Press, 2015).

14 Jocko Willink and Leif Babin, *Extreme Ownership: How U.S. Navy SEALs Lead and Win* (New York: St. Martin's Press, 2015).

15 Jocko Willink and Leif Babin, *Extreme Ownership: How U.S. Navy SEALs Lead and Win* (New York: St. Martin's Press, 2015).

16 United States Secret Service. "In Remembrance: Forty Years Since the Assassination Attempt on President Regan" https://www.secretservice.gov/reagan40thanniversary.

17 Andrew R. Johnson, "Johnson & Johnson and the Tylenol Crisis," *University of Oklahoma Department of Communication*, accessed on April 18, 2025, https://www.ou.edu/deptcomm/dodjcc/groups/02C2/Johnson%20&%20Johnson.htm.

18 ABC News, "Employers Evacuate Staff, Restrict Travel to China Amid Coronavirus Fears," January 28, 2020, Describing Honda, Nissan repatriating workers from Wuhan. URL: https://abcnews.go.com/Business/employers-evacuate-staff-restrict-travel-china-amid-coronavirus/story?id=68584011.

19 ABC News, "Employers Evacuate Staff, Restrict Travel to China Amid Coronavirus Fears," January 28, 2020, Describing Honda, Nissan repatriating workers from Wuhan. URL: https://abcnews.go.com/Business/employers-evacuate-staff-restrict-travel-china-amid-coronavirus/story?id=68584011.

20 CDC—National Center for Immunization and Respiratory Diseases, "Interim Guidance for Businesses and Employers to Plan and Respond to COVID-19," February 26, 2020, https://stacks.cdc.gov/view/cdc/85488.

21 Clare Duffy, "Amazon to End On-Site Covid Testing for Warehouse Workers," *CNN Business*, July 19, 2021, https://www.cnn.com/2021/07/19/tech/amazon-covid-testing/index.html.

22 Paul McKay et al., "Technological and Environmental Risks Take the Top Two Spots in the 2025 WEF Risk Report," *Forrester Blog*, January 24, 2025, https://www.forrester.com/blogs/technological-and-environmental-risks-take-top-two-spots-in-2025-wef-risk-report.

23 Stanley McChrystal and Anna Butrico, *Risk: A User's Guide* (New York: Portfolio, 2021).

CHAPTER 2

From Executive Protection to Executive Presence

The journey from protector to strategist is rarely linear. It's a quiet evolution, one marked not just by new responsibilities, but by a fundamental shift in how value is delivered. Sun Tzu wrote, "Strategy without tactics is the slowest route to victory. Tactics without strategy is the noise before defeat."[1]

Many protectors arrive at this same crossroads, where skill must become strategy. Many professionals enter the security field through operational excellence, but only those who learn to translate risk into relevance find their seat at the decision-making table.

That transition demands more than competence; it requires credibility, business fluency, and the ability to lead across functions without formal authority. It means letting go of the illusion that proximity equals influence, and instead cultivating trust, foresight, and the language of leadership.

To ground this leadership evolution, this chapter draws on a composite case study, available in both amalgamated form and as individual examples, such as protector-to-leader TJ Klomp, who rose from law enforcement and protective operations to guide physical enterprise security at Amazon. Their stories reveal not just what changes, but what must endure: discipline, discernment, and a deep commitment to protecting what matters most.

NAVIGATING LEADERSHIP: MODELS FOR TRANSITIONING FROM EP TO SECURITY EXECUTIVE

For practitioners aiming to move from operational roles (such as executive protection (EP)) into strategic leadership, certain leadership models or frameworks can provide a pathway to emulate and arrange a pathway to success. Here are three actionable models, along with a brief description and their relevance to this career transition, that resonate with chief

DOI: 10.4324/9781003670704-3

security officers (CSOs), protection managers, and EP professionals. These frameworks offer established, transferable skills that empower leaders in related roles outside of EP to excel.

Servant Leadership

This model inverts the traditional hierarchy by putting the leader in the service of their team. "Servant leaders possess a serve-first mindset, focused on empowering and uplifting those who work for them, serving instead of commanding, and showing humility instead of brandishing authority."[2] For an EP professional, this approach leverages their instinct to protect and support—not just toward their principals, but toward their team and stakeholders. By adopting servant leadership, emerging security leaders build trust and credibility beyond tactical skills, as they demonstrate a prioritization of the growth and well-being of their team and the organization. This style can facilitate a smooth transition into senior management by fostering high-trust teams and collaborative relationships throughout the enterprise.

Mission Command

Originally a military leadership philosophy, mission command centers on decentralized decision-making guided by a clear intent. The U.S. Army defines mission command as "the Army's approach to command and control that empowers subordinate decision-making and decentralized execution appropriate to the situation."[3] In practical terms for corporate security, a CSO employing mission command provides a clear strategic vision (the "intent") and then trusts their teams, such as protective details and regional security managers, to execute with autonomy. This framework is accessible to EP professionals with law enforcement or military backgrounds, as it builds on their experience with clarity of mission and empowering the front line. By practicing this philosophy, a leader transitioning from tactical roles can avoid micromanaging and instead delegate effectively, demonstrating the strategic oversight expected in senior positions while still ensuring cohesive action toward the organization's security objectives.

Adaptive Leadership

The framework of adaptive leadership emphasizes flexibility, learning, and innovation in the face of complex challenges. It "focuses on mobilizing individuals and organizations to embrace change by fostering learning, resilience, and collaboration."[4] This model is highly relevant for security leaders because the security environment (threats, technologies, global risks) is constantly evolving. An EP professional transitioning to a CSO role will encounter new strategic challenges, from cybersecurity convergence to corporate governance issues that cannot be solved with hard skills alone. Adaptive leadership encourages you to step back from the comfort of standard operating procedures (SOPs) and continually adjust your approach, just as you would adapt to dynamic situations during a protection assignment. By being an adaptive leader, a former tactical specialist shows they can handle uncertainty and drive change, qualities that enterprise executives value. It means tackling not just technical problems but also the "adaptive" issues like shifting company culture around security or influencing policy, thereby solidifying their role as a strategic leader.

Each of these leadership models provides a pragmatic playbook for security professionals aiming to broaden their impact. By internalizing principles of serving others, empowering teams with clear intent, and remaining flexible and growth-oriented, an EP veteran can transform into a holistic leader. These frameworks help bridge the gap between hands-on protective expertise and high-level strategic influence, guiding professionals to not only excel in the field but also in the boardroom.

THE IMPERATIVE: CONSTANT EVOLUTION

Rather than rigidly adhering to a single leadership model, the most effective security leaders cultivate a polymathic approach, *continuously learning and adjusting their management style to match evolving demands.* Security challenges and corporate dynamics are rarely static; thus, leaders who comfortably draw insights from multiple disciplines can respond swiftly and decisively. By understanding diverse frameworks, from servant leadership and mission command to transformational and situational leadership, leaders can integrate these principles into a versatile and adaptive toolkit, strategically applying the most effective method for each scenario.

General Stanley McChrystal underscores this necessity in *Team of Teams*, stating succinctly: "Adaptability, not efficiency, must become our central competency."[5] McChrystal suggests that in complex and unpredictable environments, such as today's converged security landscape, leaders and their teams must prioritize flexibility and rapid adjustment over rigid efficiency. Likewise, corporate security settings increasingly demand that leaders move fluidly between tactical precision and strategic foresight. The implication is clear: *leaders must continually reassess their assumptions, broaden perspectives, and refine their approaches to maintain effectiveness amid rapid change.*

Central to flexibility in leadership is emotional intelligence (EQ), which enhances a leader's ability to navigate uncertainty, build trust, and foster resilience. Daniel Goleman, a foundational voice on EQ, emphasizes: "Leadership is not domination, but the art of persuading people to work toward a common goal."[6] Emotionally intelligent leaders intuitively sense shifts in organizational culture, stakeholder expectations, and threat dynamics, enabling them to anticipate and quickly implement needed adjustments in leadership style. Thus, EQ is the essential skill that allows a leader to authentically embrace the flexible mindset critical to thriving in today's fluid and complex security roles.

Just as a situation dictates the tactics on the ground, your organizational environment will offer cues on how to evolve your leadership and communication styles to achieve what's necessary for success.

THE SHIFT FROM TACTICAL OPERATOR TO STRATEGIC ADVISOR

In the early stages of a protector's career, success is measured by precision: advance work done right, logistics executed flawlessly, the principal safe and unaware of the risks mitigated behind the scenes. The protector is tactically excellent, disciplined, detail-oriented, and reactive by necessity.

But stepping into a leadership role requires an expanded skillset. A CSO or Director of EP is no longer judged by physical presence or proximity to risk, but by how well they translate security concerns into strategic decisions. They must anticipate issues weeks or months in advance, brief senior executives in terms they understand, and design protective programs that enable business growth.

This shift isn't natural for everyone. Many protection professionals find comfort in structure, SOPs, muscle memory, and operational control. But leadership in the boardroom operates on ambiguity, influence, and vision. As one security executive put it, "You're no longer being asked to carry out the mission, you're being asked to help define it."

That means transitioning from a *security enforcer* to a *business enabler*. From asking, "How do I prevent this threat from reaching the principal?" to "How does this threat impact our business goals, and what's the smartest way to address it without slowing momentum?"

ESSENTIAL MINDSET SHIFTS

Transitioning from tactical operator to strategic advisor demands more than merely learning new skills; it requires foundational shifts in mindset. These shifts are profound, reshaping not only what a leader does but also how they think, communicate, and influence others.

The first crucial shift is from reactive problem-solving to proactive strategy. Tactical roles frequently condition professionals to quickly solve immediate threats, mitigating risks in real-time with precise action. Strategic leadership, however, demands anticipation and prevention, a forward-looking approach that identifies risks well before they become visible. Leaders must move beyond reacting to events and toward shaping conditions that prevent incidents altogether. As Dan Heath succinctly captures in his book *Upstream*: "The need for heroes arises from the failure to prevent a crisis."[7] The mindset of strategic leadership focuses precisely on that prevention, not heroism after the fact.

One major challenge professionals face during this shift is overcoming deeply ingrained tactical communication habits. Credibility in tactical roles often derives from visible expertise and decisive action, whereas strategic credibility demands nuanced understanding and persuasive communication aligned closely with business objectives.

Another essential mindset shift involves moving from enforcing compliance to influencing stakeholders. The tactical mindset naturally gravitates toward compliance and control, relying on positional authority and prescriptive processes. Boardroom leadership requires influencing through relationships, persuasion, and alignment with organizational goals. Security executives must master the subtle arts of influence and negotiation, reshaping their communications to highlight how security initiatives support larger business objectives. As former General and United States Secretary of State Colin Powell advised, "Leadership is solving problems. The day soldiers stop bringing you their problems is the day you have stopped leading them."[8] Similarly, when security teams and stakeholders willingly align with strategic goals without coercion, true leadership influence has been achieved.

A significant challenge in adapting to the executive mindset is transitioning from a control-oriented posture to one of flexible influence. Many protection professionals initially struggle to accept ambiguity and calculated risk as essential aspects of strategic leadership, often defaulting instinctively to a risk-elimination mindset rather than risk management aligned to business priorities.

Ultimately, the move from tactical operator to strategic advisor is underpinned by adaptability, openness to continuous learning and reinvention. Leaders must cultivate comfort with ambiguity, recognizing that leadership at higher levels often means making decisions with incomplete data and accepting calculated risks. Embracing this ambiguity not as a limitation but as an opportunity to innovate and adapt is what truly sets strategic leaders apart.

FROM INSIGHT TO IMPACT: PRACTICAL MOVES FOR EMERGING LEADERS

Understanding the mindset shift is foundational, but implementing it requires deliberate, tactical action. Many protectors ready to evolve their roles ask the same question: *What do I do next?* The following are practical steps that help translate insight into influence.

Learn the Business as Your New "Area of Operation"
Treat your company like a new operational environment. Study how it generates revenue, who its customers are, and what its quarterly objectives look like. Begin with investor calls, internal town halls, and basic business press releases. You don't need to become a CFO, but you do need to understand the forces that shape executive decision-making. Protection doesn't sit outside that ecosystem; it's embedded in it.

Build Business Fluency into Your Briefings
Before recommending any new measure, ask: "What business goal does this protect or enable?" Reframe your proposals in a language your executive team already uses. If you're presenting risk data, tie it to revenue exposure, regulatory impact, or reputational harm. This translation effort is often the turning point in becoming a trusted advisor.

Create Early Wins with Strategic Partners
Don't wait to be invited; proactively approach Human Resources (HR), Legal, and Operations teams to ask where their pressure points are. Security leaders who can solve others' problems quietly and without ego build fast credibility. That might mean stepping in to support an emerging insider risk issue, helping HR navigate terminations, or working with Facilities to address access control pain points.

Track Your Leadership Development Like You Would a Protection Detail
Keep a simple leadership journal or scorecard. Record what you've learned, where you've been influenced, what resistance you've met, and how you've adapted. The discipline of reflection sharpens your strategic awareness and helps you map your transition from operator to leader in real-time.

CASE STUDY: TJ KLOMP—FROM TACTICAL EXPERTISE TO STRATEGIC ENTERPRISE LEADERSHIP

TJ Klomp's journey from tactical protector to enterprise security leader offers a real-world template for how EP professionals can evolve into trusted strategic advisors. Beginning his career in law enforcement, Klomp developed a deep operational foundation, including crisis response, situational control, and frontline leadership. However, when he entered Amazon's corporate security environment, he quickly recognized that the skillset that had made him effective in the field wasn't enough to create a long-term impact at scale.

Amazon's pace was relentless, its risk environment multifaceted, and its expectations high. Rather than focusing solely on EP logistics, Klomp leaned into protective intelligence, developing methodologies that could anticipate and neutralize threats before they materialized. He helped shape an approach that fused physical security, emergency management, and data-driven intelligence into a unified capability, built not just to respond to incidents but to prevent them through early insight and strategic coordination.

More than adopting new tools, Klomp needed a mindset transformation. He began forging relationships beyond the security function, actively engaging with Legal, HR, Facilities, and business leadership to understand their objectives and pain points. He reframed security not as a constraint, but as an enabler, positioning protective measures as safeguards for business continuity, leadership effectiveness, and brand resilience.

One pivotal moment came when his team's intelligence-led posture enabled Amazon to navigate protest activity and reputational threats with minimal disruption. Rather than treating the event as a crisis, Klomp's team managed it as part of ongoing business operations, protecting people while enabling the company to stay on mission. That approach earned his team broader influence and validated their strategic value.

Over time, Klomp's responsibilities grew to include global physical security, emergency response, and organizational resilience, all rooted in the same principle: protect the individual AND the mission. He operationalized that principle by embedding security into Amazon's business rhythm, ensuring that executive safety, continuity planning, and emergency readiness became integrated elements of enterprise strategy.

What made Klomp stand out wasn't just his operational credibility; it was his ability to adapt, collaborate, and translate. He spoke the language of the business, prioritized relevance over rigidity, and led without ego. In doing so, he embodied the modern protector-leader: one who doesn't just react to risk, but helps the organization think smarter, move faster, and operate with confidence in an unpredictable world.

This journey echoes those of others who've made similar transitions, such as Susan Goggins of Coinbase, Former LyondellBasell CSO Scott McHugh, or ExxonMobil Shane Steward, and many unnamed professionals transforming corporate security from within, without the need for visibility or accolades.

What they all had in common was this: *they made themselves relevant to the business, not just the threat.*

BUILDING CREDIBILITY BEYOND TACTICAL SKILLS

When tactical professionals step into leadership roles, one of their first challenges is establishing credibility beyond their operational reputation. In protection work, credibility comes from presence, experience, and decisiveness. In corporate leadership, it's more nuanced. You're expected to influence peers without authority, advise the C-suite, and communicate risk in a way that resonates with business stakeholders.

Success means transition from being "the enforcer" to being "the advisor." That shift begins with listening.

Credibility in the boardroom isn't earned by demonstrating tactical prowess, it's earned by showing you understand the business. That means knowing how the company makes money, what its core risks are, what keeps the CEO awake at night, and how security fits into that picture.

Start with language. A protector might say, "We need to increase EP coverage because the threat environment is escalating." A leader says, "Our current exposure profile increases reputational and operational risk. We can reduce that by 30% through targeted coverage aligned with our business continuity priorities."

One states an observation, and the other is an informed business risk with a mitigation plan.

This difference is not semantics. It's leadership.

According to a joint Wharton-ASIS study, the most common failing among corporate security leaders is "inability to translate technical risk into business impact."[9] Tactical expertise got them in the door, but those who couldn't adapt their message didn't last.

SPEAKING THE LANGUAGE OF BUSINESS

To lead effectively at the enterprise level, protectors must learn to speak business. That means shifting from security-first thinking to risk-first and opportunity-aligned framing. You don't have to be a finance expert, but you do need to understand concepts like EBITDA, operational efficiency, exposure, and enterprise risk management.

Protection leaders must learn to ask:

"What are our business goals this quarter?"
"Where are our most valuable assets?"
"What would it cost if a key executive were disrupted for 48 hours?"

The answers help shape a narrative. Instead of proposing a new residential security measure because "it's best practice," you align it to business impact: "This initiative reduces executive exposure risk, ensuring leadership continuity during market-critical periods."

In 2021, the Security Executive Council found that security proposals with business-aligned language were 42% more likely to be approved by CFOs.[10]

Michael Gips, ASIS International's former Chief Global Knowledge and Learning Officer, put it plainly: "Security professionals must use the language of business to describe their operations and make the case for the budgets needed to support them."[11]

That doesn't mean abandoning your tactical instincts. It means translating them into business outcomes.

ADAPTING TO THE EXECUTIVE THOUGHT PROCESS

Executives think in terms of value, growth, continuity, and brand equity. They care about risk, but only as it impacts those variables.

To influence at the executive level, protectors must adapt their mindset:

From Certainty to Ambiguity

There's rarely a perfect solution. Executives expect trade-offs and calculated risks.

From Security-Centric to Business-Integrated

Security is a lens, not the driver.

From Command-and-Control to Influence-and-Enable

You won't often have direct authority. You must earn alignment through trust, clarity, and shared goals.

This mindset also means accepting that *not every risk will be mitigated*. Your job is to frame options and guide informed decisions, not demand perfection. Security exists to enable the business, not encumber it.

In one major financial firm, a security director proposed canceling a public event due to threat chatter. The executive team asked: "What's the risk if we proceed with security in place?" She responded with a scaled mitigation plan and clear contingencies. The event went ahead, and her security team was granted additional resources. No incident occurred. That leader earned trust, not because she eliminated risk, but because she helped the business make a confident, informed decision.

Leadership is not about control. It's about enabling others' decision-making and giving them the ability to move forward with eyes wide open.

CASE STUDY: EVOLVING INFLUENCE—THE PROTECTOR'S PIVOT—BUILDING CREDIBILITY, CULTURE, AND CROSS-FUNCTIONAL TRUST

(Note: This composite case study draws from experiences of three senior corporate security leaders who've transitioned from operational EP into strategic, enterprise-level roles. Specific names and organizations are omitted for confidentiality.)

The transition from operational protector to security executive rarely follows a clear path. Three experienced protection leaders, from technology, oil and gas, and consumer goods sectors, illustrate the necessary shift from tactical proficiency to strategic influence.

Initially, each measured success through precise execution, ensuring logistics, safety, and discreet handling of threats. Operational control and immediate effectiveness defined their roles.

However, advancing within global corporations revealed that operational skills alone were insufficient. Success now required shaping perceptions, building cross-functional trust, and integrating security with broader business strategy.

A crucial lesson emerged early: credibility in senior leadership demands more than tactical expertise. As one former US State Department executive-turned-CSO described, "Credibility in the boardroom comes from aligning security with business outcomes and communicating in the language of stakeholders."

Learning the language of business became critical. These leaders immersed themselves in understanding corporate finances, operational objectives, and market pressures. Security was no longer framed simply as "threat mitigation" but as ensuring "operational continuity" and "stakeholder confidence."

In one case from the oil and gas sector, geopolitical tension in a key market tested one leader's ability to reframe risk. Rather than reducing executive travel, he presented the issue in terms of maintaining market stability and investor trust. Security became seen not as restrictive, but as strategically vital to organizational resilience.

Equally important was the deliberate effort to cultivate trust and influence across departments like HR, Legal, IT, Operations, and Corporate Communications. Initially viewed solely as tactical enforcers, these leaders found success by becoming empathetic partners and risk advisors. One leader at a consumer goods firm deliberately shifted his approach from imposing security policies to collaborative problem-solving, thus facilitating solutions that achieved both security and operational alignment across the enterprise.

In a tech firm facing public controversy, the security executive proposed measured responses that balanced executive safety with public visibility and brand reputation. Rather than canceling engagements, he offered a strategic framework that preserved executive trust, market perception, and operational continuity.

Internally, these executives prioritized mentoring their teams to think strategically. They emphasized broader business acumen among junior managers, encouraging cross-functional projects and business-oriented education. One noted, "Strategic security requires teams who see their role as safeguarding enterprise strategy, not just physical safety."

Over time, each solidified credibility by consistently demonstrating strategic insight. They became trusted advisors, known for proactive risk management and alignment with organizational priorities. Reflecting on their journeys, these leaders identified three fundamental insights: they learned to embrace ambiguity at the strategic level and translate risks clearly through the lens of business impact; they focused on becoming effective translators and facilitators who communicate in terms meaningful to stakeholders; and they acted as integrators, navigating organizational complexity and aligning security with shared enterprise goals.

Ultimately, transitioning from operational protector to strategic leader demands humility, adaptability, and cross-functional trust. As one leader summarized, "At this level, you're safeguarding the entire organization's future, not just individuals. That's the measure of true leadership evolution."

LEADING THROUGH CROSS-FUNCTIONAL INFLUENCE

No protector becomes a strategic leader in isolation. The security function touches almost every part of the enterprise: HR, Legal, IT, Facilities, Communications, and more. Success depends on your ability to build alliances across departments and influence peers who may not report to you.

This is where "soft power" becomes essential.

Soft power is built on credibility, consistency, and relevance to enterprise goals and stakeholder concerns. It means showing up in the rooms where risk is discussed, not just where security is deployed. It means learning what your peers care about and helping them succeed. You're not just asking Legal to help you with policy enforcement, you're helping them mitigate liability. You're not just coordinating with IT for digital security, you're jointly protecting enterprise value.

One global CSO referred to it as "co-authoring risk." The most successful protective leaders *don't just present a security view*, they bring together perspectives across functions and enable smarter decisions.

To do that, you must:

Be Approachable and Visible

Don't hide in your silo. Walk the floor. Visit teams that have nothing to do with security. Attend cross-functional meetings, even if you're not on the agenda. Visibility builds familiarity, and familiarity builds trust. If they only see you when something's wrong, they'll associate security with disruption, not enablement.

Offer Value Before Asking for It

Help others solve their problems. One CSO began every stakeholder meeting by asking a single question: "What's the one thing that would make your job safer or easier?" That simple prompt opened the door to collaborative wins, such as jointly developed SOPs with HR or shared risk dashboards with IT. Protectors who give first earn the license to lead later.

Speak in Shared Outcomes

"We both care about continuity and trust." Language matters. Say "continuity," not "compliance." Say "protecting brand trust," not "enforcing policy." The more your messaging overlaps with other business functions, the more traction your priorities gain. You're not a separate function; you're a co-author of enterprise risk posture.

In a 2023 Security Executive Council report, 87% of senior executives said cross-functional collaboration was now a core expectation of security leadership.[12]

EVOLVING PROFILE OF THE PROTECTOR-LEADER

The next generation of protector-leaders won't be defined by the longest resumes or the hardest edge, but by a more adaptive mix of strategic, relational, and operational capability. The leaders who will excel are those who think like executives who understand the business, communicate like trusted advisors who can translate complexity into clarity, plan with the precision and foresight of tacticians, and influence with the subtlety, credibility, and steadiness of diplomats. These qualities reflect a shift from a purely protective posture to a role that demands judgment, partnership, and strategic alignment. This evolution in skill and mindset creates a natural bridge into the broader charge facing modern protection leaders.

THE PROTECTOR'S NEW CHARGE

Stepping into leadership doesn't mean leaving your operational instincts behind. It means building on them, learning to frame risk as strategy, to advise without ego, and to lead without needing to be the loudest voice in the room.

True leadership in protection today is about visibility, trust, and alignment. It's about protecting the enterprise by understanding it deeply, its people, culture, vulnerabilities, and aspirations.

The next generation of protector-leaders won't be the ones with the longest resumes or the hardest edge. They'll be the ones who know how to think like an executive, communicate like an advisor, plan like a tactician, and influence like a diplomat.

This shift isn't theoretical. New risks emerge daily, ones that don't fit yesterday's playbook. The most trusted security leaders aren't the ones with the most tactical accolades or the longest resumes. They're the ones who adapt quickly, communicate with clarity, and lead through uncertainty with calm conviction.

That kind of leadership demands continuous learning, not just in threat models or security frameworks, but in EQ, influence, and business fluency. It means adjusting your leadership style as your environment changes. What works in a founder-led startup may not be effective in a publicly traded enterprise. The most effective protector-leaders shift posture, tone, and approach while staying grounded in principle.

As one Ultra High Net Worth office CSO put it: "You don't lead with your retired badge, you lead with awareness of the business, of your team, and of what's coming over the horizon." These are the leaders who bridge risk and relevance and earn the trust not just to protect, but to lead.

NOTES

1 Sun Tzu, *The Art of War*, translated by Samuel B. Griffith (Oxford: Oxford University Press, 1963).

2 https://www.asisonline.org/security-management-magazine/articles/2017/03/the-art-of-servant-leadership/.

3 https://www.armyupress.army.mil/Journals/Military-Review/English-Edition-Archives/January-February-2025/Leadership-Theory/.

4 https://thedecisionlab.com/reference-guide/management/adaptive-leadership.

5 Stanley McChrystal, *Team of Teams: New Rules of Engagement for a Complex World* (New York: Portfolio/Penguin, 2015).

6 Daniel Goleman, *Emotional Intelligence: Why It Can Matter More Than IQ* (New York: Bantam Books, 1995).

7 Dan Heath, *Upstream: The Quest to Solve Problems Before They Happen* (New York: Avid Reader Press, 2020).

8 Colin Powell and Tony Koltz, *It Worked for Me: In Life and Leadership* (New York: Harper, 2012).
9 Wharton-ASIS International Executive Education, "Strategic Security Leadership: Bridging Operational Expertise and Executive Influence," 2021, https://www.wharton.upenn.edu.
10 Security Executive Council, "Aligning Security Proposals with Business Objectives: Best Practices for Strategic Buy-In," 2021.
11 M. Gips, "Why CSOs Fail in the C-Suite. Security Management Magazine," 2022, https://www.asisonline.org/security-management-magazine/articles/2022/why-csos-fail-in-the-c-suite/.
12 Security Executive Council, "Cross-Functional Collaboration in Enterprise Risk Management: Emerging Standards for Security Leaders," 2023, https://www.securityexecutivecouncil.com/.

CHAPTER 3

Defining Leadership in the Protection Profession

Building on the foundation laid in Chapter 1, Leading in the New Risk Landscape, and the personal and professional shifts explored in Chapter 2, From Executive Protection to Executive Presence, this chapter marks the culmination of Section I: Strategic Evolution in Protective Leadership. Here, we define and explore the multidimensional traits and skills that distinguish effective leaders in the protection profession, traits that enable a seamless progression from tactical proficiency to strategic influence.

Stepping into leadership is not the destination, but the beginning of a more demanding, nuanced journey. Effective protection leadership requires far more than a new title or expanded scope of responsibility. It demands the recalibration of identity, mastery of diplomacy, operational discipline, emotional intelligence (EQ), strategic clarity, and the ability to influence at the highest levels of an organization. These capabilities empower protector-leaders to anticipate and shape outcomes in an increasingly complex threat landscape.

Protective leadership has been historically forged at the intersection of military doctrine, business strategy, classical philosophy, and modern management practice. In the chapters ahead, we will examine how to apply these principles as actionable competencies, but here we take a final step in building the strategic mindset, offering practical insights and real-world examples that cement the protector-leader's role as a trusted strategic advisor.

WHAT IS LEADERSHIP IN THE PROTECTION PROFESSION?

Leadership in protection transcends merely giving orders or managing logistics. It involves creating clarity amid uncertainty and enabling

DOI: 10.4324/9781003670704-4

people to move forward safely and decisively. Trusted protector-leaders clearly perceive threats, candidly communicate risk, and wisely guide stakeholders toward solutions.

Leadership, fundamentally, is about influence. John Maxwell famously stated, "Leadership is influence, nothing more, nothing less."[1] In protection, influence manifests subtly, in private briefings, crisis negotiations, quiet discussions, and calm presence amidst chaos. This situational leadership involves nuanced adaptation to shifting cultural and interpersonal dynamics, making protector-leaders effective bridge-builders between tactical realities and strategic imperatives.

Understanding what leadership means in the protection profession is only the starting point. To fully appreciate its demands, we must examine how it differs from more conventional leadership roles and why those differences matter in today's environment.

UNIQUE DEMANDS OF LEADERSHIP

Leadership in protection occupies a unique space between military structure and corporate fluidity. Unlike traditional leadership roles focused primarily on productivity or profit, protection leaders measure their success by preventing incidents and crises mitigated. Peter Thiel, in his influential work *Zero to One*, emphasizes that successful leaders differentiate themselves by embracing unique strategies to create meaningful impact.[2] In protection, this means combining military decisiveness with diplomatic finesse.

Protection leaders frequently navigate ambiguity under intense scrutiny. Success often remains unseen, defined by the absence of adverse events. Dan Heath articulates this concept in *Upstream*: "Success is not a story we tell well... we don't always see the people who kept those disasters from happening."[3] This makes protective leadership uniquely challenging yet strategically invaluable.

These unique pressures demand more than just courage or operational skill. They require a combination of dimensions that, together, define the protector-leader's effectiveness.

FOUR DIMENSIONS OF PROTECTION LEADERSHIP

Strategic leadership in protection is inherently multidimensional, demanding a balanced mastery of skills that extend beyond tactical competence. Leaders in the protection profession must navigate complex situations and communicate effectively with diverse stakeholders, often simultaneously managing urgent tactical crises, strategic considerations, and nuanced emotional dynamics.

The following four dimensions, Operational Vigilance, Dynamic Decision-Making, Emotional Composure, and Strategic Credibility, serve as critical pillars of this multidimensional leadership approach. Each dimension builds upon and reinforces the others, collectively enabling protector-leaders to anticipate threats, adapt swiftly to changing circumstances, maintain clarity under pressure, and credibly align protective initiatives with organizational goals. Understanding and developing these dimensions equips leaders with the comprehensive skill set necessary to transition from tactician to influential strategic advisor, capable of effectively safeguarding both people and organizational purpose.

Let's now examine each of these dimensions individually, starting with Operational Vigilance, the foundational skill that enables leaders to proactively anticipate and address evolving threats.

OPERATIONAL VIGILANCE

Operational vigilance is foundational to protective leadership, encompassing continuous situational awareness, rigorous attention to evolving threats, and proactive safety measures. Leaders' adept at operational vigilance will anticipate vulnerabilities rather than react passively to incidents. As former Secretary of Defense James Mattis emphasized, "The most important six inches on the battlefield is between your ears,"[4] highlighting that true vigilance originates from a disciplined, strategic mindset that consistently evaluates and anticipates risk.

Modern protection leadership also demands proactive engagement with emerging technologies and innovative practices. Artificial intelligence, advanced threat analytics, cyber-physical systems, and predictive intelligence platforms have significantly reshaped the strategic protective landscape. Protector-leaders must actively seek, evaluate, and integrate relevant innovations, continually enhancing their strategic agility and operational vigilance. As Clayton Christensen outlined, "Disruptive innovation can hurt if you are not the one doing the disrupting."[5] Leaders who strategically harness technology reinforce their vigilance and proactively position protection as an integral driver of organizational success and resilience.

Historical Example

During the Cuban Missile Crisis, President Kennedy's advisors continuously monitored developing intelligence, demonstrating operational vigilance by maintaining readiness and crafting strategic options that avoided catastrophic escalation. This proactive vigilance significantly contributed to the crisis's peaceful resolution.[6]

Contemporary Example

Executive protection teams regularly leverage geopolitical intelligence platforms (e.g., OSAC and ISOS briefings) to maintain operational vigilance, adjusting protective measures proactively in response to emerging global threats.

While vigilance establishes foundational readiness, effective protective leadership also requires agility in processing information. This leads directly to our next dimension: Dynamic Decision-Making, a critical skill for navigating uncertainty and rapidly changing circumstances.

DYNAMIC DECISION-MAKING

Dynamic decision-making involves rapidly processing diverse and often incomplete data sets to form effective responses. This capacity integrates active listening, critical analysis, and agile adaptation to changing circumstances. Military strategist Colonel John Boyd's concept of the "OODA Loop" (Observe, Orient, Decide, Act) illustrates dynamic decision-making by emphasizing agility, speed, and adaptability as core advantages in fluid environments.[7]

Historical Example

During Operation Neptune Spear, the mission to capture or kill Osama bin Laden, dynamic decision-making was crucial when a helicopter malfunction forced commanders and SEAL operators to swiftly adapt their extraction plans. This agile pivot demonstrated rapid information synthesis, critical analysis, and immediate action that ensured mission success despite unforeseen complications.[8]

Contemporary Example

In 2020, as global travel restrictions rapidly changed due to COVID-19, protection leaders dynamically adapted security and evacuation strategies, using real-time updates and cross-border intelligence sharing to safely evacuate executives from affected regions.

Quick, effective decision-making is vital, yet even the best decisions falter without clear emotional management. Thus, our third dimension, Emotional Composure, is indispensable, providing protector-leaders with the stability to execute decisions calmly amidst crises.

EMOTIONAL COMPOSURE

Emotional composure represents the leader's capacity to remain calm, steady, and clear-minded in highly stressful and ambiguous situations. Leaders demonstrating strong emotional composure stabilize teams, ensuring effective collective responses under pressure. Daniel Goleman underscores EQ as the ability "to manage ourselves and our relationships effectively," emphasizing composure as a pivotal attribute of influential leaders.[9]

Historical Example

During the Apollo 10 mission, flight director Gene Kranz famously maintained extraordinary emotional composure when calmly directing his team to systematically resolve a potentially catastrophic oxygen tank explosion. His steadfast composure influenced the team's ability to effectively manage stress and devise innovative solutions, ensuring the safe return of the astronauts.[10]

Contemporary Example

By maintaining emotional composure, protector-leaders stabilize not only immediate responses during crises but also establish trust and confidence among stakeholders. This trust directly supports their capacity to influence strategic decisions, underscoring the critical relationship between emotional composure and strategic credibility.

Emotional composure enables protector-leaders to remain steady and trustworthy under pressure, creating a foundation of confidence. However, composure alone is insufficient for sustained strategic impact. Leaders must also translate this trust into actionable influence at the organizational level, bringing us to the essential dimension of Strategic Credibility.

STRATEGIC CREDIBILITY

Building directly upon emotional composure is the critical dimension of Strategic Credibility, the ability to persuasively align protective strategies with broader organizational goals, ensuring security measures resonate clearly at the executive level. Leaders build credibility not merely by operational effectiveness but by clearly demonstrating an understanding of strategic business impacts, translating complex security issues into relevant business language. Former Secretary of State Colin Powell noted, "Leadership is solving problems," highlighting that strategic credibility hinges on a leader's ability to provide clear, actionable solutions that resonate with stakeholders.[11]

Historical Example

In World War II, General Dwight D. Eisenhower exemplified strategic credibility by effectively aligning complex military strategies with political and economic considerations necessary for coalition success. Eisenhower's clear communication secured buy-in from political leaders and facilitated unprecedented collaboration among diverse allied forces.[12]

Contemporary Example

The corporate protection leader overseeing the executive security program recognized that increasing digital exposure of executives (through public speaking events, social media activity, and leaked personal data) was creating elevated targeting risks. Instead of framing the issue purely as a security concern, the leader presented a cross-functional proposal that combined digital footprint reduction, reputational risk monitoring, and discreet personal data remediation. By aligning this initiative with the company's brand protection strategy and executive wellness program, the leader secured buy-in from Communications, HR, and Legal. This broader, integrated approach demonstrated strategic credibility, addressing safety, brand integrity, and executive productivity in one coordinated solution.

Strategic credibility is the final dimension in our model, but leadership effectiveness is never the sum of isolated parts. The true strength of a protector-leader lies in the seamless integration of operational vigilance, dynamic decision-making, emotional composure, and strategic credibility into a single, adaptive leadership style. When these dimensions operate in harmony, leaders can fluidly transition between tactical command, strategic advising, empathetic team leadership, and high-level organizational influence. This integration transforms individual competencies into a complete capability, one that enables protector-leaders to safeguard people and purpose with agility, precision, and lasting impact.

THE POWER OF INTEGRATED LEADERSHIP

The four dimensions, operational vigilance, dynamic decision-making, emotional composure, and strategic credibility, are complementary pillars that, when combined, form robust, effective protective leadership. Mastery requires continuous personal and professional development, enabling protector-leaders to move fluidly among roles as strategic advisors, operational commanders, empathetic managers, and influential communicators. General Stanley McChrystal reinforced this in Team of Teams, observing that "A leader's role is no longer just to command

and control, but also to shape the environment," emphasizing integrated multidimensional fluency as essential in contemporary leadership.[13] This level of leadership fluency ensures protector-leaders can manage risks, navigate complex dynamics, and safeguard both people and organizational purpose with exceptional skill. Together, these four dimensions create the architecture of effective protective leadership. But architecture alone is not enough, it must be supported by the traits that give it strength, adaptability, and presence in daily practice. In the next section, we'll explore the core traits that bring these dimensions to life, enabling protector-leaders to apply them consistently and credibly in real-world situations.

CORE TRAITS OF PROTECTION LEADERSHIP

Effective protective leadership demands a unique blend of personal and professional competencies. The transition from tactical operator to strategic influencer isn't defined merely by adopting new tools or techniques, but rather by cultivating distinct leadership traits that inspire trust, manage complexity, and strategically guide organizational decisions. Protector-leaders who embody these core traits elevate their effectiveness from operational response to proactive strategic guidance, positioning themselves as indispensable advisors who bridge security expertise with executive leadership.

Each of the following traits, Command Presence, Diplomacy, Operational Excellence, EQ, Active Listening, Strategic Framing, Identity, Influence, and Self-Regulation, is integral to protective leadership. Together, these attributes enable leaders to navigate complex organizational dynamics, communicate clearly across diverse stakeholders, and sustain strategic resilience even amidst uncertainty and risk.

Each core trait enhances leadership effectiveness distinctly. Beginning with Command Presence, protector-leaders project the authority necessary to guide teams decisively through crises.

Command Presence

Command presence projects authority, clarity, and decisiveness, particularly in crisis scenarios. The U.S. Marine Corps describes command presence as "the projection of confidence, competence, and decisiveness that inspires others during critical moments."[14] Retired Navy SEAL Jocko Willink succinctly states, "Calm is contagious."[15]

During the Second World War, Winston Churchill's long-serving bodyguard, Walter H. Thompson, exemplified command presence by maintaining a constant, composed vigilance under conditions of extreme risk. Tasked with protecting Churchill during the Blitz, wartime conferences abroad, and numerous assassination plots, Thompson's steady demeanor and visible assurance not only safeguarded his principal physically but also bolstered Churchill's own confidence to appear publicly and lead decisively in moments of national peril.[16]

Diplomacy

Diplomacy allows leaders to subtly navigate internal complexities and resolve sensitive interpersonal dynamics. Robert Greene's The 16 Laws of Power reinforces that understanding and influencing people subtly is critical for effective leadership.[17] Effective diplomacy proactively resolves potential conflicts and strategically manages relationships across complex organizational structures.

An essential component of effective diplomacy in protective leadership is high cultural intelligence (CQ) which is the ability to navigate diverse cultural landscapes adeptly. Leaders with strong CQ demonstrate enhanced empathy, adaptability, and nuanced communication skills, fostering meaningful relationships with diverse teams and international stakeholders. Erin Meyer, in *The Culture Map*, emphasizes the importance of cultural fluency for global leaders: "When interacting with someone from another culture, try to watch more, listen more, and speak less."[18] Protector-leaders operating globally must develop a detailed understanding of cultural contexts, customs, expectations, and communication styles. This cultural sensitivity ensures protective strategies remain respectful, contextually appropriate, and widely adopted within diverse organizational environments.

Operational Excellence

Operational excellence involves meticulous planning, disciplined execution, continuous improvement, and resilience. According to McKinsey & Company, operational excellence enhances security effectiveness and positively impacts broader organizational performance.[19] Effective leaders construct reliable frameworks that ensure consistent performance, independent of individual heroics.

The planning and execution of the D-Day invasion in 1944 showcased unparalleled operational excellence. Allied commanders coordinated a massive and complex operation across land, sea, and air, integrating logistics, intelligence, and timing with precision, achievements that turned the tide of the war in Europe.

Emotional Intelligence (EQ)

Daniel Goleman defines EQ as "the ability to manage ourselves and our relationships effectively."[20] Protector-leaders leverage EQ to empathize rapidly, manage stressful dynamics, and facilitate decision-making under pressure. EQ directly enhances diplomatic effectiveness and fosters team cohesion.

On November 22, 1963, U.S. Secret Service agent Clint Hill demonstrated extraordinary emotional composure during the assassination of President John F. Kennedy. Assigned to protect First Lady Jacqueline Kennedy, Hill reacted instantly when shots rang out, leaping onto the presidential limousine, shielding both Kennedys with his own body as the vehicle accelerated toward the hospital. His instinctive and selfless action, performed amid chaos and mortal danger, reflects the ultimate standard of composure under fire for protective professionals.[21]

Active Listening

Active listening requires fully absorbing, comprehending, thoughtfully responding, and remembering information communicated. This skill reduces misunderstandings, builds trust, and provides critical contextual understanding. Leaders practicing active listening display humility and openness, deepening their credibility and influence.

Franklin D. Roosevelt's "fireside chats" during the Great Depression and World War II exemplified active listening on a national scale. By responding directly to public concerns and explaining policies in plain language, he bridged the gap between government and citizens, fostering trust and unity.[22]

Strategic Framing

Strategic framing translates tactical complexities into meaningful business consequences. Effective protector-leaders communicate security impacts clearly, aligning them with executive priorities, continuity, reputation, and strategic stability. Strategic framing allows security considerations to become integral elements of executive decision-making.

In 1961, President John F. Kennedy reframed the space race not simply as a technological competition, but as a matter of national purpose and human achievement.[23] His clear articulation of the moon-landing goal galvanized political will, secured funding, and inspired a generation to rally behind a challenging yet transformative objective.

By prioritizing ethical considerations, protector-leaders not only mitigate reputational risk but strengthen organizational integrity, inspire deeper trust from stakeholders, and solidify their strategic influence. Ethical self-regulation thus becomes a cornerstone of protective leadership identity, reinforcing credibility and ensuring sustained strategic impact.

General Dwight D. Eisenhower, as Supreme Allied Commander in World War II, skillfully balanced military strategy with coalition politics. His ability to regulate personal frustrations, maintain unity among diverse Allied leaders, and project a consistent vision kept the coalition aligned through the war's most critical campaigns.[24]

Possessing these traits is essential, but even the strongest capabilities require validation. The most effective leaders ensure their strengths are measurable, visible, and aligned with organizational goals.

METRICS FOR STRATEGIC SUCCESS

Effective protective leadership extends beyond immediate operational outcomes and crisis prevention. True strategic leadership demands precise metrics capable of quantifying intangible aspects such as organizational impact, resilience, and credibility. Peter Drucker is credited with observing, "What gets measured gets managed," a maxim that captures his broader principle that measurement drives focus and performance.[26] Douglas Hubbard further reinforces this by stating, "If it matters, it can be measured."[25] Hubbard's principle encourages protector-leaders to rigorously define meaningful metrics, even for seemingly intangible elements like stakeholder confidence or organizational resilience.

Leveraging Hubbard's methodology, protector-leaders should apply three critical questions to determine effective metrics:

What decisions will this measurement inform?
How much uncertainty is acceptable?
What is the cost of measurement compared to the value of reduced uncertainty?

Using these criteria, practical strategic metrics might include:

Stakeholder Satisfaction and Confidence Surveys
Utilize structured expert judgment and Bayesian statistics updating to assess internal stakeholder trust and perceived effectiveness rigorously. Hubbard's expert calibration method can significantly reduce biases inherent in subjective feedback.

Frequency and Effectiveness of Cross-Departmental Collaboration
Measure cross-departmental interactions to evaluate organizational cohesion and integration of security within the broader business. Applying Hubbard's interval estimation techniques ensures measurement accuracy while quantifying collaborative effectiveness.

Adaptive Response Times to Emerging Threats

Track and measure how swiftly and effectively the organization adjusts to new incidents or emerging threats. Bayesian modeling can provide quantifiable insight into agility, responsiveness, and continuous improvement over time.

Retention and Promotion Rates of High-Potential Team Members

Monitor the success rate of mentorship, development pathways, and succession planning efforts. Using Hubbard's approach, leaders can calculate confidence intervals to objectively assess leadership development effectiveness and its strategic impact.

Even well-intentioned measurement programs encounter common pitfalls that must be avoided. The most frequent missteps include concentrating on simple activity counts rather than meaningful outcomes, neglecting to establish baselines or comparative context that give the data relevance, and failing to account for stakeholder perception when validating or socializing internal metrics. Hubbard's decision-focused approach, emphasizing calibration, context, and iterative refinement, helps avoid these traps and ensures that metrics inform action rather than just record activity.

Mini-Case Study

A corporate protection team sought approval for a dedicated protective intelligence analyst to anticipate and mitigate travel risks for executives. Instead of relying on general security arguments, the team presented data showing that early intelligence efforts in the previous 18 months had prevented nine potential disruptions, saved approximately 120 executive work hours, and avoided $240,000 in travel rebooking costs. Framing the proposal in terms of business continuity and cost avoidance secured budget approval in a single meeting, demonstrating the power of decision-relevant metrics in influencing executive decisions.

Implementing these rigorous measurement methods ensures that protector-leaders can confidently demonstrate their strategic value, enhance proactive accountability, and maintain clear alignment between tactical execution and overarching organizational objectives. Presenting clear, decision-relevant metrics not only demonstrates operational performance but also builds Strategic Credibility, the ability to communicate value in terms executives understand and trust.

Metrics provide external proof of leadership effectiveness. Yet the internal discipline of identity, influence, and self-regulation forms the core of how those results are achieved and sustained.

IDENTITY, INFLUENCE, AND SELF-REGULATION

Transitioning into leadership necessitates a profound psychological shift, from tactical validation to strategic enablement. Leaders must relinquish ego-driven measures of success for outcome-focused validation, embracing ambiguity and regulating personal emotional responses. Stanley McChrystal highlights this transformation in Team of Teams: "A leader's role is no longer just to command and control, but also to shape the environment."[26]

At the heart of this shift lies ethical decision-making, the consistent practice of integrity, moral courage, and principled judgment under pressure. Ethical leadership extends beyond legality and compliance; it encompasses nuanced, values-driven decisions that shape organizational culture and trust. McChrystal emphasizes, "Character is the essential core of leadership." Protector-leaders consistently demonstrate moral clarity, making transparent decisions, publicly owning their choices, and fostering cultures that empower ethical courage across their teams.

By prioritizing ethical considerations, protector-leaders not only mitigate reputational risk but strengthen organizational integrity, inspire deeper trust from stakeholders, and solidify their strategic influence. Ethical self-regulation thus becomes a cornerstone of protective leadership identity, reinforcing credibility and ensuring sustained strategic impact.

COMMON LEADERSHIP PITFALLS

The path from tactical operator to strategic leader is rewarding but also laden with challenges. Navigating this transition demands self-awareness, humility, and a willingness to continually learn from successes and setbacks alike. While the traits and dimensions of protective leadership we've explored lay a strong foundation for success, recognizing the cognitive biases that underlie common leadership pitfalls are equally vital.

These pitfalls often stem from unconscious biases, mental shortcuts, or blind spots that can impede judgment and decision-making. For protector-leaders, one particularly relevant bias is the Dunning-Kruger Effect, a cognitive phenomenon wherein individuals with limited experience in certain strategic areas may mistakenly overestimate their competence.[27] This misplaced confidence can undermine effective leadership transitions, creating vulnerabilities within protective operations and strategic planning.

Recognizing and actively addressing these pitfalls, and the biases underpinning them, is crucial for sustained leadership credibility and effectiveness. Let's explore each pitfall, understanding its roots, consequences, and how to thoughtfully navigate and overcome them.

Resistance to Adaptive Change

Variation is constant, especially within protection professions. Leaders resistant to adapting new strategies, tools, or mindsets risk becoming obsolete. Often driven by status quo bias, a preference for familiar methods, this resistance can blind leaders to emerging threats. Historical examples abound where leaders, overly confident in proven strategies, failed to recognize evolving dangers, resulting in preventable organizational vulnerabilities. Protector-leaders must consciously cultivate adaptability, intentionally seeking innovation, fresh perspectives, and embracing strategic responsiveness.

Over-Reliance on Tactical Experience

While tactical proficiency provides essential foundational skills, exclusive reliance on past tactical successes can inadvertently trigger the Dunning-Kruger Effect. Leaders may falsely assume their past performance guarantees future strategic competence, creating critical blind spots. Strategic credibility requires clearly connecting tactical skills to broader organizational goals and understanding when tactical expertise alone is insufficient. Protector-leaders should regularly seek feedback, training, and mentorship, continuously calibrating their self-assessments to more accurately reflect evolving strategic responsibilities.

Failure to Delegate

Delegation is not merely about managing tasks, it's a cornerstone of effective leadership and organizational growth. Leaders hesitant to delegate often exhibit biases such as the illusion of control, believing outcomes are more predictable when personally managed. This reluctance stifles professional development, creates operational bottlenecks, and diminishes team capacity. Protector-leaders must consciously build trust in their teams, viewing delegation as a strategic opportunity to foster growth, initiative, and collective accountability.

Poor Translation of Risk

Effective strategic communication is crucial, yet many leaders falter by communicating risk primarily in technical or tactical terms. This habit often arises from expert bias, where leaders mistakenly assume others share their specialized understanding. This can alienate executives whose language revolves around continuity, profitability, and reputation. Protector-leaders must actively practice strategic framing, translating security concerns into relatable business impacts to ensure protection initiatives resonate with executive stakeholders.

Neglecting Broader Stakeholders

Successful protection leadership requires engaging key internal stakeholders, human resources, legal teams, communications departments, and others influencing security policies. Leaders neglecting these relationships may inadvertently suffer from silo bias, underestimating the influence of external departments. Such oversight can result in unforeseen barriers. Protector-leaders should actively cultivate cross-departmental relationships, understand organizational dynamics, and ensure comprehensive stakeholder engagement to secure strategic alignment.

Misalignment with Organizational Culture

Even robust protective strategies fail if they clash with organizational culture. Leaders who overlook this alignment may fall prey to confirmation bias, selectively interpreting feedback to support existing strategies rather than objectively evaluating cultural compatibility. Protector-leaders must consistently align security practices with organizational values, fostering security cultures that employees willingly embrace, ensuring long-term effectiveness and compliance.

Paralysis Due to Fear of Failure

Fear of failure can paralyze leaders, stifling innovation and strategic growth. This fear often reflects loss aversion bias, wherein leaders disproportionately weigh potential losses over potential gains. While protective risk is significant, strategic leadership necessitates calculated risk-taking, experimentation, and resilience amidst setbacks. Protector-leaders should deliberately cultivate psychological safety, framing manageable failures as valuable learning opportunities and fostering a resilient, innovative, and strategically agile environment.

NAVIGATING BIAS AND BUILDING STRATEGIC RESILIENCE

Recognition of these biases and pitfalls is foundational, but actively engaging with them differentiates truly effective protective leaders. By openly acknowledging cognitive blind spots, such as the Dunning-Kruger Effect, leaders cultivate a culture of continuous learning, humility, and strategic agility. Transparent self-assessment and purposeful strategic adjustments reinforce a leader's credibility, ensuring sustained organizational resilience and effectiveness.

Ultimately, the mindful management of cognitive biases is integral to successfully navigating the leadership journey. Awareness and humility, paired with intentional adaptive strategies, empower protector-leaders to transition effectively from tacticians to strategists, shaping resilient, responsive, and trusted organizations.

While avoiding pitfalls is important, no leader's journey is without setbacks. The difference lies in how those setbacks are approached and what is learned from them.

FAILING FAST VERSUS FAILING SMALL

In tactical protection environments, the concept of failure carries existential weight. Unlike industries where iterative failures drive innovation and growth, protective missions inherently involve higher stakes, with the ultimate potential cost being catastrophic, the injury or loss of a principal. Consequently, tactical professionals are naturally risk-averse, conditioned by the reality that a single failure may be irreversible.

Yet, transitioning from tactician to strategic leader requires recalibrating perceptions of risk and failure. Strategic leadership is not defined by the absence of setbacks, but rather by the disciplined use of controlled failures as vital opportunities for organizational learning and improvement. Eric Ries advocates the concept of "failing fast" in his book *The Lean Startup*, highlighting the strategic advantage of iterative learning from manageable setbacks.[28] Similarly, Jeff Bezos emphasizes bold experimentation and iterative failures as essential drivers of innovation, asserting that increased experimentation directly correlates with increased inventiveness.[29]

Within protection leadership, however, the notion of failing fast must be carefully reframed as "failing small." Leaders intentionally design controlled environmental training simulations, tabletop exercises, and realistic scenario drills that provide safe opportunities to test assumptions and strategic approaches. These controlled "small failures" build resilience, adaptability, and preparedness without compromising safety or organizational integrity.

Controlled failures enhance resilience, setting the stage for the broader principle of antifragility, where teams not only withstand volatility but actively strengthen through structured exposure to challenges.

Together, antifragility, the OODA Loop, and Stoic discipline form a philosophy that strengthens every protective decision. When combined with the four dimensions, they create a complete leadership model.

EMBRACING ANTIFRAGILITY

The concept of antifragility, as introduced by Nassim Nicholas Taleb, offers a powerful philosophical framework supporting strategic resilience. Taleb argues that robust organizations do more than merely survive stressors; they actively grow stronger through exposure to volatility and controlled challenges:

"Antifragility is beyond resilience or robustness. The resilient resists shocks and stays the same; the antifragile gets better."[30]

For protection leaders, antifragility translates into systematically exposing teams and procedures to realistic but controlled stressors, transforming small setbacks into deliberate opportunities for reinforcing organizational strength and adaptive capacity. This approach fundamentally shifts protective teams from being reactive to proactively resilient, anticipating threats and thriving through adaptability and continual improvement.

Antifragility prepares protector-leaders to grow from adversity, but strategic adaptation requires agility. Here, the OODA Loop framework enhances rapid responsiveness, providing tactical clarity amidst evolving threats.

THE OODA LOOP: ENHANCING AGILITY AND RESPONSIVENESS

Strategic leaders also benefit from Colonel John Boyd's OODA Loop: Observe, Orient, Decide, Act. The OODA Loop emphasizes agility and continuous iterative learning. By rapidly cycling through observation, orientation, decision, and action, protective leaders develop a strategic advantage over evolving threats. As Boyd articulated, adaptability and rapid responsiveness can consistently outpace adversaries operating within rigid or outdated paradigms.[31]

For example, executive protection teams using OODA principles can swiftly recalibrate plans during rapidly evolving crises, such as sudden geopolitical shifts or cyber threats. Continuous iteration through Boyd's loop fosters tactical agility, strategic responsiveness, and adaptive planning, ensuring teams learn swiftly and effectively from each small failure or operational adjustment.

While the OODA Loop empowers tactical agility, enduring strategic leadership also demands emotional resilience. Thus, the philosophy of Stoicism complements tactical frameworks by cultivating disciplined emotional composure and reflective insight.

STOICISM: EMOTIONAL DISCIPLINE AND REFLECTIVE PRACTICE

Complementing antifragility and the OODA Loop, Stoicism provides protective leaders with an invaluable philosophical toolset focused on emotional composure, resilience, and reflective learning. Stoic philosopher Marcus Aurelius emphasized maintaining equanimity and clear judgment in adversity:

> The impediment to action advances action. What stands in the way becomes the way.[32]

Protection leaders practicing Stoicism embrace setbacks as essential and informative rather than purely negative events. Through disciplined reflection, Stoicism encourages leaders to objectively analyze small failures, drawing strategic lessons and enhancing emotional resilience. This reflective practice ensures that every controlled setback contributes meaningfully to long-term organizational effectiveness, guiding protector-leaders toward strategic maturity and emotional strength in crisis conditions.

INTEGRATION: FROM TACTICIAN TO STRATEGIC LEADER

The deliberate integration of antifragility, the OODA Loop, and Stoic philosophy represents a structured pathway from tactical caution toward strategic adaptability. Leaders begin to see controlled failures as deliberate, critical stepping stones toward organizational resilience, continuous learning, and adaptive agility. Each element reinforces a critical aspect of protective leadership: antifragility establishes a mindset that embraces controlled volatility; the OODA Loop ensures tactical agility; and Stoicism nurtures the emotional composure needed to manage crises effectively.

Through intentional, disciplined exposure to controlled setbacks, protection leaders systematically build stronger, more agile organizations. Over time, this iterative learning approach reframes perceptions of risk, transforming teams from reactive responders into proactive strategic advisors. By cultivating an adaptive philosophy underpinned by these foundational concepts, protector-leaders master the nuanced balance required to lead effectively in environments where stakes remain perpetually high.

REFLECTIVE STUDY: NAVIGATING CRISIS

Imagine your organization faces credible reports of potential disruptions at an upcoming major industry conference, significant enough to cause concern among stakeholders but not explicitly targeting your principal. Your principal, known for bold leadership and visible advocacy of organizational resilience, firmly intends to deliver their keynote in-person, viewing their presence as symbolic of confidence and continuity. However, internal stakeholders, influenced by media speculation, shareholder anxiety, and perceived reputational risks, increasingly pressure you to recommend shifting to a virtual presentation.

Meditate on the following:

Strategically Navigate

How do you strategically navigate competing internal narratives (security concerns vs. strategic visibility), managing stakeholder relationships while preserving executive credibility and organizational resilience?

Bias Awareness

Which cognitive biases might you or your stakeholders be experiencing (e.g., loss aversion, confirmation bias, Dunning-Kruger Effect)? How do you thoughtfully address these biases in your decision-making and strategic framing?

Practical Data

What practical data points or strategic business impacts can you clearly articulate to the principal and executive stakeholders to inform a balanced decision without appearing overly risk-averse or reactive?

Having explored tactical, strategic, and philosophical foundations of protector-leadership, we now conclude by elevating the protector's deeper purpose, recognizing that effective leadership transcends mere risk management, fundamentally shaping organizational resilience and integrity.

ESSENTIAL TRAITS OF HIGH-IMPACT LEADERS

The most effective protector-leaders understand that their influence rarely comes from authority alone; it comes from the trust they earn and the strategic guidance they provide. They recognize that leadership in this space requires a constant balance between vigilance and agility, anticipating threats before they surface, responding with clarity when they do, and adapting quickly as situations evolve. They also know that credibility is built by translating security considerations into executive language, framing protective strategies in terms of business continuity, reputation, and growth rather than focusing solely on threats. These leaders rigorously measure and clearly communicate, using credible metrics to quantify intangible value such as stakeholder trust and organizational resilience, because they understand that what is measured well gains executive attention. Above all, they maintain composure, knowing that calm is contagious; their steady presence becomes an anchor for teams and stakeholders alike, enabling clear thinking under pressure and amplifying their overall impact. These qualities shape how protector-leaders operate day to day, but it is their underlying purpose that ultimately defines their impact.

ELEVATING THE PROTECTOR'S PURPOSE

Effective protective leadership manages complexity, mitigates risk, and unlocks strategic opportunities. Yet, the true calling of a protector-leader goes beyond tactics, systems, and procedures; it is rooted in purpose, integrity, and vision. Protector-leaders stand as guardians not just of individuals, but of confidence, continuity, and organizational mission. They guide quietly yet decisively, their impact resonating far beyond the boundaries of traditional protective roles.

The protector-leader's charge is profoundly selfless, often invisible, yet unmistakably essential. Your work ensures that organizational cultures thrive, executives confidently lead, and teams courageously innovate. In navigating uncertainty with humility, in responding to crises with composure, and in framing risk with clarity, you transcend mere safety, you empower strategic success.

As you embrace this charge, recognize the influence you hold: to transform tactical vigilance into strategic insight, reactive caution into proactive resilience, and protective measures into meaningful contributions to your organization's broader strategic narrative. Every challenge you face is an invitation to grow stronger, every setback an opportunity to reinforce organizational resilience, and every decision an act of purposeful stewardship.

The path ahead is challenging yet immensely rewarding. Your adaptability, strategic credibility, and emotional composure will not only safeguard lives but will shape the very trajectory of your organization. In accepting this protector's charge, you choose not merely to guard, but to inspire, guide, and illuminate the way forward.

With the mindset shifts, core traits, and multidimensional leadership frameworks explored in this chapter, we close Section I: The Landscape of Leadership and Risk. In Chapter 1, we examined the new risk landscape and the strategic role it demands. In Chapter 2, we explored the personal recalibration required to transition from tactical operator to trusted advisor. Here, we have defined the essential traits, dimensions, and philosophies that form the foundation of protective leadership at the highest level.

We now move from mindset to mastery, from understanding what leadership in protection is, to learning how to consistently apply it in the real world. We will explore the essential competencies, tools, and actionable strategies that allow protector-leaders to influence across the organization, lead in moments of crisis, and build enduring trust with principals, stakeholders, and teams. Carry these principles with you; they are the compass by which every skill and tactic that follows will be measured.

NOTES

1 John C. Maxwell, *The 21 Irrefutable Laws of Leadership* (Nashville: Thomas Nelson, 1998).
2 Peter Thiel with Blake Masters, *Zero to One: Notes on Startups, or How to Build the Future* (New York: Crown Business, 2014).
3 Dan Heath, *Upstream: The Quest to Solve Problems Before They Happen* (New York: Avid Reader Press, 2020).
4 Jim Mattis with Bing West, *Call Sign Chaos: Learning to Lead* (New York: Random House, 2019).
5 Clayton M. Christensen, *The Innovator's Dilemma: When New Technologies Cause Great Firms to Fail* (Boston: Harvard Business Review Press, 1997).
6 Graham T. Allison, *Essence of Decision: Explaining the Cuban Missile Crisis* (New York: Pearson, 1971).
7 Robert Coram, *Boyd: The Fighter Pilot Who Changed the Art of War* (New York: Back Bay Books, 2002).
8 Mark Bowden, *The Finish: The Killing of Osama bin Laden* (New York: Atlantic Monthly Press, 2012).
9 Daniel Goleman, *Emotional Intelligence: Why It Can Matter More Than IQ* (New York: Bantam Books, 1995).
10 Gene Kranz, *Failure Is Not an Option: Mission Control from Mercury to Apollo 10 and Beyond* (New York: Simon & Schuster, 2000).
11 Colin Powell, *It Worked for Me: In Life and Leadership* (New York: Harper, 2012).

12 Stephen E. Ambrose, *Eisenhower: Soldier and President* (New York: Simon & Schuster, 1990).
13 M Stanley McChrystal with Tantum Collins, David Silverman, and Chris Fussell, *Team of Teams: New Rules of Engagement for a Complex World* (New York: Portfolio, 2015).
14 United States Marine Corps, *Leading Marines* (MCWP 6–11) (Washington, DC: Headquarters, U.S. Marine Corps, 2001).
15 Jocko Willink, *Leadership Strategy and Tactics: Field Manual* (New York: St. Martin's Press, 2020).
16 Walter H. Thompson, *I Was Churchill's Bodyguard* (London: Coronet Books, 1955).
17 Robert Greene, *The 48 Laws of Power* (New York: Viking Press, 1998).
18 Erin Meyer, *The Culture Map: Breaking Through the Invisible Boundaries of Global Business* (New York: PublicAffairs, 2014).
19 Bain & Company, "Operational Excellence: Managing Performance in the Oil and Gas Industry," Bain & Company, accessed on December 14, 2025, https://www.bain.com/insights/operational-excellence-managing-performance-in-the-oil-and-gas-industry/.
20 Daniel Goleman, *Emotional Intelligence: Why It Can Matter More Than IQ* (New York: Bantam Books, 1995).
21 Clint Hill and Lisa McCubbin, *Five Days in November* (New York: Gallery Books, 2013).
22 Jean Edward Smith, *FDR* (New York: Random House, 2007).
23 Kennedy, John F. *Special Message to the Congress on Urgent National Needs.* May 25, 1961. John F. Kennedy Presidential Library and Museum.
24 Stephen E. Ambrose, *Eisenhower: Soldier and President* (New York: Simon & Schuster, 1990).
25 Douglas W. Hubbard, *How to Measure Anything: Finding the Value of Intangibles in Business* (Hoboken, NJ: Wiley, 2007).
26 Stanley McChrystal with Tantum Collins, David Silverman, and Chris Fussell, *Team of Teams: New Rules of Engagement for a Complex World* (New York: Portfolio, 2015).
27 Justin Kruger and David Dunning, "Unskilled and Unaware of It: How Difficulties in Recognizing One's Own Incompetence Lead to Inflated Self-Assessments," *Journal of Personality and Social Psychology* 77, no. 6 (1999): 1121–1134.
28 Eric Ries, *The Lean Startup: How Today's Entrepreneurs Use Continuous Innovation to Create Radically Successful Businesses* (New York: Crown Business, 2011).

29 Brad Stone, *The Everything Store: Jeff Bezos and the Age of Amazon* (New York: Little, Brown and Company, 2013).
30 Nassim Nicholas Taleb, *Antifragile: Things That Gain from Disorder* (New York: Random House, 2012).
31 Robert Coram, *Boyd: The Fighter Pilot Who Changed the Art of War* (New York: Back Bay Books, 2002).
32 Marcus Aurelius, *Meditations*, trans. Gregory Hays (New York: Modern Library, 2002).

CHAPTER 4

Leadership Mindset: From Reactive to Proactive

In the high-stakes world of executive protection (EP), the difference between safety and catastrophe often hinges on a leader's mindset. For decades, protectors operated reactively. Trained to respond swiftly to threats as they emerged, neutralizing danger with precision and discipline. However, in today's volatile risk landscape, where threats evolve faster than reflexes, reactive leadership is no longer enough. The modern protector must anticipate, prevent, and prepare, shifting from a mindset of response to one of foresight. This chapter explores that transformation: from reactive to proactive leadership, a change that redefines not just how protectors operate but how they lead.

Proactive leadership in EP is about seeing risks before they surface and shaping the environment, so they never have the chance to materialize. It's the difference between being caught off guard by a sudden protest and quietly adjusting a principal's schedule days in advance, guided by credible intelligence. This is more than refining tactics; it is a fundamental shift in how a leader thinks, decides, and acts. As Brian Gottlieb writes in *Beyond the Hammer*, "The most effective leaders don't just react to what is, they prepare for what could be."[1] For those leading EP programs, that preparation becomes the heartbeat of operational success.

This chapter builds on the protector's transformation from tactical operator to strategic advisor, showing how leaders embed a proactive mindset into every decision. We'll explore the habits and disciplines that make anticipation second nature, supported by real-world stories, structured frameworks, and practical steps. Through these pages, you'll see why foresight is not simply a competitive advantage, it is the foundation of modern EP leadership, and how you can fully step into it.

DOI: 10.4324/9781003670704-5

DEFINING PROACTIVE LEADERSHIP

To lead in this new risk environment, one must adopt a mindset that isn't simply responsive but predictive. True leadership lies not in reacting better, but in ensuring there's nothing left to react to. Proactive leadership in EP is the disciplined practice of anticipating and preventing threats before they escalate, using intelligence, foresight, and preparation to shape outcomes. Unlike reactive leadership, which responds to crises as they unfold, predictive leadership seeks to eliminate or mitigate risks at their source. It asks not "What is happening?" but "What could happen next?"

We now operate in a hybrid threat environment. Physical risks, reputational sabotage, cyber breaches, and ideological violence converge into a single operating picture. Threats emerge earlier, signal more subtly, and travel faster. The traditional model of "observe, assess, respond" is too slow. Leaders must adopt a posture of "listen, anticipate, influence." This shift is both strategic and psychological, requiring a departure from the comfort of tactical control to the ambiguity of strategic influence.

Predictive leadership is not guesswork. It is a deliberate, disciplined approach to anticipating risk, built on intelligence, pattern recognition, behavioral awareness, and scenario-planning. It requires leaders to think like strategists, not just tacticians, and to prioritize invisible prevention over visible presence. The most effective protector-leaders prevent disruption so completely that the principal never feels its presence.

THE STRATEGIC SHIFT

The shift toward predictive leadership in EP marks a fundamental transformation in how risk is managed. It begins with three key changes in approach, each reshaping traditional assumptions and demanding a more forward-leaning posture.

The first is a shift from control to influence. While tactical leadership focuses on managing movement and detail, predictive leadership centers on shaping risk posture, perception, and decision-making space. Leaders must persuade stakeholders, from principals to C-suite executives, to align with proactive measures, often without formal authority. For instance, convincing a CEO to cancel a public event due to online threats may require framing the risk in terms of reputational harm or stock volatility.

Second, the role of the leader evolves from tactical executor to strategic planner. Rather than reacting in real time, securing venues, or managing motorcades, strategic leadership looks months ahead, anticipating threats like geopolitical unrest or disinformation campaigns that could disrupt operations. This shift enables teams to shape the conditions under which protection occurs, rather than simply respond.

Third, effective leadership moves from visible presence to invisible prevention. The best outcomes are silent victories where threats are neutralized without the principal ever knowing. A rerouted travel plan based on protest intelligence, for example, ensures safety without drama, demonstrating the value of prevention over reaction.

These changes are supported by key tools and collaborative frameworks. Threat, Vulnerability, and Risk Assessments (TVRAs) serve as dynamic planning models, integrating physical, digital, and reputational risk factors in real time. A TVRA for an overseas trip might account for protest threats, cyber exposure, and media sensitivity, constantly updated to reflect evolving conditions.

Technology also plays a critical role. Protective intelligence platforms must mature beyond merely identifying threats. They need to become autonomous anticipatory systems, capable of detecting early signals like changes in social media sentiment, dark web chatter, or disinformation campaigns. These tools enable protection teams to act before a threat fully forms, such as uncovering early indicators of insider risk before it escalates into a breach of trust or data exposure.

Finally, predictive leadership thrives on cross-functional planning, a deliberate approach that integrates diverse expertise to navigate the complex landscape of EP. Within an organization, close collaboration with HR, IT, Legal, and Communications teams creates a unified posture, ensuring a cohesive response to potential threats. Whether securing online presence or coordinating physical safety measures, integrated planning ensures holistic protection and response. By fostering regular interdepartmental meetings, sharing real-time threat intelligence, and aligning goals across functions, leaders can anticipate threats, adapt to evolving challenges, and maintain a proactive stance. This synergy not only enhances security protocols but also builds a resilient framework that safeguards executives and organizations alike.

In this model, leadership is no longer defined by reaction but by anticipation and influence. The highest level of protection comes not from responding to visible threats, but from preventing them before they emerge.

CORE PILLARS OF PROACTIVE LEADERSHIP

Proactive leadership is defined as the disciplined practice of anticipating challenges, preventing issues before they escalate, and using intelligence, foresight, and preparation to shape outcomes. This approach is increasingly vital in EP, where protector-leaders must safeguard high-profile individuals from potential threats, such as physical attacks, cyber harassment, and geopolitical risks. In 2025, the security landscape is marked by rapid technological advancements, including artificial intelligence (AI)-driven analytics and cybersecurity integration, as well as evolving global threats, making proactive leadership essential.

The shift from reactive to proactive leadership is crucial for protector-leaders, as it enhances safety, reduces risks, and ensures organizational stability. Reactive leadership focuses on responding to incidents after they occur, often leading to higher costs and reputational damage. In contrast, proactive leadership anticipates threats and takes preemptive measures, aligning with the needs of modern EP.

Presented below, these core pillars of proactive leadership were developed through a comprehensive approach grounded in both theory and practice. Addressing today's evolving physical and digital security, each is defined, its importance explained, and its role in supporting the shift from a reactive to a proactive mindset for protector-leaders is highlighted.

Strategic Foresight and Planning:

Strategic foresight means more than having a plan; it means building one flexible enough to shift with reality. It is about spotting problems before they metastasize and designing the response before it's needed. In EP work, this isn't theory. It is risk-mapping, narrowing exposure windows, scenario-planning, and putting safeguards in place early. You're not just bracing for impact; you are changing the outcome.

Intelligence-Driven Decision-Making

Good instincts matter. But good data makes decisions sharper. Intelligence-led leadership leans on continuous monitoring, behavioral signals, and real-time updates to catch threats in motion, not after the fact. Whether scanning digital chatter or spotting changes in travel patterns, the goal is to act before a headline writes itself. Proactive leaders turn information into timing, and timing into safety.

Resilience and Crisis Readiness

Being resilient doesn't mean bouncing back. It means staying upright when the ground shifts. Protection leaders can't afford to freeze in the fog. They train for chaos, adapt in real time, and make high-pressure calls with clarity. Regular testing and simulations, sharp routines, and a culture that doesn't flinch in uncertainty are not pro forma actions. They are how teams stay operational when the unexpected arrives early.

Collaborative Leadership and Team Building

No protector leads alone. Coordination is the job. Whether it's syncing with venue staff, digital analysts, or local responders, collaboration is the glue that holds a protection operation together. Proactive leaders build trust, define roles, and clear the fog before it settles. The result? Fewer blind spots, faster response, and a team that moves with a shared fate, wired to the same mission. Because it is.

Ethical Integrity and Professionalism

Protection leadership runs on trust. Not just from principals but across teams and stakeholders. Ethics here is not a feel-good add-on; it is what separates trusted protectors from transactional ones. From how data is handled to how privacy is preserved, every action counts. Proactive leaders do the right thing when no one is watching; knowing credibility is their real currency.

Innovation and Technological Proficiency

If your tools are behind, so is your protection. Leaders today need to embrace change, not chase it. That means understanding how digital risks bleed into physical ones, and how new technology, such as AI, open-source intelligence, and real-time monitoring, can be harnessed to stay ahead. It is not about loving gadgets. It's about staying relevant, responsive, and ready.

Emphasizing anticipation, preparation, and adaptability, these pillars guide protector-leaders to anticipate threats, prevent incidents, and ensure safety through strategic planning and intelligence. For example, government agencies like the U.S. Secret Service and DSS exemplify these pillars through their use of advanced work, intelligence-led operations, and crisis readiness.

Recent trends for 2026, such as AI-driven threat intelligence and cybersecurity integration, underscore the importance of Innovation and Technological Proficiency. The shift from reactive to proactive leadership is not only a best practice but a leadership imperative, ensuring that protector-leaders can navigate today's complexities with confidence, ensuring safety, trust, and success in an ever-changing world.

CASE STUDY: SILENT SHIFT

Note: Names and identifying details have been changed to protect confidentiality, as the individual featured remains under an active protective detail.

When Sarah Bennett took over the security program for a rising female tech executive, Elena Vasquez, in 2023, she stepped into a storm.

Vasquez wasn't just known for becoming one of the founders of a quickly growing specialized AI firm, she had become a lightning rod for public scrutiny, particularly from activist groups who accuse her of possessing a techno-utopian vision of the AI technology she was building; specifically, her view that the value of the technology outweighs the threat of "human extinction." In the months prior to Sarah taking charge of the protection detail, there had been multiple direct and indirect threats made to the executive and the company, both online and physical. However, when she arrived, Sarah found a program that was solely built on reacting, not anticipating. And in 2025, that was a dangerous gap.

Having spent 15 years in corporate and private security by then, Sarah understood how exposure worked, how fast it traveled, and how often it was underestimated. When word came that her protectee would be giving a major keynote in Singapore at a global tech summit, Sarah didn't wait for the usual planning window. She started running scenarios months in advance, digging into risk patterns, online sentiment, and even subtle changes in geopolitical tension in the region. The idea wasn't just to build a defense, it was to quietly change the landscape around the founder, to shape the environment before it could shape her.

Part of that strategy included controlling visibility. Sarah worked with the founder's communications team to delay the public announcement of the summit appearance until just a few days out, shrinking the window of opportunity for adversaries dramatically. Behind the scenes, she coordinated with venue security, mapped safe routes through the hotel and venue, and arranged private air transport to eliminate unnecessary exposure. The new approach wasn't about reacting faster. It was about making sure there was nothing to react to in the first place.

As the conference drew closer, online threats had taken a sharper and more critical tone. Two weeks before the summit, Sarah's team picked up on a worrying spike in hostile online chatter. Even more concerning was increased speculation that the founder would be attending the conference, stemming from a fake travel itinerary for the founder and other executives, posted on a common online forum. Not taking any chances, Sarah brought in encrypted communications across all stakeholders and tightened digital hygiene with the founder's staff.

On-site in Singapore, as anticipated through protective intelligence monitoring, a small protest group tried to disrupt the founder before her speech; however, Sarah and her team were prepared for this possibility. Her team calmly executed a pre-planned diversion while quickly rerouting the founder backstage with zero disruption to the event. No panic, no improvising. Just execution.

Through the planning and execution of this trip, success was not predicated on the technology Sarah used or the drills her team had run. It was the atmosphere she created. There was trust between Sarah as a leader, her team, venue security, and the foreign law enforcement counterparts. Everyone knew their lane, and more importantly, knew how it connected to the broader picture. The keynote went off without incident.

In the end, the founder's confidence in the protection program deepened. But, more than that, Sarah had quietly redrawn the map. What once was a vulnerable, reactive posture of the EP team was now a forward-leaning, resilient operation. One that not only identified potential threats but also stayed two steps ahead of them.

RECOGNIZING NARRATIVE WARFARE

This model is critical in today's operating environment, where digital threat convergence has created what researchers call assassination culture—an emerging threat environment where memes, misinformation, and ideological incitement normalize violence against corporate leaders. A 2025 study by the Network Contagion Research Institute revealed that nearly one in three Americans believed it was "somewhat justified" to target high-profile executives like Elon Musk with violence.[2] Following the 2024 murder of UnitedHealth Group's CEO, "Luigi Mangione, the alleged shooter…has become a folk hero to some on social media."[3]

This assassination culture underscores the urgency of predictive leadership. Physical risk is now often preceded by digital narrative, where influence campaigns escalate into reputational damage or targeted violence with little warning. Proactive leaders monitor these narratives using protective intelligence resources to detect early signals of incitement. They also collaborate with communications teams to counter hostile narratives, preventing escalation from digital to physical threats.

The rise of assassination culture also highlights the need for behavioral awareness. Leaders must study adversary behavior, being aware of the rhetoric used by extremist groups or the tactics of lone actors, to anticipate potential risks. For instance, the attacker of the UnitedHealth CEO was driven by a personal grievance amplified by anti-corporate ideology, a pattern detectable through narrative monitoring. By understanding these behavioral cues, leaders can act before threats materialize.

CHALLENGES OF THE MINDSET SHIFT

Transitioning to predictive leadership presents several challenges, particularly for EP professionals trained in tactical precision. As C.S. Lewis stated, "You can't go back and change the beginning, but you can start where you are and change the ending."[4]

First, embracing ambiguity is difficult. Reactive leadership responds to clear threats with defined actions such as securing a perimeter, neutralizing an attacker. Predictive leadership requires sometimes acting on incomplete data, trusting intelligence tools, and making decisions with uncertainty. This can feel counterintuitive to those accustomed to controlling every detail of a protective operation.

Second, organizational resistance is common. Stakeholders accustomed to reactive security measures may question the value of proactive investments, such as intelligence platforms, scenario training, or cross-functional planning. Leaders must overcome this by framing proactivity in business terms. For example, instead of requesting "more intelligence tools," a leader might say, "Investing in predictive analytics reduces our exposure to reputational and operational risks by 20%, ensuring business continuity during market-critical periods."

Third, resource constraints pose a challenge. Proactive leadership requires time, budget, and expertise, often investments that compete with other priorities. Leaders must demonstrate return on investment, such as averting a $5 million crisis through early threat detection, to justify resources. For instance, a protective intelligence platform costing $50,000 annually could prevent reputational harm with multimillion-dollar consequences, a compelling case for the C-suite.

Finally, cultural inertia within teams can hinder proactivity. EP professionals may resist moving beyond tactical roles, preferring familiar routines like advance work or physical security. Leaders must foster a cultural shift through training and incentives while encouraging teams to embrace predictive thinking. As Dan Heath writes in *Upstream*, "The need for heroes arises from the failure to prevent a crisis."[5] Proactive leaders must prioritize prevention over heroism, requiring patience, discipline, and a willingness to act before certainty.

REAL-WORLD APPLICATION: THREAT-INFORMED LEADERSHIP

Predictive leadership isn't just about staying ahead of problems. It's about knowing how to look for them, how to read the signs, and realizing when to act before the stakes get too high. That's the core of threat-informed leadership. Using intelligence not as a sideline feature of your operation, but as a guiding force in shaping decisions. It's how leaders shift from reacting to shaping what happens next.

This isn't theoretical. It's an approach built on three words that carry weight when put into practice: gather, analyze, act. Simple words, but not easy work.

You start by gathering. The signals are everywhere. Buried in open sources within the digital domain, surfacing through dark web channels, hidden in sentiment shifts among employees, or tucked into the fine print of travel logs. Leadership today demands more than awareness. It requires systems that pull in information from places others overlook. Flight tracking data, for example, can expose timing vulnerabilities in an executive's itinerary. Monitoring social media may feel like noise until it's not. Platforms like Ontic or strong internal dashboards can help make that gathering intentional and consistent, not scattershot.

Then comes analysis. This is where sharp leadership separates itself. "Most decisions are not binary, and there are usually better answers waiting to be found if you do the analysis and involve the right people."[6] Not every spike in online chatter is a call to act. Not every anomaly is a threat. It takes experience and good judgment to filter what matters from what doesn't. Behavioral patterns, emerging trends, and a deep understanding of the landscape turn raw data into insight. If a sudden swell of online anger connects back to a known threat actor, it's no longer background noise. It is a blinking red light.

But none of it matters if it stays in the intel report. Acting on what you've learned is where leadership shows up. Threat-informed leaders bring that intelligence into the decision-making process. They influence travel schedules, manage communications strategy, and shape executive exposure with clarity and speed. That might mean reworking an itinerary in response to an emerging protest or advising stakeholders when a quiet risk starts to gain momentum. The key is decisiveness.

What ties it all together is positioning. This kind of leadership doesn't live in fear. It lives in preparation. Just like General McChrystal compares effective risk management to an immune system, with "the circulatory system of communication, the nerves of technology, and the reflexes of planning working in sync to protect the mission."[7] Threat-informed leadership doesn't just preserve safety. It reinforces the credibility of the leader and the mission itself. It's how you create the room to adapt, so when the unexpected comes, you're already moving.

CASE STUDY

Note: Names and identifying details have been changed to protect confidentiality, as the individual featured remains under an active protective detail.

In early 2025, Isabela Moreira assumed leadership of the EP program for Atlântica Energia, a global oil and gas company, based in Brazil, facing mounting geopolitical tension. The company's CEO, André Moreira, was set to travel to West Africa to sign a high-profile offshore exploration agreement with a host nation's government. The deal not only promised significant revenue, but it also attracted criticism from environmental activists and stirred unrest among local communities concerned about economic displacement.

Before Isabela's arrival, security planning for executive travel was handled in a linear fashion: book the trip, conduct a site advance, and react to whatever emerged. Intelligence was considered a supplement, not a driver. Isabela immediately shifted the approach. Three months before departure, she initiated a dynamic threat and vulnerability risk assessment, merging traditional protective measures with deep-dive geopolitical analysis, maritime security intelligence, and social sentiment mapping in Portuguese, Spanish, English, and the region's dominant local language.

The early findings were sobering. Activist groups in the capital were preparing a coordinated demonstration timed to coincide with Moreira's arrival. Intelligence analysts also picked up chatter suggesting that local militia factions, emboldened by a recent uptick in offshore piracy, might view the company's vessel movements as an opportunity for leverage. Complicating matters, leaked internal memos about the exploration deal were circulating online, adding fuel to the activist narrative.

Isabela moved quickly to build a multi-layered security plan. She partnered with the company's shipping operations to reroute supply vessels, reducing predictable patterns that could be exploited. She secured a private hangar for the CEO's arrival to avoid public airport exposure. Working with corporate communications, she advised delaying the official press release until after Moreira's departure, limiting the time activists had to mobilize in-country.

Two days before the trip, protective intelligence confirmed that protests were indeed planned at the central government complex where the signing ceremony would take place. Isabela coordinated with local law enforcement to establish a secure alternate venue inside a naval operations facility, framing it to stakeholders as a logistical upgrade rather than a security concession. The signing went ahead in the new location without incident, while the protest drew media attention elsewhere in the city.

In the post-operation review, Isabela highlighted that the outcome was not achieved through physical security alone. It was the result of integrating maritime intelligence, local and international sentiment analysis, and cross-functional decision-making into the planning cycle. By identifying risks early and quietly reshaping the event's environment, she turned what could have been a volatile flashpoint into an uneventful, business-as-usual engagement.

The operation became a blueprint for Atlântica's new travel security model, one in which threat-informed leadership did not just protect the principal but also preserved the company's reputation and operational momentum in a challenging global arena.

DEVELOPING THE THREAT-INFORMED LEADERSHIP MINDSET

In EP today, leadership is not judged only by how well you manage risk after it appears. It is measured by whether you can see it coming and influence the outcome before it reaches your principal. A threat-informed mindset is not a checklist or a fixed framework. It is a way of thinking and working that blends strategic foresight with disciplined execution. It is alive, constantly adapting, and it thrives on leaders who are willing to look far beyond the next crisis.

It begins with an almost relentless habit of scanning the environment. Leaders must watch for cultural shifts, political changes, and technological leaps that could alter the threat picture without warning. For example, this means more than reading the World Economic Forum's Global Risks Report once a year. It means staying engaged in real time by joining professional associations or industry forums, tracking the early signs of disinformation campaigns, particularly those whose velocity is driven by AI, and following climate activism, as well as monitoring geopolitical tensions. The goal is to connect those patterns back to your principal's reality.

As one author on risk once put it, the costliest way to handle a crisis is to wait until it is at your feet. The leaders who stay safe are the ones who spot the "gray rhinos," a term used to refer to highly probable, high-impact neglected threats, while they are still on the horizon and move early to meet them on their terms.[8] If you know that climate protests are beginning to target certain energy executives, you can adjust travel plans and event participation before the risk becomes immediate.

There is another layer to this approach. Most threats first emerge as stories rather than physical acts. They often spread through social feeds, extremist message boards, or obscure online communities. A threat-informed leader treats narrative monitoring as seriously as physical surveillance. What is being said about your organization or your principal? Who is repeating it? Reputational warfare played into the assassination of the UnitedHealth CEO. That case made clear the importance of spotting and addressing hostile narratives early through data removal, carefully timed messaging, or other steps that strip momentum from the threat.

This mindset changes how a team operates. Standard operating procedures have value, but modern threats require agility. Monthly scenario drills prepare teams for protests outside an event, a sudden doxxing campaign, or a cyber breach that exposes travel plans. These drills should include security, IT, legal, and communications teams so that each part of the organization knows its role. A simulated doxxing campaign is a good simulation. It is not handled by security alone. It calls for immediate action from technical teams, legal counsel, and communications staff to protect both safety and reputation.

A truly threat-informed leader sees all security domains as interconnected. Physical protection, cybersecurity, and reputation management are part of the same system. A reputational attack can quickly escalate into a physical threat. Quarterly meetings bring together a consortium of internal stakeholders, including HR, IT, legal, and communications teams, to ensure everyone is aligned on the same risk picture. Unified awareness allows for a coordinated response rather than a patchwork of reactions.

The human factor is also central. Understanding the behavior of your principal and of potential adversaries gives you insights that technology cannot match. If your principal begins appearing at more controversial events or if activist rhetoric becomes sharper, you can adjust protective measures before the risk escalates. Protective intelligence combined with intuition allows leaders to separate background noise from real warning signs.

Finally, a threat-informed leader must protect both their own resilience and that of the team. Anticipating and managing threats in high-stakes environments is a constant mental load. Leaders should plan rotations during long crises, as we did during the Ukraine evacuation, and create space for recovery after high-stress assignments. The ability to stay calm and clear-headed is not only a personal strength but also a survival skill for the entire operation.

Shifting to this mindset is not always easy. Some executives will question the cost or the need for intelligence and scenario training. The solution is to present proactivity as a business advantage. It reduces downtime, limits disruption, and preserves reputation. Once leaders understand that this approach safeguards both people and the mission, the question changes from why to how soon it can begin.

BUILDING ORGANIZATIONAL SUPPORT

The personal discipline of threat-informed leadership is powerful, but its impact is limited if it stays in the leader's head. To truly change outcomes, the mindset must spread through the organization until it becomes part of how people think, plan, and act. Predictive thinking should not be a skill reserved for the top. It should be a shared language from the front line to the boardroom.

This requires deliberate design. As leadership strategist Denise Lee Yohn notes, "to achieve the desired culture, everyone must have a clear, consistent, common understanding of it, and everyone must work together in a deliberate and coordinated effort to cultivate it."[9] In EP, that kind of shared understanding is what transforms individual awareness into collective readiness. It's what allows every part of the organization to recognize risk, communicate clearly, and act in sync when it matters most. Those dynamics are shaped by training, communication, incentives, and the right technology. They determine whether a team consistently spots trouble early or stumbles into it unprepared.

Training and education form the base. A team skilled in protective intelligence, scenario-planning, and cross-functional coordination is far better prepared to anticipate and respond. A half-day session on narrative monitoring can teach personnel how to detect hostile online campaigns before they trigger physical consequences. OSINT analysis, behavioral awareness, and crisis communication practice expand capability and sharpen instinct. When these skills are part of regular work, proactivity stops being a leadership directive and becomes the team's default habit.

Communication ensures those habits have direction. Intelligence has more influence when it is shared in ways that connect to business priorities. A quarterly risk briefing that links a potential threat to specific financial or reputational consequences captures attention. Showing that a prevented doxxing incident avoided a $5 million loss reframes the conversation from "security expense" to "business value."

A healthy culture rewards people for acting before the problem becomes urgent. Recognizing a team member who identified an emerging protest risk or drove a cross-functional solution shows that vigilance matters. The form of the reward is less important than its visibility and meaning. Over time, recognition reinforces a cycle in which proactive behavior is noticed, valued, and repeated.

Technology provides reach. Predictive analytics, narrative monitoring platforms, and AI-based detection systems extend human judgment. Leaders can secure investment in these tools by demonstrating their return. A $50,000 platform that protects against a $10 million reputational crisis is a straightforward argument. Piloting a tool first can build confidence before committing fully.

Risk culture provides the frame for all this work. Wucker defines it as "an organization's attitudes, risk decisions, acceptable behaviors, structures, and processes for assessing and managing risks, and the definition of acceptable risk."[10] Without that shared understanding, even the most skilled team can pull in different directions.

The payoff for embedding a threat-informed mindset across an organization is measured in more than avoided losses. It is the quiet confidence of a team that can read the field, adapt in real time, and protect the mission without hesitation. It is the difference between being caught in the chaos of a crisis and shaping events before they take form. Every day that passes without building this culture is a day when threats are moving, changing, and closing in. The leaders who choose to act now will find themselves not chasing danger but controlling the ground on which it approaches.

SUSTAINING PROACTIVITY UNDER PRESSURE

Sustaining a proactive leadership mindset when the pressure never seems to let up takes more than quick reflexes. It calls for a deep well of resilience, the agility to adapt in real time, and a steady commitment to keep growing, even when the pace is exhausting. Moving from a reactive posture to a proactive one is not a single leap but an ongoing climb. Leaders who make it to the top of that ridge don't stop; they keep building the habits and systems that keep their teams sharp, focused, and ready.

The real test comes in how you create an environment where vigilance is part of the air your people breathe, where stress is kept in check, and where everyone understands they have a role in protecting the mission. One of the most effective ways to sustain that edge is through structured debriefs after incidents, drills, or simulations. These are not "check-the-box" exercises; they are the moment to break down what worked and how to tighten the plan before the next threat. A close look at a successfully thwarted cyber-physical attack, for example, can sharpen your threat and vulnerability risk assessments, specifically the dynamic factors of your analysis, so that the lessons move into daily operations. Each review adds another layer of foresight, another tool in the kit for spotting trouble before it takes shape.

Pressure doesn't just test systems; it tests people. Leaders who stay clear-headed know that mental wellness is not a luxury. They model the habits, whether it's daily exercise, mindfulness, or stepping away from the noise for a moment, that keep stress from clouding judgment. When leaders make mental health visible and valued, through peer support or wellness initiatives, they give their teams permission to take care of themselves. This is not simply about morale; it is about keeping the decision-making engine running clean under the strain of high-stakes work.

A proactive culture also thrives on constant refinement. Processes need to be tested, evaluated, and adapted. That means gathering feedback from across the organization, even from departments that don't normally sit at the security table. A conversation with HR about cross-functional planning might reveal blind spots in communication or coordination that could stall a crisis response. When leaders treat improvement as an ongoing loop rather than an annual checklist, the organization stays nimble enough to keep pace with emerging threats.

And no leader can carry the full load alone. Empowering the team is not just about workload; it is about ownership. Assigning junior analysts to monitor social media chatter, for example, frees senior leaders to focus on strategic planning while giving newer team members a stake in the mission. The more the responsibility is shared, the more deeply proactivity becomes embedded in the organization's DNA.

As Juliette Kayyem reminds us, "You have to have persistent preparedness, so you're not ratcheting up and down all the time. You are preparing for some disruption."[11] That discipline is built one habit, one honest debrief, and one empowered teammate at a time. Leaders who commit to this way of working don't just hold the line under pressure, they shape an environment where readiness is second nature, and the team thrives no matter what comes their way.

LEADING AHEAD OF THE THREAT

Shifting from a reactive to a proactive leadership mindset in the EP world is not a simple gear change. It is a deliberate journey, one that demands intentional action to stay ahead of an unpredictable threat landscape. For protective leaders, this transformation begins with cultivating predictive thinking, leveraging intelligence as a decision-making compass, and embedding vigilance and resilience into the culture so deeply that they become instinct.

Predictive thinking starts with a habit of asking, '*What could happen next?*' This is not idle speculation; rather, it is a structured discipline. A leader preparing for a principal's overseas trip might map out a week's worth of plausible disruptions: political demonstrations, digital intrusion attempts, and hostile press coverage. Documenting these possibilities sharpens foresight and forces the mind to anticipate rather than react. Over time, this practice rewires reflexes, turning impulsive responses into well-considered strategies.

Protective intelligence is the second anchor. It's not enough to collect raw data; the leader's role is to turn it into insight. This might mean monitoring real-time social sentiment, flagging extremist chatter, or tracking geopolitical events that could ripple into the principal's orbit. It also means justifying the investment. Presenting how a threat-monitoring platform costing $50,000 might prevent a multimillion-dollar disruption. When intelligence is credible, timely, and connected to the organization's priorities, it becomes the engine for informed action.

Regular threat and vulnerability risk assessments keep this engine tuned. The best leaders treat TVRAs as living documents, updated quarterly or after significant events. They merge static factors, like the principal's visibility and work locations, with dynamic elements such as travel patterns or shifting online narratives. Sharing findings in a way that links risks to business outcomes. Underscoring how a security breach could impact revenue or reputation transforms these assessments into tools that the entire organization values.

Agility under pressure is essential. Leaders who rely solely on rigid standard operating procedures leave their teams exposed when the unexpected happens. Scenario-based training bridges that gap. Monthly drills simulating cyber breaches, public protests, or sudden evacuations prepare teams to pivot quickly while maintaining mission control. In these moments, the leader's influence sets the tone, creating a space where raising an early warning is not just accepted but expected.

In the digital age, narratives often move faster than events themselves. Monitoring online sentiment, extremist messaging, and activity within hidden forums provides an early signal when rhetoric may escalate to action. A spike in hostile commentary about an executive, for example, can be the cue to adjust travel or quietly alter exposure before a threat crosses into the physical realm. Assigning a team member to track and contextualize these patterns each day ensures they are not lost in the noise.

Staying informed is not optional. Leaders must remain plugged into reliable streams of global risk intelligence, pulling from professional briefings, sector-specific analysis, and trusted threat reporting channels. The goal is to turn this information into shared awareness, delivering concise internal updates so every team member, from the newest analyst to the most senior advisor, understands the changing landscape and can anticipate its implications for the mission.

The example set by the leader is the culture's true north. Sharing "silent victories" reminds both the team and the C-suite that the absence of crisis is not a coincidence. Behavioral awareness training reinforces this mindset, teaching staff to notice the subtle indicators that often precede trouble, such as changes in adversary behavior or shifts in a principal's daily pattern.

But even the most forward-leaning posture will crumble without resilience. Sustaining proactivity under relentless operational pressure means managing both the tempo and the toll. Leaders must build in recovery. Rotating staff during prolonged assignments, holding structured debriefs to learn without blame, and modeling composure when the stakes rise. Stress management practices like mindfulness or targeted peer support are not indulgences; they are performance safeguards.

Recognition closes the loop. Publicly acknowledging the analyst who spotted a brewing protest or the cross-functional team that resolved a vulnerability before it became a crisis reinforces the behaviors that keep the organization safe. These moments, often invisible to the outside world, are the true metrics of success in EP.

Admiral William H. McRaven, in *The Wisdom of the Bullfrog*, writes, "The only easy day was yesterday. Every day you are a leader, you will be tested ... and the tests will never stop. The key is to prepare yourself and your team for the fight ahead, to anticipate the challenges, and to be ready to act before the storm arrives."[12] This captures the heart of the threat-informed leadership mindset. It is a discipline, sustained not by fear of what might happen, but by the conviction that preparation and foresight are the most powerful forms of protection.

Leaders who integrate predictive thinking, intelligence-driven decision-making, dynamic assessments, operational agility, cross-functional alignment, narrative monitoring, continual learning, visible leadership, resilience, and recognition create organizations that shape risk rather than chase it. They ensure that proactivity is not a surge of effort in moments of crisis, but a constant, steady current that carries the mission forward.

DEFINING MINDSET SUCCESS BY SILENCE

In the EP world, the highest measure of leadership rarely makes headlines. It lives in the stillness, when a principal moves through their schedule unaware of the risks neutralized in the background, when a high-profile event unfolds without a single disruption, when tension is quietly defused before it has a chance to surface. Here, success is defined not by the noise of a dramatic rescue but by the silence of nothing going wrong. That silence is not luck. It is the product of foresight and the unseen hand of leaders who choose to think several steps ahead.

Every protective leader eventually faces a turning point, a moment when their role is no longer simply about guarding but about guiding. It may be the day they convince an executive team to delay a public announcement to avoid a reputational firestorm. Or the morning they identify a growing threat and shut it down before it ever reaches the principal's awareness. This is where leadership transcends physical proximity and moves into strategic influence. The modern leader does not just stand watch; they scan the horizon, anticipate the unseen, and quietly steer the organization clear of harm.

The question for every leader in this industry is simple but confronting: are you chasing threats as they appear, or shaping a future where those threats never take root? Ronald A. Heifetz captures the essence of this choice in *The Practice of Adaptive Leadership*: "Leadership is about disappointing your own people at a rate they can absorb."[13] In EP, that means making the hard calls before the danger is visible, sometimes changing plans, limiting access, or altering course in ways that may frustrate in the moment but protect in the long run. The payoff is not applause; it is the absence of harm.

This is the call to action. Take one deliberate step today that pushes you further into the proactive space. Deploy a new intelligence capability to spot early indicators of risk. Conduct a fresh threat and vulnerability assessment that links directly to your organization's priorities. Build a relationship with another department that could be pivotal in a crisis. None of these actions will make the evening news, yet together they form the foundation of a leadership legacy defined by prevention rather than reaction.

Your principal's safety, your team's confidence, and your organization's resilience depend on your willingness to lead with clarity, discipline, and anticipation. Let each decision you make strengthen the invisible shield that protects those who depend on you. And when the day passes without incident, recognize it for what it is: the sound of success.

NOTES

1 Brian Gottlieb, *Beyond the Hammer: Lessons in Leadership and Life* (Austin, TX: Greenleaf Book Group Press, 2022).
2 Network Contagion Research Institute, "Assassination Culture: How Burning Teslas and Killing Billionaires Became a Meme Aesthetic for Political Violence," 2025, https://networkcontagion.us/reports/4–7–25-ncri-assassination-culture-brief/.
3 Peter Suciu, "Luigi Mangione Has Become a Social Media Folk Hero," *Forbes*, December 12, 2025, https://www.forbes.com/sites/petersuciu/2024/12/12/luigi-mangione-has-become-a-social-media-folk-hero/.
4 C. S. Lewis, *The Problem of Pain* (New York: HarperOne, 1940).
5 Dan Heath, *Upstream: The Quest to Solve Problems Before They Happen* (New York: Avid Reader Press, 2020).
6 Kif Leswing, "Jamie Dimon: The U.S. Has 'Serious Issues,'" *Business Insider*, April 4, 2016, https://www.businessinsider.com/dimon-us-has-serious-issues-2016-4.
7 Stanley McChrystal and Anna Butrico, *Risk: A User's Guide* (New York: Portfolio, 2021).
8 Michele Wucker, *The Gray Rhino: How to Recognize and Act on the Obvious Dangers We Ignore* (St. Martin's Press, 2016).
9 Denise Lee Yohn, "Company Culture Is Everyone's Responsibility," *Harvard Business Review*, February 8, 2021, https://hbr.org/2021/02/company-culture-is-everyones-responsibility.

10 Michele Wucker, *The Gray Rhino: How to Recognize and Act on the Obvious Dangers We Ignore* (New York: St. Martin's Press, 2016).
11 Juliette Kayyem, interview by Lauren Fulton, "Juliette Kayyem on Disaster Management & How to Fail Safer," *The Verse*, April 1, 2022, https://www.theversemedia.com/articles/juliette-kayyem-how-to-fail-safer
12 William H. McRaven, *The Wisdom of the Bullfrog: Leadership Made Simple (But Not Easy)* (New York: Grand Central Publishing, 2023).
13 Ronald A. Heifetz, *Alexander Grashow, and Marty Linsky, The Practice of Adaptive Leadership: Tools and Tactics for Changing Your Organization and the World* (Boston, MA: Harvard Business Press, 2009).

CORE INSIGHTS

The Landscape of Leadership and Risk

As the threat landscape accelerates and the work demands greater clarity, the following insights distill the mindsets that move protector-leaders from reacting to shaping. They are practical habits that steady judgment in volatile moments, turn intelligence into decisive action, and anchor the shift from tactical execution to strategic influence.

The landscape explored in this section is not simply a context for leadership; it is the proving ground that forges it. The modern protector now operates at the intersection of intelligence, influence, and foresight, where success is measured as much by what never happens as by what is managed in plain sight. To lead in this era is to hold calm under uncertainty, translate complexity into direction others can follow, and recognize early signals before they become events. Section 1 traced that evolution: from guarding to guiding, from presence to prevention, and from managing risk at the edge to shaping outcomes at the center, leading with relevance, foresight, and quiet authority.

As you carry this perspective forward, these core insights serve as the foundation for developing the protector-leader capable of navigating and shaping the modern risk landscape.

CORE INSIGHTS

- **Think like a strategist, not a responder**
  Leadership begins when protection moves beyond tactics and starts shaping outcomes.

DOI: 10.4324/9781003670704-6

- **Understand the business as deeply as the threat**
  Credibility comes from fluency in how the enterprise operates, decides, and absorbs risk.
- **Translate risk into relevance**
  Executives act on impact, continuity, trust, and reputation, not on threat descriptions.
- **Lead through relationships, not authority**
  Influence grows from cross-functional trust, shared purpose, and consistent clarity.
- **Stay adaptive and composed**
  Modern protection requires emotional intelligence, agility, and the ability to thrive in ambiguity.
- **Let intelligence guide decisions before events do**
  Predictive thinking, early signals, and data-driven judgment are now the protector's decisive advantage.

SECTION 2

Introduction—The Protector as a Leader

Leadership in the protective profession begins where the noise fades and the inner voice takes over. It starts with the choices made when no one is watching; the quiet discipline of character that steadies judgment and builds credibility long before anyone sees the results. From this foundation, leadership expands outward. It shapes the way protectors guide their teams through uncertainty, how they respond when the plan fractured, and how they cultivate the next generation to carry the mission forward with confidence and integrity.

As protectors grow, their influence must grow as well. The demands of the modern threat landscape require more than technical skill or command presence; they require the ability to speak with clarity in the rooms where decisions affect people, reputations, and organizational futures. Trust becomes the currency that moves a protector from operational executor to strategic partner, capable of advising the C-suite with the same steadiness they bring to the field.

This section follows that progression. From the leadership of the self, to the leadership of teams, to the leadership that earns a seat beside the principal. It explores how character becomes culture, how crisis calms into confidence, and how the protector evolves into an advisor whose influence strengthens not only the people they guard, but the organizations they serve.

DOI: 10.4324/9781003670704-7

CHAPTER 5

The Protectors' Code

Every protector knows the quiet before a movement. Sitting in a vehicle, listening to your own breath, you feel the weight of what is about to unfold. It is here that leadership becomes real. Not in the crisp lines of your suit or the way your earpiece sits, but in the decision to act with integrity no matter what comes. The people around you may never notice that choice in the moment, but they will feel it in how you lead. This is where trust is earned, long before the motorcade pulls away or the principal steps into view.

Today, leadership in executive protection is not measured solely by who appears the most prepared or who commands the loudest. It's about the courage to admit uncertainty and the humility to serve without needing applause. Sarah Gillard, CEO of Blueprint for Better Business, captures this shift: "Great leaders have historically been celebrated for technical expertise, but when you ask people about the leaders who have really made an impact on them, it has been about ... how they made them feel."[1] This isn't a profession where leadership can rest on tradition or the glint of medals. It's a field where a single lapse, such as a forgotten detail or a selfish judgment, can shatter reputations and trust in an instant.

Nowadays clients and teams expect more than protection from physical danger; they demand psychological safety and authenticity. Reputation travels at the speed of rumor, and credibility is no longer inherited from rank; it must be earned anew each day. As one leadership expert notes, "Credibility is an essential leadership trait because it is the foundation upon which relationships and trust are built. Without credibility, leaders cannot effectively influence others or drive results."[2] Quiet influence, built day by day through small acts of decency, becomes the true anchor when the spotlight blazes and mistakes loom large.

So what does it take to become a protector-leader worthy of deep trust and confidence? It begins with character. Built through habits of honesty and moral courage. Forged through the discipline to steady a team when uncertainty strikes. It is guided by ethics, the compass that points true when choices turn gray. And it is grounded in humility, the

DOI: 10.4324/9781003670704-8

rare strength to listen, to learn, and to place service above ego. When these qualities are lived consistently, they transform leadership from a title into a presence. They create credibility that outlasts pressure. Influence that does not need to be demanded. And trust that becomes the protector's most enduring shield.

THE PROTECTOR'S COMPASS

At the heart of personal leadership in executive protection lies a principle that is easy to overlook in a profession fueled by urgency and adrenaline: live your values out loud, even when no one else is watching. In a role where every movement is scrutinized and every mistake magnified; it is tempting to focus only on visible actions. How sharp your suit looks or how quickly you react to a threat. Yet those surface details, while necessary, are not the foundation of leadership. What ultimately defines a protector-leader is the invisible architecture of character, credibility, and trust.

The protector who embraces this principle becomes the steady anchor of a team. Their influence does not depend on formal authority or proximity to power. It emerges in the small, consistent choices that others quietly notice and draw strength from. Consider the way a leader calms a nervous executive before a high-stakes event, or how they own a mistake without deflecting blame, or how they choose the less convenient path because it is the right one. These moments rarely make headlines, yet they become the very fabric of credibility. As the FBI has observed, "as leaders, our credibility will rise or fall on the decisions we make and the actions we take daily."[3] In this work, credibility is oxygen; essential, invisible, and immediately felt when it is lacking.

Not defined by tactics alone, a leader in executive protection is shaped by something greater. While a protector may be flawless in planning logistics or conducting an advance, without character, they cannot inspire trust. And without trust, there is no true leadership; only supervision. Character is not an inherited trait, but a dynamic quality shaped by habit, discipline, and the willingness to hold oneself accountable under pressure. It grows stronger when tested in moments where the easier path is tempting but the principled one is required. The Harvard Business Review captures this reality clearly: "character is the core of leadership—an essential fusion of values, ethics, integrity, and morals."[4] Without that core, even the most skilled protector risks being reduced to a technician. Functional, but not trusted as a leader.

What makes this particularly vital in protection is the weight of unseen consequences. In many professions, mistakes can be repaired with apologies or new strategies. In executive protection, errors are not only operational risks; they are credibility fractures that ripple outward. A detail may recover from a logistical misstep, but the trust lost in the process can linger for years, undermining the protector's voice in critical conversations. This is why integrity cannot be treated as a passive trait. It must be actively safeguarded and renewed, decision after decision.

The links between character, credibility, trust, and influence are not abstract. Like a chain, they are sequential and deeply practical. Character fuels credibility. Credibility builds trust. Trust enables influence. Break one link, and the chain collapses. A protector may still perform duties, but they will not command the confidence necessary to advise, guide, or lead in moments of real consequence. Leadership in this field is not about how loudly you speak but about how consistently you live by your values, so that when you do speak, others listen.

Ethics, then, is not an accessory to effective protection; it is its compass. Protectors often operate in gray areas or under pressure; the compass of character is what keeps decisions aligned with principle. This is why personal leadership cannot be reduced to a checklist or a set of rules. It is about who you are when no one is looking and who you remain under the spotlight of crisis.

The implications for protector-leaders are sobering. Your greatest asset is not your technical training, your intelligence contacts, or even your years of experience. Your greatest asset is your character, expressed in daily actions and safeguarded like the life of your principal. Without it, you cannot sustain credibility. Without credibility, you cannot build trust. And without trust, you cannot lead.

For those in executive protection, this is not abstract philosophy. It is survival. A protector who leads with character ensures not only the safety of the individuals they serve but also the resilience of the team and the integrity of the mission. The true measure of leadership in this profession is not found in the noise of dramatic interventions but in the quiet consistency of principled choices that, together, create an unbreakable foundation of trust.

NEW CORE OF LEADERSHIP

Every era demands its own kind of courage from those who protect. In the early decades of executive protection, courage was expressed through a kind of stoic toughness. The model protector was measured by how well they executed instructions, maintained command presence, and displayed unshakable confidence. Leadership was binary: you were either giving orders or taking them. Admitting uncertainty or vulnerability was an absolute weakness. The priority was discipline, not dialogue. In that world, the protector who could keep emotions hidden, follow rigid protocol, and maintain order without question was considered the ideal.

That approach worked in a time when hierarchies were rigid, information flowed slowly, and threats were often visible and predictable. Reliability, not reflection, was the mark of a competent professional. Leadership was transactional, predicated on compliance and repetition rather than on trust or influence. That way of leading has collapsed under the weight of today's realities.

Today, the environment is radically different. Threats are asymmetric. Blending digital and physical domains. A single lapse in judgment can be captured on a phone, shared online, and dissected in public within minutes. Protectors are scrutinized not only by their principals but also by peers, executives, employees, journalists, and even strangers with social media accounts. In this environment, authority cannot be imposed. It is earned.

The modern protector-leader is not a figure of intimidation but a presence of credibility. They no longer rely solely on the strength of their voice or the weight of their position. Their influence comes from a quieter place: the ability to listen deeply, adapt quickly, and act with integrity. They know that people follow not because they are told to, but because they trust the person leading them. As the U.S. Naval Institute emphasizes in its teaching of leadership and ethics, "leaders are constantly judged not just by results, but by the standards they uphold and the example they set."[5]

This is not a cosmetic shift. It is transformative. In the traditional model, when a mistake happened on a detail, the instinct was to conceal it. Leaders would minimize the issue, quietly adjust, and move on. The priority was to avoid embarrassment and maintain the appearance of perfection. But in the new model, credibility grows not from hiding mistakes but from owning them. A leader who acknowledges a missed detail, accepts responsibility, and uses it as a lesson strengthens, rather than weakens, their authority. This openness signals to the team that accountability is not about punishment but about learning. It tells team members they are safe to speak up when they see something, admit when they are overextended, or share ideas to improve. Over time, that transparency shifts a unit's culture from compliance-based silence to one of psychological safety, mutual respect, and collective problem-solving.

Consider the difference in outcomes. Under the old approach, a seasoned detail leader may hold a spotless operational record but still bleed talent. Team members leave not because the work is too demanding, but because they often feel unheard or undervalued. Fatigue, burnout, and unspoken concerns erode performance until mistakes happen anyway. Contrast that with a younger leader who fosters open, direct dialogue. A leader who takes five minutes after an operation to ask what could have been done better or encourages even the most junior member to voice concerns. Or even wilder, a leader who quickly admits their own blind spots. The result of this is a team that invests more deeply in one another, innovates on the fly, and feels trusted enough to go the extra mile.

The long-term advantage of this shift is undeniable. Teams that operate on quiet influence and earn trust are not only more cohesive but also more resilient when a crisis strikes. When the pressure is highest, these teams pull closer together instead of fracturing. They respond faster because they trust one another enough to share information openly. They adapt more effectively because they are not afraid to raise new ideas. Their leader's credibility becomes the glue that keeps them aligned under pressure. As Forbes reminds us, "credibility is the cornerstone of leadership, built not only on competence but on the trust that leaders act consistently with values and standards."[6]

This new model of leadership does not diminish a protector's authority. It amplifies it. A leader who blends decisiveness with humility, who balances confidence with openness, earns a deeper, longer-lasting kind of influence. Their authority is not tied to their title or their ability to command compliance but to the trust they've cultivated day after day. That trust endures long after the radios fall silent and the protective detail ends. It becomes part of the leader's reputation, the story told about them in rooms they aren't in, and the credibility that follows them from one assignment to the next.

The protector's strategic shift, then, is a move away from command-and-control leadership toward trust-and-influence leadership. It is not about being softer; it is about being stronger in ways that matter most. Being resilient in crisis, adaptable in uncertainty, and showing credibility in every interaction. And in today's world, credibility is the one currency a protector cannot afford to lose.

CORNERSTONES OF PROTECTOR-LEADERSHIP

Character, ethics, and integrity: these three words form the organic foundation of protector-leadership. These are not slogans or lofty abstractions. They are disciplines lived out in real time, often in moments where no one is watching, and tested most when the pressure is greatest. For protectors, these principles are not window dressing to professionalism. They are the hidden framework that sustains trust, the difference between being seen as merely skilled and being regarded as truly dependable.

It is important to recognize that these traits do not exist in isolation. They overlap, reinforce, and expand one another. Together, they create a system of credibility that not only defines individual leadership but also shapes the culture of the entire team. To understand how this system works, we must explore each element in depth. How are they cultivated? How are they tested? And how they play out in the daily realities of executive protection.

Leadership in protection begins long before the crisis. It begins with the choices made when things are quiet, when there is no spotlight, and when no one seems to be taking notes. That is where character lives.

Character is the impulse to step toward responsibility when others step away. It is to tell the full truth when a softer version might be easier. And giving credit to a teammate even when you could quietly claim it yourself. These habits may look small in the moment, but over time, they become the measure of the leader. They define how others predict you will respond under pressure. In this way, character is not about performance but about predictability. Your team, your principal, and even your adversaries know who you are by the choices you make repeatedly.

The U.S. Army captures this reality with precision: "Character is the essence of who a person is, what they believe, how they act, and what they value. It is the foundation of trust, and trust is the bedrock of leadership."[7] For protective work, this means character is forged in the grind of advance walkthroughs, late-night reports, and last-minute changes. It is revealed in how consistently you show up with discipline and humility. Strong character is not built in a crisis; it is revealed by it. And once revealed, it becomes the basis upon which others decide whether to trust your judgment when the stakes are at their highest.

During an overseas assignment, an advance agent found himself tempted to skip a final sweep of a venue because of fatigue and pressure to meet the schedule. Instead, he followed through. That last check uncovered a blocked emergency exit that could have compromised the entire operation. His consistency under pressure built more credibility with the team than any tactical move that day. But character alone is not enough. Even the strongest personal habits need a compass to point them in the right direction. That compass is ethics.

Where character is built in habit, ethics is tested in ambiguity. Protection rarely offers the luxury of simple right-or-wrong decisions. A principal may ask you to keep something quiet that impacts security. A teammate may suggest a shortcut to save time. You may face a confrontation where escalation feels justified, but restraint is better suited to serve the mission. In these moments, your technical training cannot answer for you. Only your ethical framework can.

Ethics is the protector's compass in the fog. It ensures that choices serve more than immediate convenience or personal gain. Ethical leadership means rising above expedience to do what sustains the team, the client, and the profession over the long term. As Harvard's Division of Continuing Education notes, "Errors, bad behavior, and poor decisions are magnified in leadership. Leaders set the standard for the culture around them, and their behavior ripples across their teams and organizations."[8] For protectors, this ripple is profound. A single ethical lapse, such as ignoring a minor threat report or overlooking a conflict of interest, signals to the team that standards are not being consistently upheld.

By contrast, every ethical stand taken under pressure models courage. It says, "We will do what is right, even if it costs us comfort." That kind of modeling fosters a culture where people speak up, where silence doesn't smother the truth, and where clients trust not just the skill of their protectors but also their judgment.

Ethics guides decisions, but it must be paired with consistency. Without follow-through, even the most principled intentions collapse. This brings us to the principle that carries both character and ethics into visible action: integrity.

Integrity is where character and ethics are proven, or in some cases, laid bare. It is the protector's reputation for consistency, the alignment of words with deeds, and the daily demonstration that promises mean something. Without integrity, character remains private, and ethics remains theoretical. With integrity, both become visible, credible, and actionable.

The FBI underscores this point with a sharp warning: "As leaders, our credibility will rise or fall on the decisions we make and the actions we take daily. Credibility is built over time but can be destroyed in an instant."[9] For protectors, that instant may be as simple as failing to honor a commitment, breaking confidentiality, or downplaying a detail that later proves costly. The erosion of trust begins small, but once credibility cracks, it is almost impossible to repair.

Conversely, integrity has a cumulative effect. Each time a protector follows through, delivers on a promise, or stands by their word under pressure, they reinforce their reliability. Over time, this becomes a shield of credibility. One that teammates and principals instinctively lean on when uncertainty arises. Integrity transforms trust from a fragile commodity into a durable resource.

Yet even integrity is not sufficient on its own. If character shapes the inner core, ethics points the direction, and integrity demonstrates alignment, then leadership requires all three to work in concert. It is their integration that makes a protector whole.

To stop at defining character, ethics, and integrity individually would miss the deeper truth. In isolation, these principles cannot function. They are not parallel tracks but interconnected disciplines that create a single, unified system.

Character without ethics risks becoming self-serving. Ethics without integrity collapses into empty words. Integrity without character becomes brittle, a façade that crumbles when put to the test. But, when fused together, the three form a framework that sustains credibility in ways no single trait can.

The U.S. Naval Institute captures this truth: "Character is the essential core of leadership. It must be evident not only in decision-making but in the example, leaders set, because standards are not taught by words alone; they are taught by conduct."[10] In practice, this means the protector-leader is not just reciting principles but embodying them. Always maintaining consistency between inner compass, moral direction, and outward example.

For executive protection, this integration is not abstract. It translates into how teams operate. A leader with character ensures decisions are steady. A leader with ethics ensures those decisions align with values. A leader with integrity ensures that alignment is visible in action. When these forces converge, teams inherit not just direction but confidence. They trust their leader not because of rank or command, but because they see similarity between words and deeds.

This integration, once lived day after day, creates a culture where people instinctively do the right thing. Making right choices even when no one is watching. Why, because they have seen it modeled. It creates resilience not just in the leader but in the team. And it transforms leadership from a title into a presence. A presence that is quiet, consistent, credible, and whole.

CASE STUDY: EARNING TRUST UNDER PRESSURE

It was still dark when the protective detail for a major oil and gas company gathered in a small hotel conference room on the outskirts of Lagos, Nigeria. The principal, a high-profile CEO, was due to speak at an investor forum later that morning. The region had seen significant labor unrest, and vague threats online hinted at potential protests. The team knew the day would test more than routes and contingencies. It would test their ability to function as one.

The detail leader kept the briefing short and sharp, ending with a reminder that carried weight: "If you see something, call it. No hesitation. We'll sort it out together." It set the tone that this wasn't about rigid hierarchy; it was about trust.

During the motorcade, a disagreement surfaced. Two agents monitoring communications clashed on whether to adjust the departure time from the hotel as crowd activity picked up near the venue. Normally, in a tight environment, such disagreements might get buried. But instead of shutting it down, the leader asked them to talk it through on the spot. The exchange revealed a blind spot in the original plan: a secondary access road was already backed up with delivery trucks. The dialogue, tense but constructive, prompted a quick adjustment that kept the principal out of a choke point.

Later, as the event concluded, a protest erupted with violence near the main entrance. With minutes to react, the team shifted to the alternate exit. A young agent in the follow-up vehicle noticed the crowd spilling toward that gate and quickly suggested rerouting through a service lane she had spotted during the advance. The detail leader backed her call immediately. It worked. The motorcade cleared smoothly, and the principal never sensed the disruption.

That night, in the hotel lobby, the team gathered for a quick debrief. Nobody pretended it had been flawless. They talked about the tension on comms, the protestors' movement, and how close the crowd had come to the exit route. The youngest agent was publicly credited for speaking up. Another admitted he'd hesitated too long before raising a concern, and the leader acknowledged his own role in nearly dismissing the route timing debate. The tone wasn't critical. It was candid.

From the sidelines, the principal had noticed more than the security bubble. He saw a team that communicated openly, adapted quickly, and treated one another with respect. Over the following weeks, the principal's confidence deepened. Not just in the security plans, but in the people that were protecting him.

The lesson for the team was clear. Candor and humility were not liabilities; they were force multipliers. They turned tension into solutions and hesitation into initiative. By modeling consistency, encouraging feedback, and recognizing contributions, the leader proved that quiet influence builds the kind of credibility no amount of checklists could measure.

SHIFTING DEMANDS OF MODERN LEADERSHIP

The protector's code cannot be frozen in time. It shifts in response to society's expectations and the nature of modern threats. Also, it moves with the way leadership itself is evaluated. The world we live in now asks more from leaders than technical skill. People expect leaders to show competence while also showing humanity. Younger generations want more than authority; they want authenticity and mentors who model values. Clients, colleagues, and even bystanders with phones in their hands are always watching. In this environment, the social license to lead is granted not only by the principal you serve but also by every person who sees you act.

The wider landscape reinforces this truth. Across sectors, from business to government to security, credibility has become the single most precious resource. Forbes notes that "credibility is the cornerstone of leadership, built not only on competence but on the trust that leaders act consistently with values and standards."[11] This is particularly relevant in executive protection. A single lapse in conduct, however small, can echo far beyond the moment. It can be replayed, discussed, and magnified in ways that undermine trust and erode the influence you worked years to build.

Cultural shifts have made this even more pressing. The pandemic years brought a new focus to mental well-being and resilience for others. Organizations are being judged not only on results but on how those results are achieved. Leaders who once could operate behind closed doors are now expected to be transparent, accountable, and willing to embody the values their teams live by. As former Boston Police Commissioner William Bratton has written about effective leadership, "true leaders embrace change, take responsibility during crisis, and lead with passion that inspires others to follow."[12] That insight resonates deeply in a profession where visibility is constant and credibility is the real currency.

For protectors, this changing environment carries sharp implications. It means your professional credibility is not just about running a secure motorcade or writing a precise risk assessment. It is about how you conduct yourself in moments of tension, how you treat your team when nobody else is around, and how your example sets the tone for others. In a networked world, where trust can be built or lost in seconds, the protector's code is not only a private ethic but also a public strategy. Those who live by it will stand out as trusted advisors and guardians whose influence extends beyond protection into leadership itself.

BARRIERS TO CREDIBLE LEADERSHIP

The journey to becoming a protector-leader rooted in character, ethics, and integrity is anything but linear. It is a path marked by friction, tested by external pressures and the quiet battles within. The traits that make a leader truly credible are also the ones that are hardest to cultivate. They demand honesty, humility, and consistency in a world that often rewards the opposite.

One of the most persistent barriers is the false belief that strength and humility cannot coexist. Too often, protectors inherit a model of leadership that equates authority with control and humility with weakness. They are taught that showing vulnerability erodes respect, and that seeking feedback reveals doubt. Yet research consistently refutes this assumption. Humility is not self-deprecation. It is a discipline of balance. It acknowledges limitations without surrendering confidence and drawing on the strengths of others without diminishing your own role. Forbes captures this clearly: "Great leaders are not necessarily the most charismatic or forceful; they are those with the character to build trust, admit mistakes, and continually learn."[13] In the protective field, this translates into being willing to listen to a junior team member who sees something you missed. Having the modesty to admit to an error before it turns into a larger vulnerability. That is not a weakness. That is credibility in action.

A second challenge is organizational culture. Too many environments still prize outcomes over process, compliance over character. Leaders are measured by the absence of incidents rather than by the trust they create or the culture they sustain. This narrow lens makes it easy to sideline character as something "unmeasurable" or "soft." Yet military research demonstrates the opposite: when character is treated as observable and reinforced through standards, it elevates trust and performance. As the U.S. Naval Institute emphasizes, "a work environment that rewards deceit or tolerates ethical shortcuts erodes not only credibility but mission effectiveness."[14] Toxic cultures do not just discourage the growth of these traits; they punish them. The protector who speaks up against corner-cutting, who refuses to bend an ethical line, risks being marginalized if the system does not reward their stance. Over time, this discourages honesty, normalizes cynicism, and leaves teams brittle when real crises come.

The pressure to conform compounds these barriers. In cultures where shortcuts are celebrated and blame is deflected; transparency becomes a risk. Feedback dries up. Protectors retreat into silence, learning to "go along to get along." This is where leaders must act deliberately, modeling openness by admitting mistakes, asking for critique, and recognizing not only flawless execution but also moments of ethical courage. Such as when a teammate raises a concern early, or one who apologizes and corrects a misstep. By celebrating these acts, leaders begin to chip away at cultures that otherwise calcify into mistrust.

Another obstacle lies in the relentless pace of protection itself. Schedules are tight, margins are narrow, and time for reflection often feels nonexistent. Yet growth in these traits requires intention. Just as muscles strengthen through consistent training, character and integrity are strengthened through repeated practice: moments of self-examination, structured debriefs, mentorship conversations, and deliberate acts of feedback. Without space for this discipline, even the best intentions wither. Protectors who never pause to reflect or recalibrate risk becoming technically sharper but ethically stagnant.

Finally, there is the deeply human challenge of fear. Fear of being seen as inadequate. Fear of not fitting in. Fear of losing credibility by admitting uncertainty. This fear keeps many from practicing the very traits that would ultimately make them stronger. Overcoming it requires courage. The courage to see humility as a form of strength, to treat ethics as non-negotiable even when it costs something. Recognizing that integrity is not about perfection but about consistency.

The truth is that the obstacles to developing character, ethics, and integrity are not going away. If anything, they are intensifying as scrutiny grows and pressures mount. But within those challenges lies the very opportunity for growth. Protectors who rise above the noise, who resist the pull of toxic norms, and who choose daily to act with humility and consistency are the ones who will not only endure but lead. Their example becomes a quiet defiance against a culture that too often rewards the wrong things. Establishing a guidepost for those who want to follow a better way. Despite these barriers, protectors can cultivate credibility through everyday practice. It is in the small, unscripted moments of fieldwork that character, ethics, and integrity are forged into lasting leadership habits.

LEARNING IN THE MOMENTS THAT MATTER

Writing policies or scheduling an annual training block will not develop character, ethics, and integrity. Growth does not live in binders or PowerPoint slides. It happens in the trenches of daily life. Specifically, life's unscripted moments when decisions are raw, and emotions are real.

Picture a shift leader at the end of a punishing day on the Presidential Protective Division (PPD). The detail had just wrapped up a long West Coast trip, full of multiple high-profile stops, where nerves and patience for all were stretched thin. The weight of global attention pressing on every move. A new agent on the shift snapped verbally at one of his shift mates. His exhaustion was evident, and his tolerance had evaporated. Everyone noticed. The agent knew it, too.

Instead of running straight through the checklist-driven debrief, the shift leader asked the team to pause. Later, away from the larger group, he sat down with the rattled agent. No lecture. No critique sheet. Just a personal story. He spoke about his own early days on PPD, the first time he lost his composure among the convergence of fatigue and pressure, and he raised his voice over the radio. He remembered walking away humiliated, replaying it for hours, wondering if his reputation had been damaged beyond repair.

In sharing that story, he offered more than sympathy. He showed the younger agent that mistakes, if owned with humility, are not career-ending. They can be turning points. He made clear that credibility is not earned by never stumbling, but by how you recover.

For that young agent, the lesson was indelible. It was not about technical checklists or tactical maneuvers. It was about what leadership really looks like on the most visible stage in the world. He walked away knowing that credibility is built in the recovery, and that even the leaders he looked up to had once been in his shoes.

Processes that build protector-leaders start with small, repeatable habits. These can be as simple as asking one reflective question at the end of a shift: "Who did we help grow today?" Or holding informal "rounds" where team members highlight not only operational wins but acts of courage or restraint that might otherwise go unnoticed. When people hear that calm under pressure is valued as much as tactical precision, they begin to recognize that leadership is not about being the loudest voice but about being the most dependable presence.

Good systems don't emerge by accident. They need rhythm and structure, but also room to breathe. The most effective process typically involves three key elements: honest self-reflection, real-time application, and candid peer feedback. Some leaders keep a weekly journal, jotting down one choice they made where integrity guided the outcome. Others build shared traditions, like story circles, where teammates openly recount near misses, poor calls, or the quiet decisions that could easily be overlooked. These stories are not about shaming but about anchoring. They remind everyone that mistakes happen, and what matters is what you do next.

Embedding these practices across an organization requires more than slogans. It means recruiting for values as much as for technical skills. Reinforcing those values from the first day. A new hire should not only hear about procedures but listen to seasoned protectors tell stories of times they admitted mistakes, protected a teammate's dignity, or chose discretion over bravado. These stories shape culture far more than posters or policies. They show what the organization truly values.

Training also must evolve. A tick-the-box session in a classroom will not prepare protectors for the real dilemmas they will face. Instead, training should be woven into the rhythm of work—short, scenario-based discussions during roll call, reflective check-ins after client travel, or open forums where protectors can raise difficult ethical questions. As one law enforcement leader noted, "credibility in leadership is built day after day, and once lost, it is almost impossible to regain."[15] Protectors must recognize that credibility is not a technical skill, but rather the sum of daily choices, and training should remind them that every interaction either builds or erodes trust.

When these processes take hold, something more profound occurs. Teams begin to trust themselves and one another, not just in predictable routines but in the unpredictable storms of protection. Stories emerge of moments when someone admitted a mistake and the team rallied to rectify it, or when a protector said no to a shortcut and gained the respect of both the client and colleagues. These stories become part of the collective memory. They guide the next recruit, remind veterans of what matters, and keep leadership grounded in the daily discipline of character.

The payoff is not perfection. It is resilience. Teams built on these habits do not fracture under pressure because they know they can rely on one another's honesty and steadiness. They perform better not because they never falter, but because they know how to respond when they do. This is what a true process looks like. Not a program that sits on a shelf, but a living culture that makes character, ethics, and integrity visible in action.

EMBEDDING IN ORGANIZATIONS

Embedding values and credibility through dramatic speeches at an all-hands meeting will never happen; we guarantee it. It happens in the steady rhythm of daily life; in the quiet way protectors work together and hold one another accountable. The strongest teams are defined by how consistently their leaders model the standards they expect from everyone else.

From the very first day, new protectors absorb cues from those around them. A rookie does not learn culture from the onboarding packet; they learn it from the way a senior leader handles a mistake, or from the tone a shift leader sets when tensions are high. Credibility is passed down like an inheritance, not through flawless performance, but through honest stories of when things went wrong and how character shaped the response.

Onboarding becomes the first chance to plant these seeds. Rather than a rigid recitation of rules, the best organizations invite new members to sit with seasoned protectors and hear real turning points. One story might involve a conversation with a principal that went sideways but was salvaged through humility and follow-up. Another might recall a tense interaction with a client's family that was eased not with authority, but with patience and restraint. These lived examples communicate something written rules never can: that credibility comes from consistency, honesty, and care. As Thayer Leadership notes, "intentional leaders model behaviors that shape culture every day, recognizing that their conduct teaches more powerfully than their words."[16] This sets the tone for everything that follows.

Training also shifts when values are truly embedded. It no longer ends when the classroom door closes. Real incidents become living case studies. Teams gather after a challenging movement not only to review logistics, but to surface the moments where character was visible. A protector who spoke up despite fear, someone who admitted to a shortcut, or a colleague who quietly supported a teammate in distress; these acts are acknowledged, discussed, and remembered. Recognition in these settings is not ceremonial. It is reinforcement that character is both the minimum expectation and the highest standard.

The culture of an organization is tested most during a crisis. A protest erupts during a movement. A detail member falters in front of the client. A sudden change in itinerary forces improvisation. These are the moments when habits built in quieter times are revealed. The U.S. Army emphasizes this truth: "character must be cultivated daily, because under stress leaders fall back on habits, not intentions."[17] Protectors who practice humility, accountability, and ethical courage when the stakes seem small will draw on those same habits when the pressure surges.

An organization that makes credibility and values an integral part of its daily fabric earns more than just compliance. It earns loyalty, resilience, and trust. The proof often shows up in the unexpected feedback from a principal who notices not only the seamless logistics but also the way the team cares for one another and maintains calm in the hardest moments. That is the real legacy of embedding values. Not a plaque on the wall, but a culture of credibility that endures long after the assignment ends.

WHEN PRESSURE BECOMES THE TEST

The true test for a protector-leader is never in a static environment. It is in the moment when comfort disappears, pressure mounts, and the margin for error narrows to almost nothing. This is the space where leadership is revealed. Skill and planning matter, but character is what sustains both the mission and the trust that underpins it.

Pressure has always been part of protection. The real measure of a leader is not whether stress arrives but how they meet it. Under strain, pretense falls away, and people revert to habit. Leaders who have cultivated humility, discipline, and steadiness in quiet moments carry those traits into the storm. Leaders who rely on bravado or shortcuts will ultimately fall back on those, and the cracks will show. As the U.S. Naval Institute reminds us, "we teach leadership and ethics because in the absence of an ethical foundation, no amount of training or discipline can compensate when leaders are tested."[18]

The rhythm of protection provides endless opportunities to practice. A grueling day, an urgent call, and a last-minute schedule change are moments when composure is tested. Not by policy, but by habit. The protector who pauses to debrief honestly, admits a shortfall, or gives credit away when the pressure eases is preparing their character for the next surge of stress. These acts may feel small, but over time, they form a reservoir of credibility the team can draw on when conditions collapse.

Sustaining character under pressure requires deliberate practice, not wishful thinking. The military has long understood this, training leaders through cycles of challenge, reflection, and accountability. Adversity is not avoided but designed into the process. Leaders are expected to ask the hard questions after every test: *Where did I act with courage? Where did I fall short? What hidden strength did I see in my team?* These routines are not bureaucracy. They are the guardrails that keep character alive in the storm. As one Naval Institute study concluded, "when organizations reward character, they sustain credibility; when they reward shortcuts, they corrode it."[19]

For protectors, the same principle applies. Sustaining credibility means using after-action reviews not just to critique logistics, but to illuminate choices of character. Who spoke up when silence was easier? Who showed restraint in a heated moment? Who admitted an error quickly enough for the team to adapt? These stories become more than feedback; they become part of the team's collective memory, a living archive that guides the next generation.

Credibility also extends outward. Principals and executives watch not only how secure they feel, but how their protectors carry themselves under stress. A leader who balances confidence with humility will inspire more trust than one who hides behind authority. Commissioner Bratton, reflecting on decades of law enforcement leadership, put it clearly: "The credibility of a leader comes not from the shield they carry but from the trust they earn, day after day, by being visible, accountable, and willing to listen."[20] For protectors, this is the essence of quiet influence. An authority rooted not in command but in trust.

Resilience in this context is not simply gutting it out. It is the ability to adapt, recover, and keep values intact even when everything feels unstable. Teams that practice humility and reflection in daily routines do not fracture when the pressure climbs. They adapt because they already know honesty is safe, feedback is expected, and accountability is part of the culture. Character, in these moments, is the ballast that keeps the vessel steady.

The future of protector-leadership will not be defined by those who project toughness, but by those who possess the discipline to maintain their character under stress. Humility, accountability, and credibility are not abstract ideals. They are the quiet strengths that, when pressure peaks, prove to be the difference between a team that breaks and a team that endures.

TAKEAWAY: CONSISTENCY AND QUIET INFLUENCE

What makes a team exceptional is rarely flashy; it's built in the small, steady habits that compound over time. It shows up in the way protectors carry themselves every single day. Trust grows in hallway conversations, in honest debriefs after the adrenaline fades, and in the ease with which feedback flows across a team. When conflict arises, don't avoid it. Let those moments become fuel for dialogue and stronger bonds. The goal isn't perfection. It is progress.

Consistency matters most. Show up. Follow through. Own the small things even when nobody else sees. Recognize the quiet wins, the moments when someone stepped up with integrity, or when a teammate showed calm restraint instead of escalating tension. Every debrief should hold space for lessons, not just logistics. When mistakes occur, they should be viewed as building blocks, not stains to be hidden. That shift in mindset transforms setbacks into opportunities for growth and makes accountability a shared responsibility, rather than a punishment.

Trust with principals is built the same way. It doesn't require flawlessness; it requires openness. If something is uncertain, state it clearly. If a detail is missed, acknowledge it and show the path forward. That candor prevents surprises and strengthens confidence. Over time, it creates a foundation where principals know they can rely on their protectors not just for security, but for honesty.

Quiet influence carries equal weight. Protectors who lead with small, steady gestures earn a kind of trust that endures beyond the day's assignment. These habits become the heartbeat of the team, a rhythm of reliability and care that reinforces the mission. As the warrior ethos states, "true strength is not found in bravado, but in the discipline to endure, adapt, and place the team above the self."[21]

Practical leadership, then, is less about the dramatic moment and more about the steady practice of consistency, humility, and care. When protectors embody these values in their daily lives, they shape a culture that withstands pressure and thrives even when tested.

THE PROTECTOR'S CHARGE

The measure of a protector-leader is not found in the noise of sirens, the flash of cameras, or the rare moments when plans unravel in public view. It is revealed in the silence. The steady, unbroken flow of a day where risks are neutralized before they surface, where confidence radiates from the calm presence of the team, and where trust is quietly cemented in every choice made without fanfare. Success in this profession is not about being remembered for what you stopped, but being trusted because of what never happened under your watch.

That kind of trust cannot be faked. It cannot be borrowed. Rather, it is earned through character, ethics, and integrity practiced daily, especially when no one else is looking. It grows in the way you handle tension within your team, the way you admit your own mistakes, and the way you make decisions that prioritize values over expedience. Credibility is not a label; it is a light you tend, one decision at a time, knowing that the smallest lapse can extinguish it in an instant.

Harvard reminds us that "character is the core of leadership—an essential fusion of values, ethics, integrity, and morals."[22] That truth defines the protector's path. Your authority is not derived from your badge or title. It is in your presence and the culture you build for those who serve beside you.

So here is the charge: live your code. Do not hide behind silence when your voice can guide. Do not cling to perfection when humility would build greater trust. Do not wait for a crisis to prove your values. Show them now, in the daily rhythm of protection, in the conversations no one will ever record, in the quiet decisions that slowly carve your legacy.

When the pressure comes, your team will not remember the words on a policy sheet. They will remember how you carried yourself, how you treated them, and how your credibility gave them the courage to stand tall. That is leadership. That is influence. That is the protector's code lived out loud.

The world is watching, even in the moments that feel invisible. Step forward with character. Anchor yourself in ethics. Guard your integrity with vigilance. Protectors who live this way do more than shield their principals; they shape the future of leadership itself.

The final word is not about guarding others. It is about guarding your own code, because in the end, that code is the one thing no one can take from you. The one thing that, if lived faithfully, will outlast every assignment, every mission, and every storm.

NOTES

1 Oxford Character Project, *Good Leadership in UK Business* (University of Oxford, September 2023), https://oxfordcharacter.org/uploads/files/Good-Leadership-in-UK-Business_Sep-2023.pdf.

2 "Credibility: An Essential Leadership Trait," *Forbes*, November 25, 2024, https://www.forbes.com/sites/forbesbooksauthors/2024/11/25/credibility-an-essential-leadership-trait/.

3 Federal Bureau of Investigation, "Leadership Spotlight: Credibility," *FBI Law Enforcement Bulletin*, 2020, https://leb.fbi.gov/spotlights/leadership-spotlight-credibility.

4 Harvard Business Publishing, "The Case for Leadership Character," *Harvard Business Review*, 2023, https://www.harvardbusiness.org/insight/the-case-for-leadership-character.

5 United States Naval Institute, "Why We Teach Leadership and Ethics at the Naval Academy," *Proceedings* February 2000, https://www.usni.org/magazines/proceedings/2000/february/why-we-teach-leadership-and-ethics-naval-academy.

6 Leon E. Moores, MD, DSc, FACS,, "Credibility: An Essential Leadership Trait," *Forbes*, November 25, 2024, https://www.forbes.com/sites/forbesbooksauthors/2024/11/25/credibility-an-essential-leadership-trait/.

7 Army University Press, "Evaluating Character," *NCO Journal*, September 2020, https://www.armyupress.army.mil/Portals/7/nco-journal/images/2020/September/NCOER/Evaluating-Character.pdf.

8 Harvard Division of Continuing Education, "What Is Ethical Leadership and Why Is It Important?" 2023, https://professional.dce.harvard.edu/blog/what-is-ethical-leadership-and-why-is-it-important.

9 Federal Bureau of Investigation, "Leadership Spotlight: Credibility," *FBI Law Enforcement Bulletin*, 2020, https://leb.fbi.gov/spotlights/leadership-spotlight-credibility.

10 United States Naval Institute, "Why We Teach Leadership and Ethics at the Naval Academy," *Proceedings*, February 2000, https://www.usni.org/magazines/proceedings/2000/february/why-we-teach-leadership-and-ethics-naval-academy.

11 L. E. Moores, "Credibility: An Essential Leadership Trait," *Forbes*, November 25, 2024, https://www.forbes.com/sites/forbesbooksauthors/2024/11/25/credibility-an-essential-leadership-trait/.

12 William Bratton, "Create Change, Embrace Crisis & Lead with Passion," Inc.com (2016), https://www.inc.com/william-bratton/william-bratton-create-change-embrace-crisis-and-lead-with-passion.html.

13 Joyce E. A. Russell, "Maybe We Should Select Leaders Based on Their Character," *Forbes*, October 1, 2024, https://www.forbes.com/sites/joyceearussell/2024/10/01/maybe-we-should-select-leaders-based-on-their-character.

14 U.S. Naval Institute, "The Cycle of Leadership," *Proceedings*, February 2016, https://www.usni.org/magazines/proceedings/2016/february/cycle-leadership.

15 Federal Bureau of Investigation, "Leadership Spotlight: Credibility," *FBI Law Enforcement Bulletin*, 2020, https://leb.fbi.gov/spotlights/leadership-spotlight-credibility.

16 Thayer Leadership, "Intentional Leadership," Thayer Leadership (n.d.), https://thayerleadership.com/leadership-blog/intentional-leadership.

17 Army University Press, "Evaluating Character," *NCO Journal*, September 2020, https://www.armyupress.army.mil/Portals/7/nco-journal/images/2020/September/NCOER/Evaluating-Character.pdf.

18 United States Naval Institute, "Why We Teach Leadership and Ethics at the Naval Academy," *Proceedings*, February 2000, https://www.usni.org/magazines/proceedings/2000/february/why-we-teach-leadership-and-ethics-naval-academy.

19 United States Naval Institute, "The Cycle of Leadership," *Proceedings,* February 2016, https://www.usni.org/magazines/proceedings/2016/february/cycle-leadership.
20 U.S. Department of Justice, "Office of Community Oriented Policing Services, Bill Bratton: A Profile in Law Enforcement Leadership, The Beat Podcast," May 2024, https://cops.usdoj.gov/html/podcasts/the_beat/05–2024/The_Beat_bratton.pdf.
21 U.S. Army, "Developing the Warrior Ethos," *Military Review,* 2008, https://www.armyupress.army.mil/Portals/7/military-review/Archives/English/MilitaryReview_20080430_art004.pdf.
22 Harvard Business Review, "The Case for Leadership Character," *Harvard Business School Publishing,* 2023, https://www.harvardbusiness.org/insight/the-case-for-leadership-character.

CHAPTER 6

Crisis Leadership and Legacy Building

FROM ONE PROTECTOR TO A PROTECTIVE PROGRAM UNDER PRESSURE

Every protective program begins with a decision (sometimes deliberate, sometimes reactive) that is responding to the statement "someone needs to keep them safe." In the earliest stages, this might mean a single trusted individual traveling with the principal, scanning the crowd, managing logistics, and ensuring the day passes without incident. At this point, the mission is intensely personal, the chain of command short, and success is often measured in what doesn't happen.

But protective leadership is not forged on quiet days; it's forged in **crisis.** It's in the moments when the itinerary collapses, when a credible threat emerges mid-flight, or when the principal becomes the center of a sudden reputational storm. In those moments, what you've built, or failed to build, shows immediately.

As the principal's profile grows, their travel becomes more complex, and public exposure more visible, the threat picture becomes layered. Suddenly, one person's vigilance is no longer enough. The conversation shifts from *a protector* to *a protective effort.* And soon after, it shifts again from an effort to a *program* capable of sustaining operational excellence even when the leader is across the globe or entirely out of contact.

This is dual evolution work; *shaping yourself into a leader who can command calmly in chaos and shaping others into a team that thinks and acts independently when it matters most.* It's about building a unit that can absorb shocks without losing momentum, embedding protective strategies into the organization's broader resilience framework, and leaving behind a program so capable and trusted that it thrives long after your watch has ended. Years later, in a high-threat evacuation of a regional office, a team executed flawlessly despite the original leader

 DOI: 10.4324/9781003670704-9

being half a world away. All proof that what had been built was more than a function, but part of a heritage.

Legacy building in this context isn't about plaques or titles; it's about **the readiness you leave behind.** A crisis-ready culture, decision-making discipline, and integrated protective capability *are* your legacy.

FORMING A CRISIS-READY TEAM: APPLYING TUCKMAN'S MODEL IN PROTECTIVE LEADERSHIP

In the formative stage of any protective program, leaders often underestimate how critical the *team development cycle* is to long-term success. A team's early behaviors, how they handle disagreements, how they respond to first contact with stress, how they absorb (or resist) guidance, will echo through its future performance.

Bruce Tuckman's model (**Forming, Storming, Norming, Performing, and Adjourning**) remains one of the most reliable lenses for understanding how teams grow.[1] In the protective environment, these stages are compressed, repeated, and stress-tested under conditions where failure can have immediate consequences for safety, reputation, and mission continuity. Recognizing which stage your team is in helps a protective leader choose the right interventions, from clarifying mission scope during Forming, to running red-team drills during Storming, so the team reaches Performing before a real-world crisis demands it.

FORMING

In protection, forming begins the moment your first operators assemble. Early emphasis is on:

- **Clarity of purpose**—defining mission scope, roles, and reporting lines
- **Baseline capability assessments**—identifying both the technical and soft skills each member brings
- **Early integration** with external partners (e.g., corporate security, HR, or IT) so your team is not an island from day one

At this stage, you set the tone for professionalism, discretion, and adaptability. You also set expectations for how operational work will intersect with *organizational resilience goals*, framing, from the outset, that your protective mission is part of a larger system of risk management, not a standalone silo.

Vignette: In a hostile environment deployment for a global NGO, a newly formed protection team faced a flash protest outside their compound. Because the leader had established clear role assignments in week one, the team executed its rally point plan without confusion, moving the principal to safety before the crowd reached the perimeter. That decisive performance, so early in their lifecycle, built immediate trust with both the principal and the host nation's security liaison.

STORMING

In a high-performance protective detail, the storming phase often centers on **method disagreements**, such as which routes are the safest, how much visibility is appropriate at events, or how rigidly SOPs should be applied in dynamic situations.

Here, an effective leader can use *controlled conflict* as a development tool, such as introducing **red team/blue team exercises** where one element plans the protective posture, and other attempts to expose vulnerabilities.[2] Use these exercises not just to test plans, but to surface differences in risk perception, communication styles, and problem-solving approaches.

Vignette: At a Fortune 500 product launch, an EP team had long debated access control. A live red-team drill settled it—a faux journalist breached the inner perimeter in under three minutes, prompting the team to co-author a protocol that later prevented a real-world breach.

NORMING

Once the dust settles, the team begins to find rhythm. SOPs are no longer just written documents, they're habits.

At this stage, leaders should:

- Introduce **cross-training** to avoid single points of failure (e.g., advance leads running communication drills, drivers practicing extraction scenarios, etc.).

- Begin **integrating the team into the organization's larger resilience exercises**, such as crisis management drills or insider threat tabletop simulations, so they understand their role in the enterprise's full risk picture.

Vignette: A detail supporting a global tech CEO participated in a joint cyber-physical crisis exercise with the company's security operations center (SOC) and PR teams. When a real hybrid threat—a data breach timed with an in-person protest—hit months later, the team recognized the indicators, alerted communication to control the narrative, and adjusted the principal's movement plan on the fly. The incident was contained in hours instead of days.

PERFORMING

A performing team can execute under pressure without the leader's constant direction, freeing the leader to focus on:

- Strategic coordination with stakeholders during incidents.
- Feeding real-time intelligence into corporate decision-making processes.
- Linking operational decisions to continuity and brand protection priorities.

Vignette: While a team leader was in transit during an overseas assignment, the principal suffered a serious medical emergency. Because the team had drilled med-evac procedures and pre-positioned contingency resources, the on-site lead coordinated with local responders, secured a med-flight, and kept the principal's family informed, all before the leader's aircraft landed. The operation's seamless execution became a benchmark for the company's entire travel risk program.

ADJOURNING

In protection, adjourning may occur when an assignment ends, a principal changes roles, or the leader transitions out. This is often overlooked, yet it is critical for legacy building:

- Capture **lessons learned** and embed them in the program's playbooks.
- Preserve **institutional relationships** with other departments and agencies.
- Ensure **knowledge transfer** so the program's capability is not tied to one person's memory or leadership style.

Many mature protective programs also maintain informal *alumni networks* of former team members. These relationships can be invaluable for intelligence-sharing, emergency resourcing, and preserving institutional memory long after personnel changes.

Vignette: Before departing a multinational financial firm, the EP manager compiled a "living" crisis operations binder containing updated protocols, contact lists, and after-action reports from every incident in the past five years. Eighteen months later, when a major regional office faced civil unrest, the on-site team used those archived playbooks to guide an evacuation that moved 42 staff members to safety without injury.

DEVELOPING THE LEADER: FROM SKILL MASTERY TO STRATEGIC READINESS

> The mind is not a vessel to be filled, but a fire to be kindled.
>
> *Plutarch*[3]

Protective leadership begins with the self. The most capable teams are shaped by leaders who invest in their own growth with the same intensity they expect from others. In high-stakes environments, this is not about collecting certifications or attending the occasional course; it's about cultivating mental agility, emotional steadiness, and judgment to lead under pressure.

Self-development in the protection profession has a dual purpose: **mastering your craft** and **expanding your capacity to make high-consequence decisions in complex environments**. The first requires technical proficiency and operational discipline. The second demands a deeper transformation, refining how you think, frame problems, and influence others when the situation outpaces the plan.

Leaders who kindle that "fire" in themselves set the tone for their teams. They move beyond reactive problem-solving to proactive readiness, shaping not just the actions taken in a crisis, but the thinking that precedes them. They are students of both **training** and **education**; drilling skills until they are instinctive, while also engaging in study and reflection that sharpen judgment when the script runs out.

TRAINING, EDUCATION, AND EXPERIENCE: THE THREE PILLARS OF LEADER DEVELOPMENT

In the protective profession, personal development isn't one-dimensional. A leader's readiness is shaped by three complementary forces: **training**, **education**, and **experience**. Neglecting any one of them creates imbalances and in crisis, imbalance is a liability.

These pillars align with research on leadership development, such as the Center for Creative Leadership's widely used 70-20-10 model, which finds that approximately 70% of leadership growth comes from challenging assignments and experiences, 20% from developmental relationships, and only 10% from formal training.[4] For protective leaders, the ratios may shift over a career, but the interplay of these three elements is constant.

TRAINING—BUILDING THE REFLEXES

Training is about hardwiring technical skills so they can be executed without hesitation under pressure. In the close protection context: motorcade drills, advance planning checklists, defensive tactics, firearms qualifications, medical response protocols. The goal is to make execution second nature so cognitive bandwidth is preserved for decision-making.

Malcolm Knowles' adult learning theory reinforces that training should be problem-centered and immediately relevant to the learner's role.[5] In protection, that means designing training scenarios that mirror the realities of the operating environment, not just abstract skill drills.

> *Vignette*: A principal's private aircraft suffered an engine failure on approach. The protective detail had drilled airfield evacuation procedures so frequently that they deployed to their rally points instinctively, secured transportation, and executed the contingency route before the principal even reached the terminal. Their ability to act without hesitation freed the leader to coordinate with airport security and corporate communication.

EDUCATION—BUILDING THE JUDGMENT

Education develops conceptual understanding and judgment—the ability to interpret complex situations, anticipate second-order effects, and choose the most strategic path forward. In the close protection context, it is studying behavioral threat assessment, understanding crisis communication principles, and learning how organizational resilience frameworks operate. This prepares both leaders and teams for scenarios where no SOP exists and where understanding the "why" is more important than knowing the "how."

As Daniel Goleman's work on emotional intelligence shows, leaders who cultivate self-awareness, empathy, and adaptability are better equipped to make sound decisions under pressure.[6] In protection, education often draws from disciplines beyond security, such as psychology, business continuity, cyber risk, law, and negotiation, broadening a leader's ability to integrate protective strategies into enterprise decision-making.

Vignette: During a global merger announcement, a protection leader spotted language in the CEO's press statement that could inflame labor unrest. Early intervention with the communications team allowed for changes and pre-positioned security—preventing reputational harm and potential violence.

EXPERIENCE—BUILDING WISDOM

Experience pressure tests both training and education in the real world. It's the crucible where theory meets reality, often in conditions that are ambiguous, fast-moving, and politically complex.

Kolb's experiential learning theory underscores that true learning is cyclical—leaders apply what they know, reflect on outcomes, form new concepts, and test them in new situations. In the protective environment, this cycle might involve analyzing a past advance to identify missed indicators, adjusting future threat assessments accordingly, and then testing those changes during the next assignment. For protective leaders, deliberately structuring this process ensures that every operation (even routine ones) becomes a platform for sharpening anticipation, decision-making, and adaptability.

Vignette: A junior advance agent was assigned to lead a protective movement in a volatile region, with the senior leader observing in the background. When a crowd unexpectedly blocked the motorcade route, the agent applied contingency routing learned in training, adjusted movement timing based on local cultural insight from their education, and avoided escalation. The experience, and the confidence it built, prepared them to lead during a real crisis six months later.

When training, education, and experience are balanced, they create leaders who are technically sharp, strategically capable, and battle-tested. Training builds speed and accuracy. Education builds foresight and adaptability. Experience fuses the two into wisdom that can be applied under any conditions. For the protective leader, this triad is not a checklist—it's a continuous cycle of reinforcement, refinement, and legacy building.

BUILDING THE TEAM'S CAPABILITY

A crisis-ready protective program is not defined by the sum of its individual skills, but by the **shared capability** that emerges when those skills are coordinated, adaptable, and tied to a clear purpose. In high-stakes environments, capability is both **technical** and **relational:** it depends as much on the trust between team members as on their tactical competence.

For a protective leader, building capability is an intentional act of design. It's not simply recruiting skilled operators or running them through standard drills; it's about shaping a unit that can function as a single organism in the face of volatility. This means embedding the right **mindset** alongside the right **skillset,** ensuring the team can adapt when the plan breaks down, and integrating them into the larger systems of the organization's resilience.

The long-term measure of success here is **transferability.** If a principal's protection detail finds itself on the far side of the world with the leader out of contact, the team should still be able to plan, decide, and execute to standard. That kind of independence doesn't happen by accident, it's cultivated through recruiting for the right attributes, developing skills through realistic and progressive training, giving people experience that tests their judgment, and connecting their work to the broader mission of the enterprise.

In short, building capability is as much about **preparing for the crisis you can't predict** as it is about refining the drills for the crises you can.

The following sections explore how to identify and develop the people, processes, and integrations that make a protective team more than the sum of its parts.

RECRUITMENT FOR FIT AND POTENTIAL

In protection leadership, technical skills are necessary but insufficient. Research in high-reliability organizations shows that adaptability, teamwork, and situational awareness often outweigh pure technical competence in predicting performance under pressure.[7]

Recruitment should therefore prioritize:

- Adaptability under stress.
- Discretion in sensitive environments.
- Learning agility, that is, the ability to absorb new methods and apply them quickly.

Behavior-based interviews and scenario testing can reveal these traits better than a resume review alone.[8]

Vignette: A candidate for an EP role at a multinational bank was asked, mid-interview, to role-play managing a principal's unexpected schedule change in a foreign city. Their ability to adapt calmly, coordinate resources, and communicate clearly under simulated pressure outweighed another applicant's longer tactical résumé, and proved decisive in the final hiring decision.

DELIBERATE DEVELOPMENT THROUGH SCENARIO-BASED TRAINING

Once the right people are on the team, capability is built through **deliberate practice**, a concept drawn from performance psychology research.[9] Skills are refined not by generic repetition, but by targeted drills that stretch ability, incorporate feedback, and simulate real-world complexity.

For protective teams, this means:

- Scenario-based exercises that force problem-solving under ambiguity
- Incorporating elements of "stress inoculation" so operators remain effective under pressure

- Rotating leadership roles in training to develop decision-making depth across the team

Vignette: In a joint exercise with corporate comms and cybersecurity, a detail rehearsed response to a hybrid threat, a doxxing campaign triggering a flash protest. The drill reinforced cross-functional coordination that later proved critical during a real reputational incident.

WARGAMING FOR STRATEGIC INTEGRATION

Wargaming (structured simulation of crisis scenarios) is a tool borrowed from the military and now widely used in enterprise risk management. For protective leaders, wargaming is the bridge between **operational drills** and **organizational integration.**

When done well, wargaming:

- Stress tests protective strategies against realistic, evolving threats
- Exposes interdependence with other departments (HR, legal, IT, facilities)
- Builds strategic adaptability—the ability to pivot when plans fail

WARGAMING BASICS FOR PROTECTIVE LEADERS

At its core, wargaming is a structured rehearsal of decision-making under realistic conditions. In the protective context, a simple wargame has three core elements:

1. **Scenario**—a plausible situation, grounded in real threat intelligence or operational history. Example: "Principal is in a hotel ballroom when an active threat incident begins in the lobby."
2. **Roles**—participants take on real-world positions (advance lead, detail leader, communications liaison, corporate crisis manager), ensuring everyone practices decision-making from their own perspective.
3. **Adjudication**—a facilitator introduces new developments ("power fails," "law enforcement response delayed") and tracks outcomes based on participant actions, forcing the group to adapt in real time.[10]

Basic protective wargames can be run in a conference room with a whiteboard and floor plan or virtually using collaboration tools. The key is **progressive complexity**; starting simple, then adding multiple threat vectors (e.g., insider threat indicators, reputational escalation on social media) as the team's capability grows.

Well-run wargames should conclude with a **structured after-action review (AAR)**, capturing what worked, what didn't, and what procedural or training adjustments are needed. Over time, this process builds a shared decision-making vocabulary and strengthens both operational reflexes and strategic thinking across the team.

For smaller or solo details, wargaming can be scaled down to focused tabletop reviews of past trips or plausible threats, walking through "what-if" scenarios with a partner or trusted colleague. Even brief, low-resource exercises sharpen anticipation and decision-making skills.

> *Vignette*: A protective detail for a global NGO ran a two-day wargame simulating a principal's overseas visit during a local political uprising. In the scenario, airport access was cut off and local police switched allegiances mid-operation. Because they had rehearsed contingency decision-making and cross-agency coordination in the wargame, the real visit months later proceeded smoothly despite actual civil unrest.

LEADING IN CRISIS

A protective leader's defining moments are rarely scheduled. They happen in the unscripted hours, when the plan fractures, the environment shifts, and every eye turns to the person in charge. In these moments, leadership is measured not by what you know in theory, but by how you **apply** it under pressure.

The ability to lead in crisis is not built overnight. It grows from deliberate preparation, rehearsed decision-making, and the confidence to act when time is short and stakes are high. Practices like wargaming and scenario-based drills are not just training tools; they are laboratories for crisis leadership, allowing leaders to stress-test their composure, decision flow, and communication style before they face the real thing.[11]

COMMANDING CALM IN CHAOS

In crisis, your demeanor is the emotional thermostat for your team and the principal. Neuroscience research shows that stress responses are highly contagious; *a leader's visible composure can measurably lower anxiety and improve performance across the team.*[12]

Command presence in crisis comes from:

- **Pre-commitment to protocols**—knowing exactly what the first actions will be in a threat scenario
- **Deliberate control of non-verbal signals**—measured tone, stable posture, and consistent eye contact
- **Disciplined breathing**—techniques like combat breathing to maintain cognitive clarity under stress[13]

Vignette: During an attempted breach at a high-profile conference, the protection leader walked (not ran) to the command post, delivering clear, three-step instructions to the on-site lead. That steadiness allowed the team to move the principal without panic, while security partners quietly neutralized the threat. AARs cited the leader's composure as the factor that kept the extraction controlled and discreet.

RAPID ORIENTATION AND DECISION-MAKING

Crises rarely present complete information. Leaders must act with partial data and shifting facts, making **decision speed and quality** equally important.

The OODA Loop (Observe, Orient, Decide, Act) remains a core framework for rapid decision-making.[14] In protective operations, it's often the difference between controlling the timeline and reacting to it. Whether redirecting a motorcade, managing an unexpected crowd surge, or responding to an emerging cyber-physical threat, cycling through OODA faster than the adversary keeps you ahead of the threat curve. A protective leader who trains their team to apply OODA in drills and advances ensures that, in a crisis, decisions are made at speed without sacrificing judgment.

In a crisis, the protective leader must:

1. **Observe**—Gather immediate facts without overloading on detail
2. **Orient**—Frame the situation against known threat patterns, organizational priorities, and constraints
3. **Decide**—Select a course of action that addresses the highest-risk factors first
4. **Act**—Implement decisively while preparing to adjust as new information emerges

Avoid decision paralysis by establishing pre-determined decision thresholds during planning. Knowing in advance the conditions that will trigger specific responses accelerates action and reduces hesitation under pressure.

> *Vignette*: When a violent protest unexpectedly blocked a motorcade route, the detail leader (already monitoring local law enforcement feeds) redirected to a pre-identified alternate route within seconds. The principal was moved without incident, and the executive assistant quietly rescheduled the next engagement, minimizing operational disruption.

BALANCING THE TACTICAL AND THE STRATEGIC

In a crisis, leaders often gravitate to the "front line" of the action. But, in a protective leadership role, **the bigger risk is tunnel vision**, focusing on tactical tasks at the expense of strategic oversight.

The protective leader's job in a crisis is to:

- **Delegate tactical execution** to trusted operators
- **Engage strategic stakeholders** such as corporate leadership, legal, communications to align operational actions with enterprise needs
- **Maintain situational altitude**—the broader the perspective, the better the coordination of resources and narrative

> *Vignette*: During a natural disaster overseas, the protection leader handed immediate evacuation control to the advance agent while they coordinated directly with the company's COO and crisis management team back in headquarters. This allowed simultaneous management of the principal's safety, corporate communications, and media monitoring, preserving both the executive and the company's public credibility.

INTEGRATING CRISIS LEADERSHIP INTO LEGACY BUILDING

Crisis leadership is not only about solving the problem in front of you, but it's also about building a team and a program that can handle the next one without you.

Every crisis is an opportunity to:

- Capture **after-action insights** and integrate them into SOPs
- Identify **emerging leaders** who demonstrated initiative
- Strengthen **cross-functional relationships** that proved valuable in response

When leaders treat crises as accelerators for capability (rather than interruptions), they reinforce both the resilience of their team and the durability of their program. This is how crisis leadership feeds directly into legacy building.

FROM LEADER TO TEAM TO CRISIS PERFORMANCE

Earlier in this chapter, the focus was on the leader, cultivating the mindset, judgment, and adaptability that form the foundation of crisis command. From there, the lens widened to the team and building shared capability, trust, and integration into the organization's resilience architecture.

Here, those two investments meet in the crucible of a real crisis. The leader's personal readiness and the team's collective capability are inseparable in determining outcomes. Where preparation ends and autonomy begins is the seamless handoff that defines a mature, resilient protective program.

The next step is to explore the cultural dimension, how leaders create an environment of trust, accountability, and continuous learning that sustains high performance between crises and across leadership transitions.

CREATING A CULTURE OF TRUST, ACCOUNTABILITY, AND CONTINUOUS LEARNING

Trust, accountability, and continuous learning are the cultural pillars that keep a protective program strong between crises. Without them, even the most technically capable team will erode under pressure or drift toward complacency. With them, teams become resilient systems that can adapt, self-correct, and perform consistently, whether the leader is present or not.

Culture begins with the leader. The US Army's Non-commissioned Officer Corps.' leadership philosophy of *Be, Know, Do* captures the essence: **Be** the character and example others trust; **Know** your craft, your people, and the mission; **Do** what is right, decisive, and necessary.[15] In protection, these three imperatives translate into the everyday signals you send about what is valued, rewarded, and tolerated. The team will mirror not only the skills you teach, but the standards you embody.

This principle echoes the martial traditions of leadership, from the samurai code of *Bushidō* to the writings of Sun Tzu and Musashi, where mastery is not simply measured by technique, but by the cultivation of virtue, understanding, and decisive action. A leader who models integrity, discipline, and curiosity shapes a team that operates the same way, even when faced with uncertainty or danger.

Edgar Schein's work on organizational culture emphasizes that culture is not formed by slogans or mission statements; it is shaped by what leaders consistently reward, tolerate, and model.[16] In protection, this means that every decision, briefing, and AAR sends a signal about what truly matters. Over time, those signals accumulate into the unwritten code by which the team operates, and that code is what endures when the leader steps away.

BUILDING AND SUSTAINING TRUST

Trust is the currency of a high-performing protective team. It's built through **competence, consistency**, and **care**. Team members trust leaders who can make sound decisions under pressure, keep their word, and look out for their people both professionally and personally.

Trust also flows upward. The principal (and organization) must believe that the protective team's advice is credible, discreet, and aligned with their interests. This means communicating with transparency, guarding confidentiality fiercely, and resisting the temptation to overstate threats or hide inconvenient truths.

> *Vignette*: A CEO's security detail discovered a credible online threat tied to a business decision. Rather than pushing for immediate, highly visible measures that might alarm stakeholders, the team quietly elevated security, coordinated with cyber investigators, and briefed the CEO in a closed-door session. The principal later remarked that the team's discretion had increased their confidence in the protective program more than any single security upgrade.

For global or multicultural teams, trust also depends on cultural awareness. Leaders who understand and respect differences in communication style, hierarchy, and conflict resolution build stronger, more cohesive teams across borders.

EMBEDDING ACCOUNTABILITY

Accountability in a protective culture isn't about punishment; it's about ownership. High-reliability organizations rely on "just culture" principles, where individuals are held responsible for their choices but are encouraged to report mistakes and near misses without fear of unfair reprisal.[17]

For protective leaders, this means:

- Setting clear expectations for performance and behavior
- Modeling accountability by owning their own decisions and errors
- Creating space for team members to speak up about risks, process gaps, or personal limitations before those issues become crises

Vignette: During a high-visibility event, an agent failed to follow a low-profile positioning protocol, resulting in unwanted press photos of the principal. In the AAR, the team lead openly acknowledged that unclear pre-event guidance contributed to the misstep. By sharing responsibility rather than placing blame, the leader preserved trust, corrected the process, and reinforced the expectation that mistakes must be surfaced to be fixed.

DRIVING CONTINUOUS LEARNING

Continuous learning is the engine that prevents stagnation and prepares the team for emerging threats. In protection, this means deliberately seeking lessons not only from incidents, but also from near misses, cross-functional exercises, and external case studies.

Key practices include:

- **Structured after-action reviews** held promptly after events, focused on facts, and resulting in actionable changes.
- **Cross-training** to develop versatility and reduce single points of failure.
- **External benchmarking** engaging with peers, professional associations, and industry briefings to import best practices and new threat insights.[18]

Vignette: After participating in a multinational corporate security summit, a protective intelligence analyst brought back insights into emerging drone threats to executives. Within weeks, the protection leader had commissioned a vulnerability assessment and updated event security protocols, a proactive move that later proved valuable during a shareholder meeting when unauthorized drones were spotted near the venue.

CULTURE AS A FORCE MULTIPLIER

When trust, accountability, and learning are embedded into the program's culture, they amplify the effectiveness of every other investment, from training and wargaming to crisis management and stakeholder engagement. Teams operating in this kind of culture:

- Communicate more clearly under stress
- Self-correct faster when errors occur
- Retain talent and attract high-caliber recruits

Ultimately, culture is part of the leader's legacy. Long after policies are updated and tactics evolve, the culture you leave behind will determine whether the program remains resilient, adaptable, and respected.

MENTORSHIP AND LEGACY

Culture becomes lasting when it's paired with intentional mentorship. A strong program doesn't just execute well in the present but builds leaders for the future. In protection, the measure of a leader's long-term success isn't only the crises they managed, but the people and systems they leave behind.

Mentorship ensures that critical skills, decision-making habits, and cultural values aren't lost when personnel move on. John Maxwell indicated, "Success is knowing your purpose in life, growing to reach your maximum potential, and sowing seeds that benefit others."[19] For the protective leader, those "seeds" are the next generation of operators, analysts, and managers who will carry forward the standards you've set.

IDENTIFYING AND DEVELOPING EMERGING LEADERS

Mentorship starts with observation. Pay attention to those who step up under pressure, who demonstrate curiosity about the broader mission, and who earn the trust of peers and stakeholders.

Once identified, give these individuals **progressive responsibility**:

- Assign them to lead advance work for a lower-risk trip
- Let them run point during a scenario-based training or wargame
- Involve them in post-incident reviews and let them present findings to stakeholders

Mentorship should also be two-way. Reverse mentorship is inviting emerging leaders to share insights on new technologies, evolving threat trends, or generational perspectives, which will ensure senior leaders are adaptable and connected to fresh ideas.

This approach not only builds skill and confidence, but it also signals trust, which is a powerful motivator that accelerates professional growth.

Vignette: A junior EP agent was given the lead on security for a board off-site, coordinating facilities, communications, and local law enforcement. Despite a last-minute venue change, the event went smoothly, earning the agent credibility and the confidence to take on more complex assignments.

TRANSFERRING INSTITUTIONAL KNOWLEDGE

Leaders often underestimate how much operational insight resides in their heads — contacts, shortcuts, risk assessments, and "why" certain SOPs exist. Without deliberate transfer, this knowledge disappears when they depart.

Strategies for knowledge transfer include:

- Maintaining a living **operations binder** with updated SOPs, contact lists, and case studies.
- Recording **after-action debriefs** in a central, searchable archive.

- Assigning shadowing **opportunities** so junior team members can learn by watching decision-making in real time.[20]

Vignette: Before retiring, a CSO compiled a digital "continuity kit" that included threat trend reports, key vendor agreements, and lessons learned from major incidents. Months later, when a new threat emerged, the incoming leader found the exact mitigation strategy in those files, saving days of research and coordination.

LEAVING A LEADERSHIP LEGACY

A leadership legacy is built in layers — not in a single project, crisis, or decision. It is the accumulation of:

- **Skills you've taught** — the technical competencies, judgment frameworks, and decision-making habits you've embedded in others.
- **Standards you've upheld** — the non-negotiables for conduct, performance, and ethical behavior that define your program's identity.
- **Systems you've built** — the processes, playbooks, and networks that keep operations running smoothly regardless of who holds the title.
- **People you've developed** — the next generation of leaders who can not only perform but also guide and mentor others.

When these elements endure beyond your tenure, you've left the program, and the people, stronger than you found them. In the protective profession, this is the true measure of legacy; *a team that can operate effectively in your absence, adapt to evolving threats, and uphold the mission without relying on a single individual.*

It's easy to think of legacy as a ceremonial concept (a farewell speech, a line in an annual report) but it's the operational resilience you leave behind. It's evident when a team flawlessly executes a crisis response six months after you've gone, or when a junior leader you mentored trains the next generation without missing a beat. Legacy is not about being remembered, it's about ensuring the mission, the standards, and the culture you've cultivated continue to thrive long after your watch ends.

THE LASTING ECHO

Leadership in the protective profession is not defined by a single skillset, a flawless crisis response, or a high-profile assignment. It is the sum of how you have developed yourself, how you have built and empowered your team, how you have led when it mattered most, and how you have prepared the program to thrive without you.

The journey begins inward, strengthening your own judgment, composure, and adaptability. It then expands outward, recruiting the right people, forging them into a capable and trusted unit, and embedding them into the broader resilience framework of the organization. In crisis, those investments converge: the leader's clarity and the team's capability form a single, decisive force that protects people, reputation, and mission.

Marcus Aurelius reminded himself, *What we do now, in the brief moment allotted to us, echoes through the quality of our lives and the lives we touch.*[21] In protection, that echo is not about fame or recognition. It is the enduring culture, the standards upheld, the systems built, and the people developed. Your legacy is measured in the decisions made with integrity when you are not in the room, when those you've led act with purpose because you prepared them to think, decide, and lead.

In the end, protective leadership is not about being the hero in the moment. It is about ensuring that every moment (planned or unforeseen) is met with competence, integrity, and unity, no matter who is wearing the earpiece or standing at the front of the room. That is how you leave a program stronger than you found it, and that is how leadership becomes a legacy.

NOTES

1 Bruce W. Tuckman, "Developmental Sequence in Small Groups," *Psychological Bulletin* 63, no. 6, 1965, pp. 384–99, https://pubmed.ncbi.nlm.nih.gov/14314073/.

2 Micah Zenko, *Red Team: How to Succeed by Thinking Like the Enemy* (New York: Basic Books, 2015).

3 Plutarch, *Moralia*, "On Listening to Lectures," in *Plutarch's Morals*, trans. William W. Goodwin (Boston, MA: Little, Brown, and Company, 1878).

4 Center for Creative Leadership, *70-20-10 Rule for Leadership Development*, CCL Insights, https://www.ccl.org/articles/leading-effectively-articles/70-20-10-rule/.

5 Malcolm S. Knowles, *The Adult Learner: The Definitive Classic in Adult Education and Human Resource Development*, 8th ed. (New York: Routledge, 2015).

6 Daniel Goleman, *Working with Emotional Intelligence* (New York: Bantam Books, 1998).
7 Karl E. Weick and Kathleen M. Sutcliffe, *Managing the Unexpected: Sustained Performance in a Complex World*, 3rd ed. (Hoboken, NJ: Wiley, 2015).
8 Mark Murphy, *Hiring for Attitude: A Revolutionary Approach to Recruiting and Selecting People with Both Tremendous Skills and Superb Attitude* (New York: McGraw-Hill, 2012).
9 Anders Ericsson and Robert Pool, *Peak: Secrets from the New Science of Expertise* (Boston, MA: Houghton Mifflin Harcourt, 2016).
10 C.3. Appleget, Robert Burks, and Fred Cameron, *The Craft of Wargaming: A Detailed Planning Guide for Defense Planners and Analysts* (Annapolis, MD: Naval Institute Press, 2020).
11 Appleget, et. al., *Craft of Wargaming.*
12 Daniel Goleman, *Primal Leadership: Unleashing the Power of Emotional Intelligence* (Boston: Harvard Business Review Press, 2002).
13 Dave Grossman and Loren W. Christensen, *On Combat: The Psychology and Physiology of Deadly Conflict in War and in Peace*, 3rd ed. (Millstadt, IL: Warrior Science Group, 2008).
14 John R. Boyd, "Patterns of Conflict," unpublished briefing slides, c. 1986; see also U.S. Army, *FM 6-0, Commander and Staff Organization and Operations* (Washington, DC: Headquarters, Department of the Army, 2014).
15 U.S. Department of the Army, *FM 22–100, Army Leadership* (Washington, DC: Headquarters, Department of the Army, 1999).
16 Edgar H. Schein and Peter A. Schein, *Organizational Culture and Leadership*, 5th ed. (Hoboken, NJ: Wiley, 2017).
17 James Reason, *Managing the Risks of Organizational Accidents* (Aldershot: Ashgate, 1997).
18 Amy C. Edmondson, *The Fearless Organization: Creating Psychological Safety in the Workplace for Learning, Innovation, and Growth* (Hoboken, NJ: Wiley, 2019).
19 John C. Maxwell, *The 21 Irrefutable Laws of Leadership: Follow Them and People Will Follow You*, 10th Anniversary Edition (Nashville: Thomas Nelson, 2007).
20 Michael Useem, *The Leadership Moment: Nine True Stories of Triumph and Disaster and Their Lessons for Us All* (New York: Crown Business, 1998).
21 Marcus Aurelius, *Meditations*, Book 6, Section 30, paraphrased from Gregory Hays, trans., *Meditations* (New York: Modern Library, 2002).

CHAPTER 7

Leading Up: Becoming a Trusted Advisor

Imagine a high-profile protectee asking, "Why should I trust you with my life?" As a protective leader, do not be mistaken, it's not just a question about securing a venue or stopping a threat. Rather, it's a challenge to prove you belong in their world. A world where every decision is dissected, every misstep can cost millions, and every moment is a balancing act between opportunity and exposure. The question posed is asking if you understand their pressures, if you can speak their language, and if you can deliver more than a guardian's vigilance. They want a partner who can stand beside them, aligning safekeeping with their vision for success.

Executive protection has always been a quiet craft. It is built on discretion and a steady pulse of vigilance that rarely makes itself known. For years, the best protectors moved in the shadows, watching crowds with a practiced eye and running contingency plans that no one ever saw. The goal was simple: nothing happens. No delays, no disruption, no drama.

As a protector, you witnessed the way a CEO floated between high-stakes meetings, unbothered by what might be waiting outside. Behind that ease was a team moving with discipline and intent, quietly holding the line. That used to be enough. Being invisible meant you were doing the job right.

But that era is over.

Today's threats do not wait quietly in the shadows. They strike from public platforms, from data breaches, from ideological corners of the internet no one saw coming. Digital vulnerabilities unravel operations in hours. Disinformation campaigns can turn executives into villains overnight. And the kind of violence once reserved for heads of state

DOI: 10.4324/9781003670704-10

has entered corporate life. Recent attacks on business leaders have sent shockwaves through boardrooms across the country. The message was clear: business leaders are not just vulnerable; they are targets.

This is the world we live in now. And in this world, the old rules don't hold. New challenges demand a new kind of professional, one who doesn't just react to threats but influences the C-suite, turning protective intelligence into strategic insights that protect revenue, reputation, and organizational resilience.

The characteristic "bodyguard" mindset, visible presence, and silent support fall short. Protection can't just be physical anymore. It must be strategic. That means integrating threat anticipation into the decision-making process, not just the security of venues. It means understanding risk as a leadership issue, not just a security concern. The modern protector isn't there to stand behind the principal. They're there to stand beside them, thinking ahead, advising up, steering outcomes before danger can shape them.

At the core of this relationship dynamic lies trust; the indispensable cornerstone of any effective executive relationship. Without it, the protector is no more than a hired hand, a cost line item susceptible to cuts and sidelining. Without trust, influence is limited, and protection risks becoming a transactional service rather than a strategic partnership. But when trust is earned, the protective professional moves into rarified territory: the executive's inner circle, a seat at the strategy table, a voice that shapes outcomes.

Earning this trust requires more than technical skill; it demands empathy and a willingness to step into the complex emotional and strategic world of executives. It requires the ability to translate security into business language. It means turning threat information into revenue protection scenarios and reputational risk assessments, and continuity plans that are understood not as constraints, but as enablers of fearless leadership.

Those who have developed this type of leadership have forged enduring opportunities; however, getting to this point in their career is hardly simple. It necessitates patience, emotional intelligence, and strategic acumen. But the impact is profound. Trusted advisors do more than guard lives; they enable legacies. They empower leaders to shape their organizations with clarity and confidence, bringing protection into the realm of organizational advantage.

Today's landscape demands nothing less. Threats never remain at rest; rather, they are constantly evolving. That reality calls for protective professionals who also evolve, who weave intelligence into the fabric of business strategy, anticipating risks and enabling success, not only responding to danger but shaping the environment in which leaders operate.

Leading up requires shedding typecasts. The classical "bodyguard" or "security guard" archetype is no longer sufficient. Instead, professionals must become thinkers, communicators, and collaborators. They must deeply understand the relentless pressures executives face, their vulnerabilities under public scrutiny, and the complexity of high-stakes decision-making. They must demonstrate that protection is not simply about preventing harm but about creating the confidence leaders need to thrive, whether negotiating mergers, addressing diverse stakeholders, or standing tall in high-risk regions.

This concept is not optional; it is essential because executives work in a crucible where geopolitical instability, digital threats, and public sentiment converge unpredictably and rapidly. A security professional who cannot translate complex insights into terms that resonate with the C-suite, like revenue protection, brand equity, and operational continuity, risks marginalization. Leading up reframes the role: it positions you as a business enabler, an essential partner in the organizational mission. This shift challenges traditional boundaries and propels you into the executive's inner circle, where your insights shape the course of your enterprise.

The practical change underpinning this transformation is a shift from reactive to proactive intelligence. Protection historically scaled up after threats materialized, guided by annual assessments too static to keep pace with a dynamic threat landscape. A report penned in January might miss a social-media-driven protest becoming a physical risk by February, leaving the organization exposed during moments it could least afford.

The future is different. It is driven by the need for real-time protective intelligence, constantly scanning digital and physical environments to foresee and mitigate threats before they escalate. Tools such as social media monitoring platforms, threat intelligence software, and predictive analytics allow rapid identification of risks and nimble strategy adjustments. This foresighted approach fosters executive trust, showcasing not just security proficiency but leadership acumen.

Leading up is more than a shift in professional responsibility; it marks a protective leader's personal growth. It demonstrates a level of maturity that reframes security from a costly obligation to a strategic asset, helping steer the organization toward success in an ever-changing and uncertain environment.

EARNING TRUST AND INFLUENCE

To truly understand the art of leading up within executive protection, it is essential to shift the paradigm from guarding physical safety to becoming a trusted partner who shapes strategy and outcomes at the most senior levels of an organization. The traditional protector's role, focused on physical awareness and crisis response, is no longer adequate in a world of layered, dynamic risks that extend far beyond the visible or tangible.

This evolution calls for a profound change in mindset. It requires moving from transactional security services, where safety is delivered through protocol and presence, toward a relational advisory role, rooted deeply in trust, influence, and business acumen. The trusted advisor occupies a uniquely challenging role that balances expertise with empathy and tactical vigilance with strategic vision.

The foundational framework for this kind of relationship was articulated with precision in *The Trusted Advisor* by David Maister, Charles Green, and Robert Galford, who describe trust as comprising four interdependent elements: credibility, reliability, intimacy, and low self-orientation.[1] Credibility refers to the protector's knowledge and expertise presented with confidence yet without arrogance. Reliability emerges from consistent actions, evidence that you do what you say you will, despite challenge or pressure. Intimacy means cultivating connection, knowing the leader's personal and professional pressures, and responding with understanding and discretion. Lastly, self-orientation must remain minimal; protectors must prioritize the principal's best interests over their own ego or convenience. When these dimensions align, the protective relationship transcends duty and becomes a partnership.

Historically, executive protection was entrenched in process and compliance, not relationship. The language of risk assessments, checklists, and operational constraints dominated communication, often alienating leaders who were seeking clarity, brevity, and actionable insight. This gap inhibited protectors from influencing decision-making in the executive suite, confining them instead to the perimeter of strategy.

Leading up requires translating complex security realities into narratives that resonate with executive concerns, such as: how will this threat impact revenue? What reputational risks could emerge? How might operational continuity be disrupted? Embedding security with these lenses converts what could be technical data into strategic business intelligence, inviting executives to engage not out of fear but as informed actors shaping risk and opportunity.

Noted Professor Brené Brown's leadership teachings underpin this approach. Her assertion that "clear is kind" emphasizes the necessity of transparent, straightforward communication that respects executive time and attention while building relational trust.[2] This clarity is not about oversimplification; rather, it is about distilling complexity into purposeful, relevant insight that empowers rather than burdens.

Ultimately, leading up is not a new task spliced onto old roles but a fundamental transformation that redefines what it means to protect and advise. It is a journey into strategic influence grounded in trust, business fluency, and mutual respect. Thus, enabling protection professionals not just to avert harm but to drive leadership confidence and organizational resilience in an unpredictable world.

THE STRATEGIC CATALYST

The journey to becoming a trusted advisor for executives begins with recognizing that the world of executive protection is undergoing fundamental transformations. These changes are not simple tweaks to existing practice; they are profound shifts that demand new ways of thinking, acting, and relating to the principal and the C-suite. Understanding and embracing these strategic shifts across the industry is critical for any professional seeking to move beyond traditional protection toward becoming a valued, strategic partner.

One of the most significant shifts is the move from a reactive posture to a proactive intelligence alignment. Historically, executive protection teams prepared and escalated their security measures only after identifying a credible threat. Annual threat assessments, while comprehensive at the time of delivery, quickly became outdated as political developments, social movements, and technological landscapes evolved. A report issued as early as January could become obsolete within weeks if it failed to capture an emerging protest fueled by rapid social media mobilization or a sudden geopolitical crisis. In this reactive model, protection teams often found themselves responding to incidents rather than preventing them, fighting fires instead of building safeguards.

Now, trusted advisors must lead with foresight, leveraging advanced tools and methodologies that enable detection and anticipation of risks before they materialize. New technology has revolutionized the way professionals gather and process information. Protective intelligence teams can continuously scan digital ecosystems, flagging anomalies and patterns that indicate brewing threats—whether they be physical, digital, or reputational. This real-time intelligence empowers the protection team to adjust strategies dynamically based on the volume and velocity of threats identified, shifting from playing defense to asserting proactive control over the risk environment.

For instance, predictive analytics enables organizations to identify patterns and anticipate emerging risks well before they manifest. By forecasting risk spikes days or even weeks in advance, executives gain a critical strategic advantage. This foresight enables them to make informed, proactive decisions, adjust travel plans, engage key stakeholders early, and mobilize resources strategically to minimize disruptions. As emphasized by *Harvard Business Review*, "To recognize risks earlier, invest in analytics,"[3] underscoring the necessity of data-driven foresight in reducing surprises, enhancing organizational agility, and ensuring operational continuity. Such capabilities align risk management with broader strategic objectives, reflecting dynamic and effective leadership in complex environments.

Another profound shift is the redefinition of security from a perceived cost center to a strategic asset deeply woven into the organization's core mission. Historically, security spending was scrutinized as an overhead expense, often perceived as a drain on profitability with intangible returns. Protectors were often isolated from conversations about organizational strategy, relegated to roles focused on logistics or incident response.

Leading up demands that protection professionals demonstrate, through sustained action and clear communication, how security underpins and enables business objectives. Protecting top executives is not merely about physical safety; it directly supports revenue generation, brand reputation, regulatory compliance, and long-term resilience. Protective teams positioned as business enablers help facilitate market expansion, foster investor confidence, and manage crises that could otherwise escalate to catastrophic losses.

One compelling illustration of this shift is seen in companies undertaking complex mergers and acquisitions. In these high-stakes moments, protection professionals play a crucial role in assessing and mitigating reputational risks while preserving operational fluidity. Their contributions early in strategic planning can prevent deal delays, avert publicity disasters, and secure client and shareholder trust, thereby protecting the firm's bottom line.

To reinforce this transformation, organizations are increasingly implementing comprehensive frameworks and advanced tools that unify physical, digital, and reputational risk management into a cohesive strategy. These solutions go beyond mere threat detection; they deliver actionable insights and real-time data visualization tailored specifically for executive decision-making across various parts of the organization. Such strategic tools enable seamless collaboration across security, operations, and C-suite leadership teams, translating complex risks into business-relevant metrics that inform proactive, coordinated responses.

Drawing from established business theories in strategic risk management and organizational design, these integrated approaches exemplify the shift from reactive control mechanisms to anticipatory, value-driven practices. This evolution reflects a higher level of organizational maturity where executive protection functions as a vital, strategic enabler within the organization, aligning risk mitigation with broader business objectives to foster resilience and sustainable success amidst uncertainty.

A MODEL OF INFLUENCE

Advancing beyond the traditional protector role toward becoming a trusted advisor involves embracing a comprehensive framework of fundamental tenets that collectively establish an effective system for influencing senior leaders and the broader executive team. These tenets transcend theoretical concepts; they represent actionable, disciplined practices that must be consistently integrated into every interaction, communication, and decision-making opportunity. By internalizing and applying these disciplines, the protective leader builds credibility, fosters deep trust, and delivers strategic value that extends far beyond physical protection.

At the core of this framework is empathy in action, a deliberate effort to deeply understand the multifaceted pressures executives face, not only professionally but personally as well. This involves recognizing the heavy burdens leaders carry and the vulnerabilities exposed when they serve as the public embodiment of an organization amid uncertainty. Empathy requires attentive listening that transcends surface dialogue to perceive underlying anxieties, aspirations, and unspoken concerns. As a Forbes leadership coach explains, "Empathy in action is understanding an employee's struggles and offering to help. It is appreciating a person's point of view and engaging in a healthy debate that builds to a better solution. It is considering a team member's perspectives and making a new recommendation that helps achieve greater success,"[4] highlighting that empathy is an active and essential leadership skill built on listening, understanding, and purposeful action. When security professionals engage with this level of presence, they move beyond transactional dynamics toward a genuine partnership rooted in mutual respect and understanding.

Credibility and integrity serve as the pillars that uphold trust. The protector's word functions as a vital currency; one earned gradually through unwavering reliability and transparency. In her capacity as a researcher who has studied human connection, Brené Brown, emphasizes "trust is built in very small moments,"[5] highlighting the importance of consistently owning mistakes and demonstrating a commitment to the leader's best interests. Each fulfilled promise strengthens the foundation of reliability, without which even the most astute strategic counsel risks being disregarded.

Business acumen forms the essential link that connects security expertise to executive priorities. Framing risk through lenses such as revenue impact, brand equity, operational continuity, and shareholder value translates protective insights into strategic intelligence. By articulating how threats could disrupt product launches, erode customer trust, or affect financial outcomes, protector advisors contextualize security challenges as integral components of business decision-making. Chris Voss, former FBI negotiator, underscores the power of addressing concerns in terms individuals care about, noting, "The most powerful word in negotiation is 'because'—it provides a reason that motivates action."[6] This quote highlights a crucial influence principle: people are more likely to be persuaded and cooperative when they understand the rationale behind a request or action, making "because" a key tool for building empathy and alignment in high-stakes conversations.

Effective communication serves as the vehicle through which trust and influence are conveyed. In high-pressure executive environments, clarity, brevity, and candor are non-negotiable. Security professionals succeed by distilling complexity into concise, relevant briefings aligned with the executive's immediate priorities and strategic vision. "Leaders who reach the top do not simply pay lip service to the importance of effective communication. Instead, they study the art in all its forms, writing, speaking, presenting, and constantly strive to improve on those skills."[7] Conversely, ambiguous or overly technical messages breed confusion and disengagement.

Adaptability remains a fundamental discipline, recognizing that both risk landscapes and business environments are in constant flux. Leading protective advisors maintain a mindset of curiosity and resilience, continuously updating their strategies in response to new threats and evolving organizational needs. As Peter Drucker famously observed, "The greatest danger in times of turbulence is not the turbulence—it is to act with yesterday's logic."[8] This highlights the imperatives of continuous learning and flexibility to remain effective in unpredictable environments.

Together, these tenets create an integrated model of influence grounded in empathy, credibility, business insight, communication mastery, and adaptability. Empathy fosters openness; credibility cultivates honesty; business acumen ensures relevance; communication transforms knowledge into actionable influence; adaptability preserves strategic value. This cohesive system enables security professionals to transcend traditional roles, becoming trusted advisors who thrive at the nexus of executive leadership and organizational resilience.

CASE STUDY: BREAKING THE WRENCH

Note: Names and identifying details have been changed to protect confidentiality, as the individual featured remains under an active protective detail.

Early one spring, a head of executive protection received an urgent call in the middle of the night. A high-net-worth executive in the cryptocurrency sector named Alexi Marceau had narrowly escaped an attempted home invasion at his vacation home. His hard-won digital fortune had always seemed secure behind air-gapped cold wallets and multi-factor authentication, but the attackers hadn't bothered with passwords or phishing emails. They came directly to his door, armed and masked, intent on using force to get what they wanted.

The reality was not just chilling but a new reality altogether. The world's criminals had evolved faster than most executives ever realized. Digital protections, once considered ironclad, no longer shielded against physical violence designed to compel compliance at the most vulnerable level: the human and their family. News of similar assaults, from Western Europe to North America, had left a trail of trauma among the industry's elite. Crypto leaders, emboldened by technology and flush with success, had become prime targets for so-called "wrench attacks." Kidnappings, home invasions, and brazen assaults aimed not at hacking devices, but at exploiting the physical person behind the assets.

Alexi, like many others, hadn't wanted to believe he was truly at risk. When his protection leader first tried to broach the subject months earlier, he met an all-too-common resistance: "Nobody knows where I live. My wallet is ironclad. And even if someone tried, I could never be coerced into giving up my keys." The conversation quickly closed, with a polite nod toward "paranoia."

But now, after barely escaping an incident that left his family shaken and his team wide awake, Alex was listening. The security leader saw the opportunity in front of him. The moment called for more than technical upgrades; it demanded the direct candor, blended with the confidence in the expertise only an experienced protector can bring.

First, the protection leader invited Alexi into a transparent conversation, not just about physical security measures, but about the new tactics criminals used: personal information harvested from company registries, coordinated attacks by local gangs working for organized crime, and the chilling reality that criminals no longer cared about firewalls. This was about leverage. In plain language, he explained recent attacks across Europe and Canada, how families had been targeted, and how attackers, when blocked digitally, simply shifted to coercion and violence.

To build trust, the protection leader shared anonymized case debriefs, illustrating how other crypto executives, many of whom Alexi knows well, successfully navigated or averted attacks by embracing uncomfortable truths and taking action before threats escalated into crises. He acknowledged Alexi's frustration and fear, allowing space for emotion while steering the discussion toward pragmatic steps rather than denial or panic.

Through a series of meetings, sometimes tense but always honest, the protection leader established his credibility and deep concern for the executive's family, not just his assets. He patiently reframed protection as a leadership issue, not a sign of weakness or paranoia. The conversations went beyond locks and alarms; they were about habits, routines, privacy practices, and contingency planning. Most critically, the discussions centered on the psychological safety of speaking candidly about risks.

Alexi eventually agreed to key changes: secure transport protocols, limited public appearances, layered residential defenses, and ongoing executive education for himself and his inner circle. The protection leader also established trusted lines of communication with law enforcement and legal counsel and conducted low-profile but effective staff briefings, making sure everyone understood why the changes mattered without instilling fear.

For the protection leader, the defining moment was not the hardware deployed, but the human transformation—guiding Alexi from denial through discomfort into proactive ownership of his vulnerability and influence. It took patience and willingness to persist through resistance and hard conversations, but ultimately, safety was redefined; implemented not as a fortress or a gadget, but as a shared fate between protector and principal.

This case, reflective of the surge in "wrench attacks" worldwide, is a testament to what it means to lead up in today's threat environment: seeing around corners, having the conversations executives would rather avoid, and standing strong when the greatest threats are not technical, but deeply personal.

BUSINESS ACUMEN FOR THE PROTECTIVE LEADER

The role of the protector, especially within the highest levels of an organization, must expand to meet the realities of a world defined by complexity, disruption, and rapid change. Today's executives do not lead in isolation; they operate within a crucible of constant exposure where geopolitical shifts, digital transformations, and public sentiment converge and mutate in real time. It is within this volatile environment that the trusted advisor in executive protection must demonstrate their fullest value.

The modern protector's mandate now includes mastering advanced business acumen. This is no longer solely about physical or discrete security measures. Instead, it requires understanding the interconnectedness of threats across domains—physical security risks intertwining with cybersecurity vulnerabilities, reputational hazards, and regulatory exposures that can either reinforce or unravel organizational stability.

To navigate this complexity, trusted advisors embrace cross-disciplinary collaboration.

> There is a correlation between the elevation of business challenges and the importance of the trusted advisor. This has upped the ante to fulfill the trusted advisor role. At a time when change has become a constant, trusted advisors must remain current, make sense of it all, and collaborate with enterprise leadership to create opportunity out of challenge.[9]

They work closely not just with security teams but also with legal, communications, finance, and operations leadership to assemble a holistic picture of risk and resilience. This synthesis empowers executives to make decisions informed by integrated threat analysis rather than siloed inputs.

For example, a protective team in a multinational pharmaceutical company anticipates that political instability in a target emerging market could disrupt supply chains and trigger regulatory scrutiny. By working with intelligence analysts and senior management, they develop a multi-layered response plan that includes contingency logistics, public affairs messaging, and enhanced physical protection. This coordinated strategy significantly reduces operational risk and reassures stakeholders through proactive communication.

Furthermore, the landscape demands the ability to interpret the implications of digital risks. The proliferation of social media and digital platforms has made corporate reputations sustainable yet fragile. Even a small misstep or misinformation campaign can escalate rapidly, impacting stock prices, customer loyalty, and employee morale. Protectors attuned to these dynamics can help the C-suite anticipate and mitigate such threats, positioning security as central to brand stewardship.

Those unable or unwilling to embrace this broader business understanding run the risk of isolation. Executive protection teams that fail to speak the language of enterprise value, or to integrate broadly with organizational risk functions, merely operate as tactical units. They remain vulnerable not just to risk exposure but to marginalization within strategic planning.

In contrast, those who master the blend of security expertise, business insight, and collaborative culture become indispensable partners in shaping strategic resilience for the entire organization. This holistic approach elevates executive protection beyond a service into a critical driver of sustainable organizational success.

CHALLENGES OF ADOPTION

The path toward becoming a trusted advisor to the C-suite is fraught with obstacles. Transformation of mindset and practices within executive protection teams, as well as acceptance by organizational leadership, often encounters resistance. This can be both overt and subtle. Understanding these challenges in detail explains how they arise and, crucially, how to navigate and overcome them.

One of the most entrenched barriers is legacy bias, a powerful cultural force within many organizations. For decades, executive protection was firmly rooted in principles of physical surveillance, predictable routines, and visible presence. Many executives, seasoned protection professionals, and even entire departments remain attached to this traditional identity. The image of the stoic guard standing watch or the security detail flanking the CEO is deeply ingrained, serving as a symbol of control and safety. It can be difficult to shift perceptions away from this viewpoint toward one that embraces strategic advisory roles, intellectual partnership, and business fluency. This resistance stems from comfort with the familiar and fear of the unknown—a natural and understandable human tendency in complex, high-risk environments. As Maria Minor explains,

> Legacy bias is a formidable barrier in organizations, where long-standing traditions and routines create comfort zones that resist new ways of thinking. Overcoming this requires acknowledging the natural human tendency to cling to familiarity, while fostering openness to innovative perspectives.[10]

That challenge, however, rarely looks the same in every company. Corporate cultures are anything but uniform. Some places are weighted down by hierarchy, where decision-making flows through tightly held channels and status keeps fresh thinking at arm's length. Others hang on to tradition for dear life. Repeating old routines because that's just how things are done around here. And sometimes, even progressive or "flat" organizations freeze up the moment you try to nudge them beyond their familiar comfort zone. If you're stepping forward as a strategic advisor, it helps to read the room. Resistance shows up with a dozen different faces, and what feels like legacy thinking in one boardroom might present as a rigid chain-of-command in another.

So, as a protective leader, how do you find your lane in the midst of all that? Sometimes, it's about nudging gently at the edges. Seek that one person who's open to a different conversation, mapping out the real power dynamics, and earning trust in steady increments. Other times, you will have to reframe what you do by connecting protection to the priorities corporate leaders already care about. And don't underestimate the power of timing. Crisis, transition, or moments when the usual playbook stops working—those are doors that, sometimes, open wider.

Communication gaps present another persistent obstacle. Executive protection specialists are often trained and socialized within security and law enforcement cultures that emphasize technical competence and operational rigor. Their language, while clear within their domain, is often thick with jargon, acronyms, and risk-based terms that fail to translate to the C-suite's strategic perspectives. Executives, in turn, expect concise, outcome-focused communication, often framed in financial metrics, competitive positioning, or reputational impact. Misalignment here leads to missed opportunities for influence and confusion. In worst-case situations, it can also lead to frustration on both sides. Bridging this divide requires developing a knack for translating intentions through a sustained effort rooted in curiosity about the world the C-suite inhabits.

Often, there is an undercurrent of fear and vulnerability that shapes leadership receptivity. Executives, especially in public or shareholder-facing roles, may resist exposing vulnerabilities or admitting gaps in understanding or control. They are pressed to project confidence and resilience, even under duress. "Leaders accept advisors who demonstrate both competence and character—a combination that creates psychological safety, enabling frank conversations about uncomfortable truths and fostering collaboration on complex challenges."[11] This makes engaging them in candid, sometimes uncomfortable conversations about risks and protection harder. A protector seeking to lead up must therefore cultivate patience and emotional intelligence. Building trust cannot be rushed or forced; it grows from consistent, respectful, and empathetic engagement. Those protectors willing to lean into discomfort, model vulnerability, and provide unwavering support have greater success in breaking through these barriers.

Overcoming the challenges of adoption demands deliberate strategies. First, invest time in consistently listening to the executive's perspectives and concerns. This listening goes beyond information gathering; it builds psychological safety that opens doors for deeper dialogue. Then, tailor communication to the executive's priorities and language, connecting security insights directly to business outcomes. Always frame risks in terms of impact, whether revenue, brand reputation, or operational continuity, rather than cryptic threat indicators.

Second, lead by example. Internal teams must model the transformation, embracing business fluency, cross-functional partnership, and proactive intelligence gathering. Leaders who consistently demonstrate credibility, reliability, and adaptability invite executive confidence.

Third, invest in education and training. Providing ongoing learning opportunities that blend security expertise with leadership development, strategic thinking, and communication skills helps embed the trusted advisor mindset broadly within the team, reducing cultural friction.

Lastly, cultivate a culture of continuous feedback and reflection, positioning failures and setbacks as growth rather than blame. This openness fosters resilience and progressively deepens trust and influence.

In the end, don't worry if progress doesn't follow a tidy path. Resistance isn't always personal; often, it's just the way organizations protect what's familiar. Spot those barriers for what they are, listen closely, and meet organizations where they are. That's how you shift not just practices, but mindsets—one well-timed, well-grounded step at a time.

MAKING TRUSTED ADVISING A DAILY PRACTICE

Transforming the concept of leading up into a tangible, actionable practice requires more than inspiration. It demands a clear, practical approach that security professionals can apply consistently in their day-to-day interactions with executives and organizational leadership. This methodology involves three interconnected and continuous steps that collectively build trust, influence decision-making, and embed security as a strategic function.

The first and foundational step is to listen deeply. Listening goes far beyond hearing words; it is an immersive process of understanding the executive's world. It acknowledges not only the spoken concerns but also sensing the unspoken fears, ambitions, and pressures that shape their behavior. Many protectors are trained to focus on tactical details, yet those who succeed in leading up know the transformative power of wholehearted listening. This requires creating a safe and confidential space where leaders feel heard without judgment or interruption. Listening deeply means asking open-ended questions about what worries the executive most, what scenarios keep them awake at night, and what success looks like from their uniquely challenging vantage point. The protector's role is to gather not only facts but to discern emotional and strategic undercurrents that may not be fully articulated. This emotional intelligence forms the bedrock of credible advisory relationships. As Greenleaf profoundly observed, "Only a true natural servant automatically responds to any problem by listening first."[12]

Within a global investment firm, for example, a new CEO confided fears about digital threats that extended beyond physical safety, concerns about phishing attacks targeting her close advisors, and potential leaks that could negatively influence market performance. The protector, by engaging in deep listening, uncovered these anxieties and was able to tailor a protective plan that addressed this asymmetric threat, thereby aligning directly with the executive's primary concerns.

The second step in this methodology is to translate and advise. Once equipped with profound insight from listening, protection professionals must convert raw data and emotions into clear, actionable intelligence framed within the language and priorities of the executive and the broader business. This translation is not merely linguistic but strategic. It involves mapping threats to their likelihood and, more importantly, consequence. Protectors articulate how each risk can disrupt business processes, threaten shareholder confidence, or undermine strategic initiatives. Importantly, this step requires proposing measured, practical actions that align security measures with business opportunities, not constraints.

Consider a multinational manufacturing client facing escalating threats amid restructuring and layoffs. The protector's analysis went beyond identifying threats from disgruntled employees to framing the risk within the business context: potential production halts, reputational damage influencing supplier relationships, and community backlash that could delay regulatory approvals. Recommendations included a combination of heightened surveillance, support programs for employees, and a communications strategy designed to foster transparency and trust with stakeholders. This business-contextualized advising secured executive buy-in and mitigated the threats and intrinsic vulnerabilities, demonstrating the power of translating intelligence into a strategic partnership.

The third step encompasses delivering and reinforcing. Ideas and plans, no matter how well conceived, fail without execution and sustained communication. Trusted advisors lead not only by designing strategies but by ensuring their diligent, flawless implementation. Delivery includes coordinating cross-functional teams, managing relationships with external partners such as law enforcement or cybersecurity firms, and dedicating attention to detail throughout daily protective operations. Furthermore, continuous reinforcement through regular updates is critical; leaders require ongoing assurances that protective measures are functioning and aligned with shifting circumstances. Updates must be concise, focused on business outcomes, and offered at a cadence that respects executive time while maintaining situational awareness.

For example, in the case of a CEO facing threats from a hostile former board member, the protector executed multi-tiered security protocols, integrating physical protection with digital monitoring and communication controls. The CEO received detailed, yet straightforward, updates regarding threat mitigations, compliance with safety protocols, and emerging intelligence. These reports quantified how interventions reduced downtime and preserved confidence among investors and employees. Through this ongoing dialogue, the protector sustained trust and reinforced their role as a strategic partner.

This process of listening deeply, translating insights, and delivering with reinforcement does not represent a linear sequence but a continuous cycle of engagement. Each phase informs the others. New intelligence fuels deeper listening; deeper listening allows refined translation; refined translation demands nimble delivery and communication. Mastery of this cycle is essential to maintaining influence and integrating protection within organizational leadership.

Incorporating this methodology into daily practice necessitates disciplined habits. Protectors must cultivate patience, listen unsupervised, and employ communication skills to distill complex insights into actionable advice. Training programs should embed these principles, supported by mentorship and coaching that encourage reflective practice and resilience.

The power of this approach is best appreciated not as a hypothetical but in lived experience. Teams who internalize and operationalize this process report increased trust from executives and experience greater inclusion in strategic forums. They shift the perception of protection from reactive cost to proactive advantage. It is a journey requiring patience, investment, and courage, but one that delivers profound organizational and personal dividends.

BUILDING A CULTURE OF TRUSTED ADVISING

To transform individual expertise into organizational mastery, the essence of leading up must be embedded systematically throughout the company's culture and operational fabric. This involves deliberate development of people, communication patterns, and values that collectively sustain executive protection as a strategic, trusted pillar. As Stephen R. Covey wisely stated, "Trust is the glue of life. It's the most essential ingredient in effective communication. It's the foundational principle that holds all relationships."[13] This underscores the critical importance of trust as the foundation for building a culture of trusted advising.

A primary vehicle for embedding trusted advising begins with education and training. Organizations must design curricula that bridge security expertise with business literacy, communication skills, and leadership principles. Training programs build fluency in the language of finance, risk management, and governance, equipping protection teams to align intelligence with enterprise ambitions. Similarly, training nurtures emotional intelligence, empathy, and courage; capacities essential for navigating the executive's world with authenticity and respect. Embedding these competencies in onboarding, leadership development, and continuous learning ensures the trusted advisor mindset permeates from frontline personnel to senior leadership.

Strategic communication and framing constitute the second pillar of embedding trusted advisor capabilities. Regular, multi-channel communications broadcast the value and strategic outcomes of protection activities beyond protective teams. Success stories are shared, demonstrating how intelligence averted crises, preserved brand equity, or enabled confident decision-making. Such visibility shifts perceptions from that of cost centers to indispensable assets. Communication protocols emphasize clarity, relevance, and alignment with organizational priorities, guaranteeing that messaging engages not only executives but stakeholders across departments, building broad-based support.

Recognition systems reinforce and reward trusted advising behaviors. By acknowledging individuals and teams who exemplify cross-functional collaboration and strategic leadership, organizations nurture aspirational models. Whether through formal awards, public commendations, or career advancement, recognition codifies valued behaviors and motivates sustained excellence. Such systems make trusted advisors visible and celebrated beyond the security function, enhancing recruitment, retention, and morale.

Technology and systems integration form the third pillar. Investment in cutting-edge platforms that unify physical and digital protection intelligence is critical. These systems facilitate real-time information sharing among protection, IT security, legal, and communications teams. Together, they enable holistic risk monitoring and coordinated response. Training and support are essential to ensure usability and adoption of these platforms, fostering transparency and collaboration. As these systems become embedded, security leaders can deliver seamless, business-aligned intelligence to executives, further deepening trust.

Underpinning all these pillars is culture building—a deliberate commitment to create an environment that values openness, learning, and mutual accountability. Organizations must foster psychological safety, where failures and near-misses are openly examined not for blame but for continuous improvement. Encouraging curiosity, experimentation, and adaptive thinking empowers professionals to anticipate and respond to evolving risks dynamically. Integrating trusted advising into organizational values, leadership charters, and performance management makes it a shared responsibility, not a niche skill.

This holistic embedding process transforms executive protection from an isolated function into an enterprise-wide center of influence and resilience, with trusted advisors positioned at the core of strategic decision-making.

RESILIENCE UNDER PRESSURE

The role of a trusted advisor to the C-suite is demanding and relentless. The pressures are perpetual, and the stakes are monumental. Executives and their protectors operate in environments marked by uncertainty and rapid change. In such a crucible, sustaining influence, composure, and strategic clarity require more than knowledge and skill; they necessitate resilience, mental stamina, and emotional endurance.

Diane Coutu, writing in the *Harvard Business Review*, puts it plainly: "More than education, more than experience, more than training, a person's level of resilience will determine who succeeds and who fails."[14] Resilience is not simply surviving through moments of hardship but mastering the mental, emotional, and physical stamina to rise repeatedly with strength and insight.

Resilience in this domain is multifaceted. It combines endurance and psychological tenacity with the competency to manage complex interpersonal dynamics under stress. Trusted advisors must maintain vigilance and effectiveness through long hours, travel, and often unpredictable schedules, all while maintaining the ability to anticipate, mitigate, and recover from a range of physical, operational, and reputational threats. Maintaining this equilibrium is indispensable for high-quality judgment and communication.

A key component of sustaining resilience is the cultivation of intentional self-care practices. This does not imply indulgence but disciplined routines that preserve cognitive function and emotional balance. Nutrition, rest, physical activity, and mindfulness techniques play foundational roles in supporting the protector's capacity to perform consistently at the highest levels.

Even more critical is the development of support networks. Trusted advisors must build connections across professional and personal spheres—a community of peers, mentors, coaches, and confidants who provide perspective, encouragement, and corrective feedback. These relationships offer a psychological buffer against burnout and isolation, fostering sustained engagement and growth.

Reflective practice also underpins sustained performance. This involves regularly examining past decisions, successes, and failures to extract lessons and refine approaches. After-action reviews, journaling, and debriefing sessions help transform experience into wisdom, allowing the trusted advisor to evolve continuously and avoid repetitive mistakes.

The discipline of adaptability complements resilience by encouraging an open mindset. As the threat landscape shifts unpredictably, so too must protective strategies and interpersonal approaches. Flexibility in problem-solving, willingness to adjust communication styles, and openness to innovation ensure that the trusted advisor remains relevant and effective through changing conditions.

Trusted advisors sustain their courage by stepping forward despite uncertain outcomes. They meet unpredictability with steady presence and unwavering commitment, leading with confidence even when the path ahead is unclear. This kind of courage isn't the absence of fear or doubt but the resolve to engage fully in the moment, embracing risk and ambiguity with a steady heart and mind.

Sustaining under pressure is neither passive nor accidental. It requires deliberate cultivation of habits, supports, and mindsets designed to equip the protector for the extraordinary demands of leading up. Excellence is sustained not by isolated acts of brilliance but by consistent, disciplined commitment to resilience in all its dimensions.

The capacity to endure and thrive under pressure ultimately protects not only the executive's safety but also the advisor's ability to influence thoughtfully and strategically, ensuring leadership strength when it matters most.

EMBEDDING LEADING UP INTO DAILY PRACTICE

The translation of the concept of leading up from theory into everyday action is seen as requiring more than awareness. A sustained commitment to specific habits, approaches, and mindsets is viewed as necessary. These practical elements are regarded as serving as foundational guideposts for professionals aiming to have trusted advising embedded into their daily responsibilities and interactions at all levels of the organization.

First and foremost, the priority must always be to listen with intent and care. This listening goes far deeper than just collecting information. It calls for presence and empathy, inviting the executive to share not merely surface concerns but the underlying emotions and aspirations shaping their leadership experience. This kind of listening builds psychological safety and forms the foundation from which influence can grow. Leaders must feel genuinely heard to begin trusting their protectors as advisors. Regular, open dialogues focused on understanding evolving anxieties and goals signal a protector's commitment to partnership over mere duty.

Equally important is the skill to frame communications in a language the C-suite values and understands. Helping executives grasp the full business implications of security matters means moving beyond technical jargon and presenting risks and mitigations in terms of revenue impact, brand reputation, operational stability, and shareholder confidence. This alignment of business acumen bridges the culture gap between protection and executive leadership. It turns abstract threat data into strategic insight, thereby compelling attention and action. The goal is to make security conversations proactive and business-oriented rather than reactive and tactical.

Consistent transparency and candor in communication also foster trust and credibility. Protectors must be willing to share the difficult truths, including potential vulnerabilities or uncertainties while at the same time conveying confidence in plans and capabilities. This openness disarms defensive tendencies and promotes collaborative problem-solving. Leaders appreciate advisors who balance realism.

The value of embracing candid, sometimes uncomfortable conversations cannot be overstated. Often, difficult dialogues build the foundation for genuine trust because they demonstrate courage and commitment. Refusing to avoid hard topics, while offering solutions and support, advances security relationships into a true partnership. The discipline to maintain these conversations, even amid stress or uncertainty, marks the difference between transactional service and trusted advising.

Incorporating real-time intelligence tools is no longer optional but vital for success. Protectors must leverage predictive analytics, social media monitoring, and integrated threat platforms to anticipate emerging threats. This equips them to inform executives before crises materialize, shaping decisions and reducing surprises. Daily briefings and timely intelligence reports aligned with business priorities exemplify how data-driven foresight enhances strategic advising.

Building and nurturing cross-functional relationships throughout the organization supports coordinated risk management. Effective trusted advisors do not operate in isolation; they connect protective operations with other key business units. These relationships ensure intelligence is comprehensive and responses are unified. The protector acts as an interlocutor, facilitating communication and collaboration across departments, advancing organizational resilience.

Celebrating and communicating successes play a critical role in transforming perceptions of security from cost centers into strategic assets. Documenting and showcasing cases where protection initiatives prevented revenue loss, preserved reputation, or enabled business continuity reinforces the advisor's value proposition. Success stories should be shared with executives and broadly within the organization, fostering wider appreciation and support.

Continuous education and training must be codified as foundational pillars. The rapidly evolving threat landscape and shifting C-suite expectations demand ongoing professional development. Training programs blending security expertise with leadership, business acumen, and communication skills keep teams equipped and confident to lead up effectively. Mentorship and coaching further deepen skill development and reinforce cultural transformation.

Finally, developing and stewarding a culture of transparency and adaptability anchors the trusted advisor role. Such cultures encourage sharing of lessons learned from failures and successes alike, promote curiosity and openness to innovation, and reward initiative and cross-functional partnership. Through cultural transformation, trusted advising becomes a shared responsibility and a defining attribute of organizational resilience.

Adopting these practical approaches and mindsets is neither accidental nor quick. It requires deliberate ongoing effort fueled by courage, empathy, and a commitment to aligning security with enterprise purpose. The result is a powerful transformation of the protector's role—from a guardian to an indispensable strategic partner poised to enable fearless leadership in a volatile world.

EMBRACING THE POWER

Embracing the power of leading up is a seminal moment in your journey as an executive protection leader. This is more than a role change; it is the opportunity to become a trusted advisor whose insights, empathy, and courage create real impact. Moving beyond being a guardian, you step into a role that shapes the future of leaders and organizations alike. This means being present, listening deeply, and speaking with clarity in ways that matter. It's about building relationships founded on trust and respect that open doors to influence.

The path to this transformation requires dedication and patience. Yes, you will face challenging conversations and moments of uncertainty. However, it is through these moments that your strength and authenticity will show with distinction. Your ability to connect security realities with business priorities will empower executives to see protection not as a limitation but as a strategic advantage. Every thoughtful conversation and trusted insight you offer fuels leadership that is ready to meet complexity with confidence.

This expanded role invites you to lead with intention, anchoring resilience deep within the culture of your organization. It calls for courage to take bold steps forward even when the terrain is uncertain. Your leadership will inspire not only safety but also innovation and growth. By embracing this calling, you will leave a legacy of transformation. One that redefines protection as a source of strength, strategy, and lasting achievement.

The future awaits your influence. Step into this evolving role with confidence and strength, knowing your work shapes outcomes far beyond what is visible. Your journey as a trusted advisor and strategic partner is just beginning. And its impact will be felt by executives, organizations, and communities for years to come. Now is the moment, your moment, to embrace the full potential to lead.

NOTES

1 David H. Maister, Charles H. Green, and Robert M. Galford, *The Trusted Advisor* (New York: Free Press, 2000).
2 Brené Brown, *Dare to Lead: Brave Work. Tough Conversations. Whole Hearts* (New York: Random House, 2018).
3 "To Recognize Risks Earlier, Invest in Analytics," *Harvard Business Review*, November 1, 2020, https://hbr.org/2020/11/to-recognize-risks-earlier-invest-in-analytics.
4 Tracy Brower, "Empathy Is the Most Important Leadership Skill According to Research," *Forbes*, September 19, 2021, https://www.forbes.com/sites/tracybrower/2021/09/19/empathy-is-the-most-important-leadership-skill-according-to-research/.
5 Brené Brown, *Dare to Lead: Brave Work. Tough Conversations. Whole Hearts* (New York: Random House, 2018).
6 Chris Voss, *Never Split the Difference: Negotiating as If Your Life Depended on It* (New York: HarperBusiness, 2016).

7 Carmine Gallo, "How Great Leaders Communicate," *Harvard Business Review*, November 23, 2022, https://hbr.org/2022/11/how-great-leaders-communicate.
8 Peter F. Drucker, *The Effective Executive* (New York: Harper Business, 2006).
9 Mark Cohen, "Chief Legal Officers: The Expanded Purview of a Trusted Advisor," *Forbes*, March 24, 2025, https://www.forbes.com/sites/markcohen1/2025/03/24/chief-legal-officers-the-expanded-purview-of-a-trusted-advisor/.
10 Maria Minor, "Does Your Workplace Culture Breed Biases? 8 Essential Tips to Eliminate Them," *Forbes*, June 18, 2020, https://www.forbes.com/sites/mariaminor/2020/06/18/does-your-workplace-culture-breed-biases-8-essential-tips-to-eliminate-them/.
11 Linda A. Hill, "For Innovation, a New Kind of Leader," *Harvard Business School Executive Education*, November 20, 2019, https://www.exed.hbs.edu/blog/leading-building-culture-innovation-linda-hill-maurizio-travaglin.
12 Robert K. Greenleaf, *Servant Leadership: A Journey into the Nature of Legitimate Power and Greatness* (New York: Paulist Press, 1977).
13 Stephen R. Covey, *First Things First* (New York: Simon & Schuster, 1994).
14 Diane L. Coutu, "How Resilience Works," *Harvard Business Review*, May 2002, https://hbr.org/2002/05/how-resilience-works.

CORE INSIGHTS

The Protector as a Leader

These section reveals a simple but profound truth: *before a protector can lead a team or influence an executive, they must first lead themselves.* Personal leadership becomes the raw material from which crisis leadership, team readiness, and strategic advisory influence are built. Character forges credibility: credibility earns trust; trust opens the door to influence. And once inside that door, protectors must communicate with clarity, think with business acuity, and act with steadiness under pressure.

Together, these chapters form a progression: **the protector's code, the protector's capability, the protector's influence.**

This evolution is not accidental; it is deliberately cultivated in daily habits, team culture, and the discipline to stay resilient when pressure tests every assumption.

As you carry these lessons forward, the following core insights anchor the protector-leader's path from internal mastery to organizational impact.

CORE INSIGHTS

- **Character is the foundation of all influence**
  Credibility starts in the daily habits that build trust long before any crisis.
- **Trust is earned through consistency and clarity**
  Small, repeated acts of honesty and follow-through create the access and influence leaders rely on.

DOI: 10.4324/9781003670704-11

- **Crisis performance depends on the systems, culture, and habits built long before pressure arrives**
  Teams revert to their training, shared standards, and disciplined preparation when stakes surge.
- **Leadership must scale beyond the individual; your true legacy is a team that performs without you**
  Legacy lives in the people, processes, and culture that endure after you're gone.
- **Modern influence requires fluency in the executive's world, not just the threat landscape**
  Advisors earn a seat at the table by translating risk into strategic business impact.
- **Resilience (mental, emotional, and operational) is now a leadership requirement, not a luxury**
  Steady judgment under pressure depends on the leader's ability to adapt, recover, and remain grounded.

SECTION 3

Introduction: Sustaining and Scaling Leadership

In a 24-hour news cycle and a threat environment shaped by velocity, scrutiny, and constant exposure, sustaining leadership has become as critical as demonstrating it. Modern protection leaders cannot be the perpetual first responder; endurance today depends on systems—trusted teams, deliberate rhythms, and habits that preserve clarity under pressure.

All of us have carried the weight of long hours, unbroken tempo, and the quiet strain that accumulates over years of service. Those lessons shaped our understanding of what leadership in this profession truly demands: not unending stamina, but the discipline to protect the protector. Resilience is no longer a personal preference; it is an operational requirement, allowing leaders to think clearly, act decisively, and build teams that endure the cadence of modern risk.

Sustaining leadership also requires the ability to make decisions when information is imperfect—to combine partial insight with sound judgment and move with confidence despite uncertainty. In our field, waiting for perfect clarity can be as dangerous as acting too soon. What matters is recognizing when there is enough insight to lead and having the systems and trust that allow teams to act with purpose rather than hesitation.

This section explores those dual foundations of sustainable leadership: the inner resilience that protects people, and the intelligence-led clarity that protects decisions. Together, they reveal a simple truth—sustaining leadership is not about doing more but about designing systems that make excellence repeatable.

DOI: 10.4324/9781003670704-12

CHAPTER 8

Protecting the Protector: Mental Health and Burnout

"Are you ok?"

In the world of executive protection, this question is routine; peers check each other for injuries or confirm physical readiness before a protective movement. A mundane question that has a reflexive confirmatory response, "yup."

But, in today's relentless environment, with its ever-mounting levels of stress and sacrifice placed on the executive protection professional, this pro forma question demands a deeper consideration. It should not simply probe for injuries or fatigue, but reach beneath the practiced composure: How are you holding up, really? What burdens have you silently shouldered, what costs have you quietly accepted to uphold your promise to protect?

There is a certain quiet pride that comes with working in executive protection, an unspoken acknowledgment among practitioners that they shoulder burdens few others can understand. The world behind the scenes is a relentless test of focus, discretion, improvisation, loyalty, and, above all, endurance. Many high performers are drawn to executive protection, believing their value stems from tireless commitment, being the first to volunteer, the last to rest, and the one who can always be counted on. But, as this commitment deepens, it takes on a life of its own. The work is never simply a job; it becomes an identity, a badge of belonging within a select circle of reliability and resolve. The needs of the principal come first, and in meeting those, protectors often set aside their own needs and, often, those of their families altogether.

At first, this approach appears effective. The toughness that enables one to handle tense confrontations and complex travel schedules seems to create a shield against ordinary human vulnerability. Sick days become rare, downtime grows suspect, and the ability to power through fatigue feels like a mark of distinction. It is only much later, often when the damage has already been done, that the true cost emerges. As the years pass and the stakes escalate, the incremental sacrifices pile up quietly. Each

DOI: 10.4324/9781003670704-13

skipped vacation, each missed family milestone, each night of disrupted sleep in a hotel room or midnight shift wear away at the foundation. Resilience becomes less a virtue and more a personal prison.

At the heart of the crisis now gripping executive protection is the collision between these ingrained habits of toughing it out and the hard limits of human psychology.

While dedicated data for the executive protection field remains scarce, it is both common and statistically sound to use broader security industry findings as a proxy when inferring the risks and pressures faced by executive protection professionals. Deducing from a 2020 study of security practitioners, which revealed that 40% exhibited symptoms of PTSD and nearly one in six faced workplace mental health challenges,[1] highlights the permissive environment for stress that almost certainly extends into the specialized world of executive protection. The shared exposure to high-stakes environments and similar demands allows these broader statistics to serve as a meaningful indicator of the mental health burdens protectors may shoulder in the absence of industry-specific research.

The occurrences of occupational burnout are just as pervasive, with the World Health Organization specifically defining it as "a syndrome conceptualized as resulting from chronic workplace stress that has not been successfully managed."[2] As protectors, we have witnessed its impact visible not just in the obvious moments of collapse, but in subtle, accumulated shifts: waning focus, increased irritability, impulsive decisions, and strained relationships at home and within the team.

This is the dangerous trap of tying one's worth exclusively to output, to the idea that value is proved solely through self-sacrifice. What begins as a healthy drive can mutate into compulsion, and daring overcommitment too often sets the stage for personal and organizational disaster. Many of the industry's most experienced practitioners admit, in private if not in public, to having lived for years inside a cycle of suppression: even when rest was desperately needed, they kept going, haunted by the suspicion that stepping back would mean losing favor or being left behind. The culture, unfortunately, has not always helped; until recently, vulnerability was equated with incompetence, and resilience was conflated with relentless suffering.

There is an alternative. A new paradigm of high-stakes leadership that insists mental health is not just a personal concern, but an operational priority. Increasingly, forward-thinking leaders are reframing the conversation. They recognize that the most reliable protector is not the one who never gets tired or never needs help, but the one who is sustained by a resilient system. A structure in which support, rest, and open dialogue are institutionalized, not improvised in crisis. Organizations that invest in well-being do not just prevent burnout or turnover; they foster teams that are sharper in the field, quicker to recover from setbacks, and more loyal over the long arc of a demanding career.

This chapter is neither a technical manual, nor a collection of slogans. It's an invitation to rethink what it means to be strong, to rediscover the dignity in asking for help, and to reclaim the humanity at the core of the protection profession. By weaving together research, real stories, and practical insights, the aim here is not just to illuminate the scale of the crisis but to offer a practical route forward for leaders and teams alike. This is what it means to protect the protector: to ensure that no one is left behind by their own loyalty, and that leadership is measured not by how well we hide our wounds, but by how well we heal together.

THE WEIGHT OF VIGILANCE

Mental health for protection professionals is not a background concern or a private struggle. It is part of the structural foundation on which all effective protection work stands. In executive protection, true mental health is not simply the absence of breakdown or dysfunction; rather, it is the sustained presence of psychological balance, adaptability, and meaning, even amid relentless pressure and shifting demands. It is a collective and ongoing responsibility, one woven into the profession's culture and support systems.

Mental health in this context demands more than responding when a crisis can no longer be ignored. It is the daily practice of intentional recovery, regular self-reflection, mutual trust, and open communication. To thrive in roles where stress is both inevitable and intense, protectors must cultivate habits that enable sustainable engagement over time, making resilience and psychological safety an industry-wide imperative, not just a personal hope.

It is said that what is carried is rarely visible. And while the world of protection credits quick reflexes and operational readiness, few acknowledge the mental burden of perpetual vigilance and responsibility. As one current United States Secret Service agent assigned to the Presidential Protective Division described, "Even during supposed downtime, our minds remain tethered to mission and constantly operating at a state of high readiness. The consequence of this is our personal relationships quietly strain under the weight of unrelenting pressure." The work infiltrates every corner of a protector's life, keeping the nervous system on edge, and if left unchecked, will erode the psychological balance so vital to sustained performance.

Burnout in this field is not sudden. It is the slow erosion of engagement and professional identity, as chronic stress and fatigue drain energy from the mission. The symptoms range from emotional exhaustion to the dangerous disengagement that can threaten not only individual well-being but team cohesion and operational outcomes. As recent research underscores, "Burnout can have profound effects on employees, including physical and emotional exhaustion, diminished job performance, increased absenteeism, lower job satisfaction, and even long-term health problems such as anxiety and depression."[3] This highlights how burnout not only saps engagement but also undercuts every element of personal and organizational functioning.

For too long, the industry has treated mental health as a private struggle or a sign of individual weakness. Yet the reality is far more complex. The nature of this work means detachment from constant responsibility is nearly impossible for most operators. The field's very culture hasn't encouraged transparency or team-based care, even as research makes clear that burnout and role engulfment are industry-wide risks.

Trust, openness, and a psychological safe harbor are not luxuries. They are required for both optimal performance and human flourishing. Organizations that invest in rest cycles, protected time off, meaningful check-ins, and counseling not only reduce burnout but also improve productivity and retention. In these supportive cultures, operators know they are "trusted professionals and valued human beings," not simply expendable resources.

Resilience in executive protection is not a triage device reserved for moments of crisis. It is a daily practice that aids in navigating adversity and chronic stress, allowing protectors to adapt and draw renewed purpose from their calling. Key research and field experience underscore that resilience rests on small choices, mindsets, and habits cultivated every day.

This means shifting one's self-talk, practicing gratitude, seeking out healthy relationships, and incorporating recovery moments into the workday rhythm. "Eat, sleep, exercise." Commit to a healthy sleep schedule, move regularly, and nourish your body. These are not optional extras but core elements that fuel focus, judgment, and emotional steadiness in the field.

Equally important is nurturing a mindset of compassion toward oneself and others: letting go of punitive self-criticism, turning to friends, family, and even animals for emotional connection and support, and allowing time for reflection or meditation. These practices do not subtract from professionalism. They are the origins of strength and perseverance, especially in high-stakes contexts.

The profession's deep sense of calling is both armor and vulnerability. Without systems for acknowledgment, support, and belonging, even the most committed will suffer harm. History teaches that cultures of resilience flourish not only on grit and sacrifice but on systems of mutual support and shared values—a lesson drawn from both military tradition and emerging organizational psychology.

Protectors are called to serve and endure in the face of adversity. It is time for the industry to invest in its mental health with equal seriousness as it invests in tactical readiness and physical safety. Such a shift means embedding care into policy and practice, not as a crisis response, but as a standing practice, and affirming that protecting the protector is the foundation of every successful mission.

THE COST OF PUSHED LIMITS

Too often, organizations and operations in the executive protection field have an ingrained ethos, "ride the horse until it dies—and then eat it," reflecting a stubborn pattern of pushing personnel and systems well beyond their limits before squeezing out whatever remnants remain. This mindset calls for a strategic reckoning with that reality, urging a decisive shift away from the entrenched norm of extracting effort without regard to the cost to mental health. The so-called "Dead Horse Theory" evokes this organizational trap: when faced with burnout and systemic exhaustion, teams often respond not by stepping back to reassess, but by doubling down until little of value remains.[4]

The result is a workforce treated not as skilled professionals but as interchangeable resources, fueling a cycle of burnout and dehumanization. As research shows, "Employees in organizational settings often feel the extremely negative experience of being treated as interchangeable machines, numbers, or resources," a dynamic that "has negative effects on employees' well-being, attitudes toward the organization and work behaviors ... causing problems such as depression, anxiety, and stress-related disorders." Such organizational dehumanization is "associated with employees' emotional exhaustion and psychosomatic strains."[5]

After organizations exhaust their collective resources, responsibility for sustainability shifts to the individual. This is where a new, quieter danger emerges: the "Competence Trap." Early in their careers, many executive protection professionals are applauded for relentless dedication: saying yes to every assignment, stretching the day, and answering the call is mistaken for both ambition and indispensability. Over time, these patterns of self-overextension fossilize into a self-worth that is intrinsically tied to output. The response to mounting fatigue is rarely to reflect or rest, but to double down with even more effort, ultimately neglecting the practices of growth, self-care, and renewal that make sustained excellence possible.

As described in The Influence Journal, "The biggest danger to high performers isn't failure — it's getting stuck in their own success."[6] The very competence that first elevates a professional becomes the invisible barrier that restricts further growth, as individuals and their organizations confuse repetition and reliability with real development. This ominous cycle leaves even the most capable protectors vulnerable, not to a loss of skill, but to the slow erosion of passion, innovation, and well-being.

The challenge is to help professionals recognize this cycle—not just as a personal failure, but as a product of powerful feedback loops, both organizational and psychological. Only through honest self-reckoning, clear boundaries, and a new ethic that values well-being alongside output can the cycle of the competence trap be broken.

By blending these insights, a critical truth emerges. Neither the organizational "Dead Horse Theory" nor the individual "Competence Trap" can be ignored without serious consequences. These realities demand an immediate strategic shift. Leadership must move beyond celebrating endurance toward systems grounded in psychological safety and honest assessment of both individual and organizational limits. The stories of agents losing touch with family, returning home as strangers, or silently bearing trauma are no longer outliers. They are a reflection of an unsustainable status quo that organizations can no longer afford to ignore. A shift is not only essential, it is the industry's urgent need for sustainability and individual resilience that redefines what it means to lead and protect.

Today, some organizations are finally beginning to recognize that pushing people past the point of recovery is not simply unfair; it is a direct operational risk. The transition is less a matter of new policies and more a new philosophy about what makes a protector truly effective. Instead of celebrating unbroken streaks of service as evidence of exceptionalism, leaders now ask what patterns actually produce the best outcomes over time, refining key performance indicators. What emerges is a simple but profound observation: teams that systematically build in rest, rotate assignments, and create space for processing critical incidents are sharper, more proactive, and make fewer mistakes. Mistakes, after all, do not only come from lack of skill but also from depleted reserves.

Take, for example, the introduction of mandatory downtime. Whereas taking leave once required a display of vulnerability, often accompanied by subtle shaming among peers, it became something that the entire leadership team tracked as diligently as readiness rosters. In high-performing organizations, a leader is as likely to be questioned about why someone hasn't used their accumulated leave as about a missed checkpoint. This reorientation does not diminish the commitment of professionals; instead, it signifies organizational maturity and a genuine commitment to sustainability.

A similar shift is being played out in how teams approach post-incident care. In the earlier model, once the immediate emergency was handled, the unspoken assumption was that everyone would simply "move on." Now, after a high-threat operation or critical stressor, details include scheduled decompression periods and structured check-ins. Policies have evolved beyond the technical; after-action debriefings are now expected to include both emotional and tactical dimensions. The debrief is less about identifying who was right or wrong and more about understanding the totality of the circumstances: psychological, cognitive, familial, and then, processing those outputs collectively. As recent research affirms that peer support provides "...the benefit of normalizing experiences through a shared lived experience. They increase understanding and foster empathy and compassion among participants, which helps build resilience and hope."[7] This integration of structured post-incident care underscores that recovery is not merely operational, but fundamentally human. It is essential to sustain both individual well-being and team performance.

It is clear that neither organizational inertia nor individual overextension can be sustained without profound consequences. The intersecting realities of the Dead Horse Theory and the Competence Trap reveal a system where both structures and people are stretched to the breaking point, ultimately sacrificing well-being, morale, and professional longevity for fleeting gains. If genuine resilience and excellence are to be achieved within executive protection, the cycle of extraction must be replaced with a new ethic—one that values human limits, nurtures growth, and sees protectors as whole people rather than expendable resources. The future of the field depends not only on recognizing these traps, but on actively building cultures of care, renewal, and collective strength.

FOUNDATIONS FOR EVERYDAY RESILIENCE

Building safeguards and a resilient system within executive protection is not just about writing new policies or launching isolated initiatives. It is a deliberate, daily cultivation of a dynamic and nourishing culture. A new cultural approach is founded on four core principles: radical awareness, protected boundaries, robust peer support, and relentless investment in professional development. When woven together, these principles provide a truly sustainable foundation for both individual well-being and collective resilience.

Radical awareness is more than looking for visible signs of stress or crisis. It is the practice of staying deeply attuned to yourself and others. As protectors are trained to scan for threats, they also search for subtle shifts in mood, behavior, or engagement that may signal underlying fatigue or anxiety. Leaders and team members alike must make authentic check-ins and honest conversations part of their routine, replacing superficial greetings with real curiosity about well-being. This shared vigilance enables early intervention, helping to address problems before they escalate into isolation or burnout. As research affirms, "Leaders, managers, and supervisors play an essential role in protecting workers from burnout. Although individual-level interventions to improve self-care and resilience can be helpful, organizations also need to make changes to address root causes of burnout."[8] Investing in wellness training, mindfulness, and practical emotional regulation strategies can amplify these effects and empower teams to manage stress proactively.

Protected boundaries demand a conscious move away from the heroics of chronic availability and self-sacrifice. In a healthy environment, excellence is redefined not by how long someone stays on the clock, but by the clarity with which they protect their time, recovery, and energy. Leaders set the tone by openly prioritizing rest and modeling appropriate limits on accessibility. Structured time off, support for personal and family needs, and permission to disconnect become organizational norms. As evidence shows, "In environments where healthy boundaries are modeled and respected from the top down, both performance and morale measurably improve."[9] Flexible scheduling policies, technology-free downtime, and visible recognition of self-care as a form of professionalism further reinforce this foundation.

Robust peer support offers resilience where it is needed most. Executive protection has long celebrated the lone wolf, but teams flourish when mentorship and mutual care are purposefully cultivated. Pairing newcomers with seasoned agents—focusing not only on tactics, but on managing fatigue, doubts, and setbacks—fosters real connection and open dialogue. Regular group check-ins, informal peer counseling, and recognition of those who help colleagues through tough moments further dismantle stigma and isolation. "Workplaces that foster supportive peer relationships can help buffer employees against stress and reduce the risk of burnout. Encouraging collaboration, camaraderie, and open communication is a protective factor for psychological well-being."[10] Formal mentoring programs, structured debriefings, and peer recognition are proven ways to embed resilience throughout the team.

A frequently underestimated concept encompasses the fourth principle, centered on the relentless pursuit of professional growth. Even in environments where teams are well-supported and rested, stagnation can quickly take root if members are not consistently challenged with new learning and development opportunities. In a high-performance culture, every protector is encouraged to cross-train, embrace new competencies, and reflect on their evolving contributions. Assignment rotations and ongoing education are viewed as vehicles for engagement, rather than punishment. They help sustain intellectual curiosity and agency, serving as vital psychological safeguards against complacency and burnout. As the Center for Creative Leadership notes, "Continuous learning is the single best investment leaders can make in themselves and their organizations, ensuring adaptability in the face of change and protecting against disengagement."[11] Facilitating regular training, promoting knowledge sharing, and meaningfully connecting growth opportunities to personal and collective goals ignites long-term motivation, adaptability, and sustained professional fulfillment.

Collectively, these four interconnected strategies build an organic system of support and sustainability. Radical awareness ensures early action; protected boundaries reinforce safety and presence; peer support guarantees no one faces challenges alone; and ongoing growth keeps spirits high and minds fresh. Fully integrated into the culture and rhythms of executive protection, enhanced by regular training, leadership modeling, protected rest, and open dialogue, they protect against burnout and forge a professional community defined by resilience, loyalty, and excellence.

CASE STUDY: A TEAM AT THE BREAKING POINT

The assignment began like any other: a weeks-long deployment protecting an executive principal during a tumultuous overseas merger. The pace was brutal. Every shift stretched long into the night, rest was sacrificed to urgent logistics, and the relentless pressure to "show up strong" overwhelmed even the best-trained professionals. At first, the team, comprised of some of the industry's most seasoned and highly competent operators, powered through. One former military operator, recently promoted, set the tone by refusing days off and always volunteering for the next high-profile task. As the operation wore on, others followed suit, believing endurance was the true badge of trust and belonging.

By the third week, subtle warning signs surfaced and complacency started to settle in. One agent began forgetting basic procedural checklists; another, usually steady, grew impatient in briefings. Meanwhile, the team's lead privately struggled with rising anxiety from issues at home and insomnia, unwilling to disclose his distress for fear of appearing weak or risking elite assignments. Even as fatigue deepened, calls for backup went unheeded. Quiet conversations about "pushing through" and the normalization of skipped meals or missed family calls became routine. The detail, locked in the competence trap, mistook adaptability and experience for limitless resilience, and no one wanted to be the first to step back.

It was only after a security gap was narrowly avoided, a lapse spotted moments before it threatened the principal, that the true cost became impossible to ignore. In the after-action review, honest feedback was finally solicited. For the first time, team members admitted their exhaustion, isolation, and the strain of performance without support.

The insight was clear: skill and commitment had become a prison, not a strength.

Recognizing the gravity of the situation, the organization chose to intervene. Leaders normalized honest check-ins, and team members were encouraged, not punished, for flagging their own strain. Mandatory downtime and decompression rotations were instituted. Peer mentors checked in after every high-pressure cycle, and professional counseling was made visible and accessible. Perhaps most transformative was a cultural shift: the bravest agents became those who modeled healthy boundaries and encouraged seeking help, reframing vulnerability as a sign of professionalism.

For the detail leader and every member of the team, burnout was finally understood as not resulting from one single event; it is the outcome of ingrained habits, cultural silence, and confusing output with worth. Teams that thrive aren't those of unsustainable endurance; they are the ones who recognize limits in time, support each other visibly, and continuously recalibrate how they define strength and excellence. For this team, the lesson is that enduring resilience is not the absence of need, but the courage to act before the costs become irreversible.

SHIFTING PRESSURES AND ISOLATION

The world of protective leadership has undergone significant changes in the past decade. The context shaping executive protection today is more turbulent, interconnected, and exposed than at any previous point in history. Political volatility is surging in many countries, while global health crises and mass movements have upended traditional assumptions about crowd behavior, threat modeling, and dynamic factors in risk assessments. In this evolving landscape, the expectations placed on protection agents stretch far beyond physical vigilance. Today's protector is expected to be a diplomat, a crisis manager, and a technology expert, all while being a grounded human. One capable of balancing empathy with quick action, even as their work is scrutinized more closely than ever before.

The modern executive protection environment intensifies traditional pressures while continuously adding new sources of stress. Longer deployments are now common, driven by improved logistical capabilities that enable agents to remain in the field for extended periods without interruption. Public exposure has surged due to social media and the availability of digital information, putting agents under a constant spotlight and increasing scrutiny from clients and the general public. The constant presence of asymmetric threats further increases the complexity of operations. As a result, agents often remain in a heightened state of readiness even after their official shift ends, with the boundaries between work and home fading rapidly in an era of instant digital connectivity. The demands of the job seldom pause; phones rarely stop ringing, and many agents find their minds racing with work concerns long after their bodies try to rest.

This environment not only demands more, but it also sharply amplifies feelings of isolation. With protectors constantly on the move, facing frequent relocations and extended deployments, social support networks become fractured or nonexistent. The operational secrecy essential to the job makes genuine connection even more difficult, leaving many protectors unable to share even everyday experiences with friends or family. As a result, protectors often rely on colleagues as surrogate family, the only ones who truly witness the toll such relentless stress and disruption extract. As the U.S. Surgeon General has highlighted, "Loneliness is far more than just a bad feeling—it harms both individual and collective well-being. Social connection is a fundamental human need, as essential to survival as food, water, and shelter."[12]

And all the while, the research grows more urgent. Global workplace studies reveal sharply rising rates of chronic burnout, anxiety, and disengagement across high-reliability, high-consequence sectors.[13] As ASIS International points out,

> The impact of burnout extends well beyond the individual, particularly when it affects security personnel. Given the high-stress nature of their responsibilities... the consequences can be significant and far-reaching. Mental and emotional exhaustion among security staff dramatically increases the likelihood of oversight, human errors, and weakened security measures. This heightened vulnerability not only escalates the risk of physical and digital security breaches but also poses serious threats to organizational integrity and public safety.[14]

Suicides among those in protective and security roles are a stark reminder that resilience cannot be left to chance or willpower alone. Mental health must become a deliberate and collective priority.

There are signs of industry-wide momentum toward change. Those leading major enterprises now routinely inquire about rest protocols and support structures alongside tactical readiness, understanding that employee well-being is essential to sustainable performance. As experts from Harvard Business Review note, "It doesn't have to be costly to redesign work to improve employees' well-being. In fact, it can often be a good investment."[15] This perspective reflects a growing recognition that protecting the effectiveness of protection professionals begins with investing in their holistic health and support systems.

This is a seminal moment. Failure to shift brings real consequences such as lost talent, reputational disaster, and operational breakdown.

Success belongs to those teams and leaders who embrace the full complexity of human sustainability, who see it as integral to readiness and longevity, not as an expendable luxury.

WEIGHT OF TRADITION: THE COST OF SILENCE

The greatest barriers to meaningful cultural change are often deeply rooted in longstanding traditions, personal pride, and the human tendency to resist shifting established ways of working. For decades, protectors have absorbed the lesson, sometimes spoken but often implied, that vulnerability is risk. The best protectors are those who never crack. The perpetual stories that circulate in the breaks between assignments —the one about the agent who quietly handled a principal's midnight crisis without complaint, or the teammate who never called in sick have institutionalized norms far more powerfully than any memo. With a damning impact. It is against this backdrop that even mentioning a need for support can feel unwise, if not dangerous.

Stigma is the first and most enduring wall. It keeps people quiet long after they know something inside is slipping. Even as organizations adopt better language and create more support channels, there are still too many whispered warnings about what happens to those who raise a hand for help. "As a result of stigma, many employees suffer in silence, often for fear that their reputation, relationships, or job status could be in jeopardy if they disclose they're struggling with their mental health or have a mental health condition."[16] Some agents believe, with justification from their own experiences or those of colleagues, that disclosure leads to lost assignments, fewer travel opportunities, or a slow fading from the circle of trust. Leaders worry about being seen as soft or unable to carry a full load. In the training classroom, resilience is celebrated as an ideal, but in the field, exhaustion is too often rewarded with applause, not intervention.

Trust, or the lack of it, forms the next barrier. Many in the field question whether management's concern is genuine or if wellness initiatives are merely window-dressing. Rumors always circulate, confidential conversations somehow make their way back to supervisors, and team rosters are shuffled for undisclosed reasons. In this climate, accessing support requires a leap of faith. Team members, especially those with years invested, may only speak up when the situation becomes dire, by which point recovery is longer and more difficult. Where leadership walks the talk when admit their own struggles, share their own stories, or demonstrate time and again that help-seeking is career-sustaining, not career-ending. The tides begin to shift. The necessity to change the culture starts at the top. "In reality, when CEOs share their own mental health experiences, they are displaying strength, courage, and self-awareness. Which, the last time I checked, are great qualities for a leader to have."[17] However, in organizations where talk far outpaces trust, resources often lie idle or are utilized only in moments of crisis.

Layered atop these cultural realities are more structural limitations. Many protection organizations operate at the bare minimum of staffing and resources. The reality is that schedules are written for the needs of the principal or client, not of the protectors; thus, they allow little margin for absence or rest. Small providers may simply lack access to counseling or robust peer support, while contractors navigating multiple clients find themselves without a "home base" for help. Add in the complexity of constant geographic mobility, language differences, or cultural barriers, and it is no surprise that real connection and the systematic response to distress are so often elusive.

Sometimes the damage is compounded by an innocent misdiagnosis. Supervisors, who are dedicated and hard-working but lack clinical training, often observe declining performance, absenteeism, or emotional withdrawal and assume that discipline or motivational issues are to blame. In their well-intentioned effort to uphold standards, they double the load or issue warnings, missing the deeper call for support. This can set up a negative spiral that silences others who might have benefited from early intervention. One seasoned protective agent, reflecting on a colleague's downward turn, put it bluntly: "By the time anyone acted, it was already too late for a gentle course correction."

Perfection can be the enemy of the good; it is the quiet saboteur running beneath all these currents. The pressures of perfection run deep in some of the most elite protective organizations in the world.

> The Secret Service has this motto: zero fail. It means you can never let your protectee be harmed. You must be perfect, every moment of every day. There are no do-overs in the Secret Service. And that level of stress is, I think, pretty unique.[18]

The reality is that stress and pressures are not exclusive to the Secret Service; whenever the stakes can be measured in lives and reputations, the pressure to deliver flawlessly at all times is immense. Many agents internalize the field's unspoken "zero fail" ethos as a matter of self-worth. Any lapse erodes confidence. Far from being a driver of excellence, chronic perfectionism breeds shame, defensiveness, and, in the worst cases, collapse. As Nadia Renata and psychologists across the field note, "perfectionism is strongly and consistently related to numerous 'detrimental' work and non-work outcomes, including higher levels of burnout, stress, workaholism, anxiety, and depression…."[19]

Breaking down the cultural barriers of stigma, mistrust, and entrenched traditions requires more than well-intentioned memos or intermittent workshops. Real change emerges when every person, from leadership to line agents, commits to reimagining what support and resilience truly mean for the protective profession. Trust is built not just by talking, but by consistent action and transparency. It is only then that organizations can foster environments where reaching for help is seen as an expression of professionalism and strength. In reality, the challenge and the opportunity for executive protection now lie in moving beyond theory into tangible practice. Translating insight and aspiration into daily operational reality, where support systems are embedded.

BUILDING A CULTURE OF AWARENESS

Translating ideals into actionable practice means distilling them to their essence and committing to constant use, not just in times of breakdown. Among the most effective approaches emerging from research and lived experience is a threefold process: recognize, support, recalibrate. For those in executive protection, embodying this model means not only identifying early signs of strain, but also supporting oneself and others through proven strategies, and continually adjusting responses to thrive in high-pressure environments.

Recognition within executive protection is far deeper than mere observation. It is a discipline grounded in attentiveness, pattern interpretation, and proactive care. In high-stress environments, recognition means deliberately tuning in to subtle shifts in demeanor, tone, and understanding that these cues often signal the first signs of stress or impending burnout. For executive protection professionals, this is not an abstract skill but a critical operational asset: effective teams actively attend to what is not spoken, noting changes in a colleague's temperament after a tough assignment, or noticing the silent tension that signals when a team member is overloaded.

Recognition is inseparable from situational awareness. It is trained through continuous environmental and behavioral scanning, advanced observation, and the ability to distinguish between routine fatigue and red flags for intervention. Leaders and peers who master this discipline understand that checking in on someone who is showing subtle changes is not an intrusion, but a hallmark of professional excellence. In elite protection teams, recognition is also embedded in team culture and operational debriefs, establishing a standard where early supportive intervention is valued as highly as tactical readiness. When consistently practiced, recognition in executive protection becomes both a guardrail against silent suffering and a powerful tool in sustaining team resilience and mission success.

Support is much more than an individual obligation. It is a shared responsibility, deeply woven into the fabric of effective teams. Executive protection is a high-stakes profession; support means consciously creating an environment where trust, psychological safety, and open dialogue are valued as essential as technical skills. This includes regular check-ins, accessible mental health resources, and peer support networks that encourage protectors to lean on each other during times of stress and to share coping strategies without stigma.

Organizationally, support is embedded when leaders institutionalize practices like structured rest cycles, protected time off, and confidential counseling services, signaling that well-being is a collective priority, not a personal weakness. Strong support cultures normalize speaking up about fatigue, encourage looking out for teammates, and equip everyone with the language and channels to ask for or offer help. For executive protection professionals, such structures are not only protective factors against burnout but key ingredients for sustained high performance. In the end this empowers teams to thrive together in the most demanding environments.

Recalibration is the mark of an organization that views wellness as a moving target and consistently updates its approach. Every major event becomes a chance not only to review tactical performance, but to ask deeper questions about how the team weathered the stress. Intrinsic agility means that policies adapt organically: rotations shift, break schedules evolve, and peer-mentoring initiatives emerge in real time, all in response to genuine insights gained from lived experience. Leaders do not wait for metrics alone; they gather feedback and then close the loop with every team member affected. The culture of recalibration means "good enough" is never the goal, and that pride lies as much in learning as in flawless execution.

The impact of this approach is witnessed in teams that, after facing challenges, grow united and respected not just for their operational skills, but also for their human strength. Its real power lies not in flawless execution, but in the daily commitment to practice these principles. As organizations move forward, embedding this mindset into their structures and culture becomes essential for sustaining excellence and well-being at every level.

REDEFINING A BENCHMARK

To ensure that lessons about mental health and resilience do not remain rhetoric, organizations must entwine them with job roles, expectations, and advancement. The reimagined onboarding for new protectors introduces the topic of stress management and well-being not as a footnote, but as a central plank of professional development. New hires learn from day one that asking for support is a marker of insight, not a flaw, and that advancement is measured not only through technical delivery but through the ability to sustain oneself and the team over time.

Training is transformed from periodic compliance workshops to ongoing cycles of learning: nuanced sessions on psychology, the impacts of chronic vigilance, and the value of social connection. Supervisors become facilitators, inviting candid dialogue and fostering a climate where voices at all levels are welcomed. Feedback is gathered in multiple formats, including anonymous channels, open forums, and private one-on-ones. Leaders must be attuned to accommodating different needs and personalities. Where possible, organizations adapt these approaches to local language and culture, flattening the barriers of distance or difference and bringing every protector into the fold.

Recognition is recalibrated. Rather than celebrating those who work without pause, acknowledgment and rewards are focused on individuals who balance operational excellence with meaningful peer support and personal accountability. Leadership evaluations place equal weight on daily stewardship of team well-being, ensuring that sustained health and a supportive culture are recognized as key measures of success. As Amy C. Edmondson writes, "When people feel psychologically safe at work, they are more likely to bring their whole selves to the job — and that includes speaking up about concerns, asking for help, and supporting one another."[20] This foundation of psychological safety transforms recognition from a reward for endurance alone into an affirmation of holistic, resilient leadership.

Technology is increasingly becoming a powerful supporting role, providing real-time data about workload spikes and recovery, generating early warnings about potential burnout flags, and making support resources as visible as any operational directive. The best organizations use these signals, in combination with human insight, to make prevention second nature rather than a last resort.

Narrative, ultimately, binds everything together. The lived stories of struggle, bounce-back, and shared support are told and retold, shaping a culture where flourishing, not just survival, is seen as proof that the system works. The difference is tangible, not only in less turnover or fewer errors, but in the confidence with which agents step forward, knowing they will not be left to falter unseen.

SUSTAINING UNDER PRESSURE

Periods of relentless strain, whether from extended deployments, demanding clients, or unyielding operational pressures, are inevitable for every agency and team. What distinguishes truly exceptional organizations is not their ability to simply survive these moments, but their commitment to embedding resilience as a daily discipline. Edmondson, at Harvard Business School, affirms, "Building the kind of organizational resilience that enables people to thrive in a world of constant change is not about a single heroic leader—it's about routines, relationships, and a climate of psychological safety that are practiced every day."[21] For these teams, resilience is woven into routines and culture, ensuring that well-being and adaptability are sustained through both everyday challenges and the most demanding circumstances.

Top leaders anticipate the grind. At the first sign that events are amplifying, an extended threat, a run of overseas travel, a high-profile controversy. Astute leaders begin doubling down on check-ins, shorten rotations even before fatigue is visible, and call in extra support wherever possible. The senior team sends the message early and often: Recovery is part of our operation, not an interruption. Agent sleep, focus, and morale are discussed as actively as logistics or intelligence. Those returning from the hardest stints are automatically placed in decompression rotations, their experiences reviewed not just for lessons on tactics, but for signals of how the next cycle can be made more survivable for all.

After every period of intense operational pressure, teams conduct a comprehensive review that goes beyond surface outcomes. Immediate, candid feedback becomes standard practice, with attention given not just to the results, but to the internal dynamics and well-being of the team. Lessons are rapidly translated into meaningful adjustments, allowing improvements to be enacted within days. Thus, ensuring growth is continuous and no insight slips through the cracks.

LIVING RESILIENCE IN PRACTICE

Resilience in executive protection is forged not by dramatic gestures or infrequent initiatives, but by the aggregation of intentional daily actions and attitudes. It emerges when leaders at every level make a habit of sincerely checking in on the mental and emotional health of their colleagues. It demonstrates that rest and recovery are as vital as vigilance or technical skill. By openly sharing their own experiences with fatigue and vulnerability, leaders model that stepping back to recharge is a mark of wisdom, not weakness. Protectors are encouraged to notice early warning signs in themselves and one another, fostering an environment where taking a break is both normalized and expected.

The battle against stigma is addressed through story and structure: sharing honest accounts of adversity, recovery, and resilience turns asking for help into a point of pride. Teams cultivate trust by making it routine to quietly flag concerns and look after one another before problems escalate. Continuous professional development is integral to the organization's culture. Annual targets include cross-training and stretch assignments that challenge stagnation and expand competence, ensuring adaptability across roles and in response to emerging threats.

Support resources are made visible, accessible, and free from unnecessary red tape. It is engagement, not bureaucracy, that becomes the measure of their effectiveness. Data from schedules, incident trends, and candid team conversations is reviewed not as a formality, but as a critical tool for spotting patterns: where fatigue intensifies, which teams may be close to burnout, and who may be at risk of falling through the cracks.

Thriving organizations close the gap between policy and everyday practice. Feedback is not only welcomed but imperative; incremental changes are enacted swiftly, and recovery and adaptability are upheld as daily disciplines. Real resilience is the product of transparent communication, collective responsibility, reinforced personal boundaries, rapid and meaningful support, and a shared bravery to continually reassess and adapt as new challenges emerge, ensuring the protector remains protected.

LIVED EXPERIENCE TO LASTING CHANGE

The real test of courage and wisdom in executive protection is not how tirelessly one stands guard, but how bravely one recognizes when old models must be laid to rest. The dead horse theory reminds us: when a horse is dead, no amount of pushing, motivating, or rewarding will bring it back to life. Nonetheless, teams often try to carry on by riding even when exhaustion and burnout have rendered them immobile. Likewise, the competence trap tempts us to overvalue relentless endurance and technical mastery, blinding us to creeping costs and eroding the very resilience we claim to cherish.

Those who write these words now, the authors of this book, do so not as distant observers but as protectors who have known, up close, the invisible burdens, the pride, and the pain that define executive protection work. The difference now is a shared resolve: to honor not just the physical readiness of every protector, but their full well-being. May we have the humility to dismount when the horse is dead, the clarity to escape the competence trap before it becomes a cage, and the empathy to ensure no one rides on alone.

This is how leadership excellence and personal welfare must move forward together from those who have witnessed and lived what stands to be lost and gained.

The choice is yours.

NOTES

1 Chris Middleton, "The Decline of Mental Health in the Security Industry," *Security Journal United Kingdom*, March 2024, https://securityjournaluk.com/decline-mental-health-in-security-industry/.

2 World Health Organization, "International Classification of Diseases (ICD-11)," 2025, https://icd.who.int/browse/2025-01/mms/en#129180281.

3 Society for Human Resource Management, "Here's How Bad Burnout Has Become at Work," April 30, 2024, https://www.shrm.org/topics-tools/news/inclusion-diversity/burnout-shrm-research-2024.

4 Holistique Training, "The Dead Horse Theory in Professional Life," 2025, https://holistiquetraining.com/en/news/the-dead-horse-theory-in-professional-life.

5 Juan A. Moriano, Fernando Molero, Ana Laguía, Mario Mikulincer, and Philip R. Shaver, "Security Providing Leadership: A Job Resource to Prevent Employees' Burnout," *International Journal of Environmental Research and Public Health* 18, no. 23 (2021): 12551, https://doi.org/10.3390/ijerph182312551.

6 The Influence Journal, "The Competence Trap: When Your Talent Becomes Your Barrier," *Medium*, April 6, 2025, https://medium.com/@TheInfluenceJournal/the-competence-trap-when-your-talent-becomes-your-barrier-caef686c7c19.

7 Fallon, P., Jaegers, L. A., Zhang, Y., Dugan, A. G., Cherniack, M., & El Ghaziri, M. (2023). Peer support programs to reduce organizational stress and trauma for public safety workers: A scoping review. *Workplace Health & Safety, 71*(11), 523–535. https://firstresponsemh.com/wp-content/uploads/2023/10/fallon-et-al-2023-peer-support-programs-to-reduce-organizational-stress-and-trauma-for-public-safety-workers-a-scoping-8.pdf

8 Centers for Disease Control and Prevention, "New Burnout Prevention Training for Public Health," *NIOSH Science Blog*, October 24, 2023, https://blogs.cdc.gov/niosh-science-blog/2023/10/25/burnout-training/.

9 Society for Human Resource Management, "Here's How Bad Burnout Has Become at Work," April 30, 2024, https://www.shrm.org/topics-tools/news/inclusion-diversity/burnout-shrm-research-2024.

10 American Psychological Association, "Workplace Well-Being: Promoting Employee Mental Health," 2023, https://www.apa.org/topics/healthy-workplaces/promoting-employee-mental-health.

11 Center for Creative Leadership, "The Importance of Continuous Learning for Leaders," 2023, https://www.ccl.org/articles/leading-effectively-articles/the-importance-of-continuous-learning-for-leaders/.

12 U.S. Department of Health and Human Services, "Our Epidemic of Loneliness and Isolation: The U.S. Surgeon General's Advisory on the Healing Effects of Social Connection and Community," 2023, 7, https://www.hhs.gov/sites/default/files/surgeon-general-social-connection-advisory.pdf.

13 World Health Organization, "Mental Health in the Workplace," 2023, https://www.who.int/teams/mental-health-and-substance-use/policy-law-rights/mental-health-in-the-workplace.

14 ASIS International, "Tackling Burnout in the High-Stakes World of Security," *Security Management Magazine*, December 31, 2024, https://www.asisonline.org/security-management-magazine/articles/2025/01/burnout/tackling-burnout/.

15 Erin L. Kelly, Lisa F. Berkman, Laura D. Kubzansky, and Meg Lovejoy, "7 Strategies to Improve Your Employees' Health and Well-Being," *Harvard Business Review*, October 30, 2021, https://hbr.org/2021/10/7-strategies-to-improve-your-employees-health-and-well-being.

16 Lyra Health, "Mental Health Stigma and How to Overcome It," April 28, 2022, https://www.lyrahealth.com/resources/mental-health-stigma/.

17 Melissa Doman, "Talking About Mental Health as a CEO," *MelissaDoman.com*, n.d., https://www.melissadoman.com/blog/talking-about-mental-health-as-a-ceo.

18 Carol Leonnig, "In 'Zero Fail,' Carol Leonnig Says Secret Service Is Underfunded and Overworked," interview transcript, *NPR*, May 16, 2021, https://www.npr.org/transcripts/997377737.

19 Brian Swider, Dana Harari, Amy P. Breidenthal, and Laurens Bujold Steed, "The Pros and Cons of Perfectionism, According to Research," *Harvard Business Review*, December 26, 2018, https://hbr.org/2018/12/the-pros-and-cons-of-perfectionism-according-to-research.

20 Amy C. Edmondson, *The Fearless Organization: Creating Psychological Safety in the Workplace for Learning, Innovation, and Growth* (Hoboken, NJ: Wiley, 2019), 18.

21 Amy C. Edmondson, *The Fearless Organization: Creating Psychological Safety in the Workplace for Learning, Innovation, and Growth* (Hoboken, NJ: Wiley, 2019), 199.

CHAPTER 9

Intelligence-Led Leadership: Data Informed

THE POWER OF INTELLIGENCE-LED LEADERSHIP

The same principles that sustain human endurance—awareness, rhythm, and recalibration—also sustain decision performance. In leadership, intelligence is resilience at scale. It is how an organization listens, learns, and adapts to pressure without breaking tempo. Where Chapter 8 explored the personal and cultural systems that protect people, this chapter turns to the systems that protect decisions: how leaders use intelligence to sustain clarity, consistency, and foresight under stress.

> In war, the simplest things are difficult. The difficulties accumulate and end by producing a kind of friction… that is inconceivable unless one has experienced war.
>
> *Carl von Clausewitz*

Leadership in the protective arena has always meant navigating friction—the unplanned variables, shifting priorities, and incomplete information that make decisions both urgent and uncertain. In today's corporate and geopolitical environment, that friction has simply multiplied. A sudden protest in a foreign city, a viral narrative targeting a brand, or a cyber breach with physical implications—each demands immediate choices with operational, reputational, and sometimes life-safety consequences.

What distinguishes an average leader from a decisive one is not access to more data, but the ability to create *decision advantage*—to have the right information, in the right context, at the right time, and the confidence to act on it. Intelligence-led leadership is the discipline of turning information into insight and insight into action. It transforms risk management from reaction to rhythm, creating the organizational equivalent of endurance: a system that sustains awareness, speed, and precision through every cycle of pressure.

 DOI: 10.4324/9781003670704-14

Michael Warner once defined intelligence as *information that has been analyzed and given meaning.*[1] *Meaning*, therefore, is what converts information into power. It is the difference between seeing events and understanding what they signify. In protective leadership, that meaning is the currency of trust—it allows security, operations, and communications teams to anticipate rather than chase events.

From here, the journey of intelligence-led leadership begins; understanding how resilience scales into insight, how feedback becomes foresight, and how the same loops that protect people can also protect decisions.

FROM REACTIVE TO PROACTIVE

For decades, protective programs were designed to react. The model was linear: receive an alert, act, restore order. That framework served well in a slower, more predictable world—one where most threats had clear boundaries and time allowed for deliberate response. But, in an age of digital velocity, disinformation, and converging risks, reaction alone is no longer a measure of readiness.

The environment that protective leaders operate in today is perpetually in motion. Physical, digital, and reputational domains overlap; incidents cascade across platforms and jurisdictions in minutes, requiring leaders to manage information as a living ecosystem, not a linear flow. Modern risk moves at a pace that demands anticipation, not just vigilance. Intelligence is the mechanism that makes that possible. It turns the feedback loops that once sustained personal resilience into organizational foresight.

Reactive leadership waits for disruption to dictate tempo. Proactive leadership sets tempo before disruption can take hold. The intelligence-led leader builds systems that detect weak signals, distill meaning, and trigger early adjustments before an event forces action. The result is not omniscience, but decision advantage—the ability to act with clarity and confidence in conditions of uncertainty.

This shift is not theoretical; it is cultural. It requires leaders to treat intelligence not as a product or department, but as a practice—a way of thinking embedded in every operational rhythm. The same routines that support human recovery in Chapter 8—observation, reflection, recalibration—become the structural routines of insight generation.

In that sense, intelligence-led leadership is not about replacing instinct with algorithms. It is about extending awareness; fusing intuition and information into a single, adaptive system. When this fusion becomes habit, organizations stop chasing the next crisis and start shaping the environment around them.

INTELLIGENCE AS LEADERSHIP CURRENCY

The modern protective leader deals in a different form of capital. It isn't measured in budgets or headcount, but in clarity. Intelligence is that currency: the ability to transform noise into meaning and meaning into influence.

Just as resilience depends on feedback and rhythm, intelligence depends on context and timing. Flood an executive team with raw data, and value collapses under the weight of confusion. Deliver one timely, contextualized insight that prevents a multimillion-dollar disruption, and its worth becomes undeniable. Intelligence-led leadership is the discipline of maintaining that equilibrium—collecting enough to understand, filtering enough to decide, and communicating enough to influence.

In this sense, intelligence becomes an influence amplifier. It elevates the security function from reactive guardrail to strategic partner, proving that protection is not a cost center but a decision enabler. A leader who consistently delivers intelligence-driven recommendations earns trust not through hierarchy, but through relevance. Each time an assessment helps executives act faster or, with greater confidence, the credibility of the entire protective function compounds.

This dynamic is exemplified by Ryan Long, whose work building a global intelligence program at a Fortune 500 company redefined how protective intelligence operates. His approach of embedding analysts directly into operational and business rhythms[2] transformed intelligence from a reactive watchtower into a proactive decision engine. By aligning outputs with enterprise priorities, his team influenced travel planning, supply chain continuity, and brand strategy, demonstrating that intelligence could inform growth as effectively as it mitigated risk. Long's model made a simple truth clear: when intelligence is tied to decision cadence, it ceases to be a back-office report and becomes a leadership tool.

In the hands of forward-leaning leaders, intelligence therefore becomes more than information, it becomes trust capital. Each loop of insight and response reinforces organizational confidence. Over time, that trust converts into speed, precision, and resilience, the same traits that define elite protective teams in the field.

CUTTING THROUGH THE FOG

In *On War*, Carl Von Clausewitz described the "fog of war" as the accumulation of uncertainty that clouds even the most disciplined plans.[3] The same fog now surrounds leadership in a world where risk moves faster than reason. For the modern protector, the objective is not omniscience, but clarity: seeing enough of the pattern to act before chaos dictates the outcome.

Clarity does not happen by accident; it's engineered through process and practice. The intelligence leader uses structure the way an athlete uses muscle memory, to move with precision under pressure. The framework that enables this is the intelligence cycle: directing collection toward what matters, transforming raw data into insight, and feeding that insight back into the next decision. It's less about surveillance and more about sensemaking, establishing a rhythm between awareness and action.

The real art lies in proportion. Knowing when to focus narrowly and when to zoom out, when to collect and when to stop collecting, when to act and when to wait. In protective intelligence, the leader must continuously balance speed and significance. A thousand alerts can paralyze; a single relevant signal can unlock decisive advantage. The goal is not to know everything but to understand what truly matters now.

Leadership in this context means being both conductor and interpreter; orchestrating cross-functional inputs from security, operations, communications, and risk teams, then translating those inputs into language executives can use. This is where insight becomes influence. A good intelligence leader doesn't overwhelm decision-makers with volume; they deliver meaning in motion, the right insight at the right moment in the right format.

When clarity becomes habit, the organization begins to operate with decision rhythm. It moves beyond crisis management into continuous foresight. In this way, the intelligence function mirrors the human resilience system explored in Chapter 8: both depend on feedback, recalibration, and trust in the process.

THE STAKES OF GETTING IT RIGHT

The true impact of intelligence-led leadership is measured not by the number of reports produced, but by the moments of clarity it creates—crises avoided, risks neutralized before they mature, and opportunities seized because a leader recognized a window others missed. Intelligence at its best converts complexity into calm, providing a rhythm of awareness and action that allows organizations to move with confidence even amid uncertainty.

One example is a Fortune 500 global intelligence program that demonstrated how a disciplined approach can earn C-suite trust and directly shape enterprise-level decisions. Another, the "Storm Over Singapore" scenario, drawn from composite experiences, illustrates how converging streams of intelligence, trust, and preparation can alter a high-stakes travel decision within minutes. Both examples, whether lived or representative, reveal the same truth: clarity is engineered, not improvised. The leaders who get it right treat intelligence as a living system—one that senses, interprets, and adapts in real time.

The stakes for getting it wrong are equally clear. Without disciplined feedback loops, organizations drown in noise, mistaking data for understanding and activity for progress. The result is fatigue disguised as foresight. Intelligence-led leadership prevents that drift by turning information into alignment and uncertainty into advantage.

Building on this foundation, the next sections move from principle to practice—showing how intelligence functions as a **strategic enabler**, how to structure people and processes around continuous feedback, and how to sustain a culture where learning is embedded in every decision rhythm.

> In protective leadership, you will never have perfect information. The goal is not to eliminate uncertainty, but to ensure that uncertainty works in your favor.

INTELLIGENCE AS A STRATEGIC ENABLER

> Strategic intelligence is the kind of knowledge that policymakers need to create wise policy in the first place.–
>
> *Sherman Kent*[4]

Intelligence delivers its greatest value not in warning alone, but by shaping strategy, turning awareness into alignment and information into influence. In protective leadership, this means aligning intelligence outputs to the organization's priorities so that the information provided is not just relevant, but indispensable to decision-makers. Strategic alignment transforms the role of the protection leader from operational responder to trusted advisor, shifting perceptions of security from a cost center to a competitive asset.

The distinction between *strategic*, *operational*, and *tactical* intelligence is not academic; it determines whether intelligence earns influence or is ignored. Sherman Kent's foundational work makes this clear: tactical intelligence addresses immediate action, operational intelligence enables coordination across functions, and strategic intelligence informs the highest-level choices about direction and risk tolerance.[5] When protection leaders operate at a strategic level, they earn a place beside finance, operations, and communications as architects of the organization's future.

DECISION ADVANTAGE THROUGH ALIGNMENT

Decision advantage is not created by data volume or speed; it comes from alignment—when intelligence speaks the same language as leadership. The most effective protection leaders understand that intelligence must reflect the priorities, pressures, and vocabulary of the enterprise. When it does, insight becomes influence, and influence becomes trust.

Alignment is what turns intelligence into a leadership tool rather than a technical function. A well-crafted briefing that connects a regional protest to market volatility, shareholder sentiment, or reputational exposure will resonate far more deeply than one that lists incident counts or threat levels. Context translates information into meaning. Meaning, in turn, drives action.

Former director of both the CIA and NSA, Michael Hayden, describes the purpose of intelligence as creating *decision advantage*.[6] In the protective sphere, this advantage comes from anticipating the decision points an executive team will face and delivering insights that allow those decisions to be made with greater speed and confidence than adversaries or competitors.

This principle is vividly demonstrated by global intelligence leaders who integrate their teams directly into business rhythms. One Fortune 500 intelligence head built a system where protective insights informed not just security posture, but travel planning, supply chain continuity, and brand strategy. His team's deliverables were aligned to operational and financial calendars—delivered in the formats, cadence, and language used by senior leadership. The result was more than trust; it was strategic access.

Alignment, however, is not a one-time achievement. It is a feedback process that requires constant listening, recalibration, and translation between worlds. Leaders must regularly engage stakeholders across departments, understand evolving priorities, and adjust intelligence outputs accordingly. Each conversation refines the system's rhythm, ensuring that what is produced remains both actionable and credible.

In practice, this means turning intelligence into a shared operating picture—one where security, communications, operations, and legal functions converge around the same situational awareness. The leader's role is to maintain coherence across that network, ensuring that insight flows both upward to decision-makers and laterally across functions. When that alignment holds, intelligence becomes the organization's nervous system—translating stimuli into coordinated action faster than competitors or adversaries can react.

In the end, decision advantage is rhythm. It's the cadence between awareness and action, between understanding and execution. Leaders who master that rhythm transform intelligence from a background process into a strategic capability—one that not only informs decisions but also defines the tempo of success itself.

LESSONS FROM A GLOBAL ENTERPRISE

One Fortune 500 global intelligence leader demonstrated how aligning intelligence outputs with enterprise priorities can earn the trust of the C-suite and shape decisions well beyond the traditional scope of security. By integrating protective intelligence into operational and strategic planning, his team became a trusted business partner to senior leadership; influencing travel plans, protecting supply chain continuity, and anticipating reputational risks before they escalated. His approach, detailed later in this chapter, shows how credibility is built through consistent delivery of actionable insights that matter to the business.

Such credibility is not built overnight. It requires consistent delivery of insights that demonstrate an understanding of the enterprise's priorities and the discipline to avoid flooding executives with information that may be interesting but is not directly useful. In this sense, intelligence becomes not just a risk management tool, *but a leadership tool.*

While strategic intelligence principles apply across many disciplines, their true impact in protection comes through protective intelligence. As Tom Kopecky explains in The Complete Collection on Protective Intelligence, it is *the proactive process of collecting and assessing information to identify, assess, and manage threats before they escalate.*[7] When aligned with enterprise priorities, protective intelligence becomes more than a security tool—it becomes a lever for influence, allowing leaders to anticipate risk, shape strategy, and contribute meaningfully to the organization's future.

Influence, however, must be earned. Decision-makers trust intelligence leaders who understand their pressures, speak their language, and consistently deliver value aligned with enterprise outcomes. As one experienced intelligence professional observed, *Intelligence without strategic alignment is trivia.* In practice, this means engaging regularly with stakeholders beyond the security function, understanding their objectives and constraints, and integrating those insights into collection and analysis priorities.

When practiced this way, protective intelligence stops being a reactive reporting function and becomes a strategic discipline—one that positions protection leaders as full partners in governance and growth. The companies that best anticipate and manage emerging risks—political, social, or digital—will not simply endure disruption; they will use it as a competitive edge. Strategic intelligence is not about predicting the future; it's about positioning leadership to shape it.

STRUCTURING A PROTECTIVE INTELLIGENCE PROGRAM

An effective protective intelligence program is not static. It must adapt to shifting organizational priorities, evolving threat landscapes and lessons learned from past operations. Its value lies not just in the volume of data it collects, but in the precision with which it connects that data to leadership decisions.

People: The Human Core of Intelligence

Every intelligence system begins with people. Technology can accelerate awareness, but judgment remains human. Analysts, operators, and leaders each play distinct roles in the cycle: the analyst interprets, the operator observes, and the leader integrates. Together they form a feedback network that gives the organization both depth and agility.

The diversity of perspective strengthens that network. A global enterprise should integrate geopolitical analysis, cyber insights, brand intelligence, and field reporting into a single collaborative rhythm. Each discipline contributes a different form of awareness; combined, they create a more complete picture than any single source could provide.

As intelligence scholar Richards J. Heuer Jr. observed, *Intelligence analysis is fundamentally about making sense of a complex world so decision-makers can act with confidence.*[8] That clarity is built by people, not platforms. The best protection leaders treat their intelligence teams not as data collectors but as interpreters of complexity: professionals trusted to bring coherence to chaos when the stakes are the highest. Tools can process data, but only people can translate information into meaning, and meaning is what leaders need most when uncertainty becomes the operational constant.

Process: Turning Insight into Action

Process gives rhythm to judgment. It defines how awareness becomes understanding, and understanding becomes action. The traditional Intelligence Cycle (direction, collection, processing, analysis, dissemination, and feedback) remains the backbone, but its strength lies in its loop, not just its steps.

Leaders must ensure that every stage feeds the next: direction informs collection; analysis informs operations; and feedback informs the next directive. When that rhythm is maintained, intelligence stops being episodic and becomes a continuous heartbeat that sustains decision cadence.

Frameworks like David Omand's SEES model (*Situational Awareness, Explanation, Estimation, and Strategic Notice*) help maintain this balance, reminding leaders that intelligence must always serve the decision-maker, not the database.[9] The question isn't "what do we know?" but "what does the leader need to know now?"

Strong processes also institutionalize reflection. After-action reviews (AARs), brief feedback loops, and periodic calibration meetings allow the system to learn from itself. As in Chapter 8's discussion of resilience, adaptability is the outcome of reflection built into rhythm.

Technology: Extending Reach, Not Replacing Judgment

Technology is the force multiplier of modern intelligence, but only when driven by purpose. Automated tools can aggregate data, map networks, or visualize risk, yet they cannot replace the leader's discernment. The most successful programs use technology to *extend human judgment*, not outsource it.

Every platform should answer a simple question: does it improve the decision rhythm? If a tool accelerates awareness, shortens analysis time, or reveals patterns otherwise invisible, it strengthens the loop. If it merely adds volume without context, it weakens it.

The goal is integration, not accumulation; using technology to connect disparate data streams into a coherent operational picture that supports fast, ethical, and informed decisions.

Feedback: The Engine of Adaptation

No structure endures without feedback. The best programs treat lessons learned as a form of intelligence in themselves, data about the system's own performance. Feedback completes the loop, transforming one decision into insight for the next.

This discipline keeps the intelligence function adaptive and self-correcting. It allows leaders to refine collection priorities, re-evaluate risk assumptions, and adjust communication styles to match executive needs. Over time, feedback becomes the organization's memory and collective learning system.

A well-structured intelligence program is not static. It moves in rhythm with the enterprise it serves; sensing, interpreting, and adjusting continuously. When people, process, and technology operate as a synchronized loop, intelligence stops being a department and becomes a reflex.

FROM DATA TO DECISION

The modern protective leader is rarely short on information. In fact, they are saturated in it, so the problem is the opposite—*too much data and too little clarity*. Internal reports, security system alerts, social media monitoring, partner briefings, and open-source feeds can produce a flood of inputs that overwhelm even seasoned analysts. Without a disciplined process, the result is informational noise—which does not drive good decisions. As Michael Morell, former Deputy Director of the CIA, has observed, intelligence is only valuable if it is received in time for the decision-maker to act on it.[10] That means speed alone is not enough; information must be processed, analyzed, and delivered in a form that matches the decision-maker's need and timeline.

FILTERING THE NOISE

The first step is triage. Not every data point carries equal weight, and part of the intelligence function's value is the ability to recognize what matters now, what may matter later, and what can be set aside. This requires a combination of technical tools, to sort and aggregate data, and human judgment to understand nuance, context, and potential second-order effects.

Intelligence programs that fail to filter risks overwhelming decision-makers can lead to "alert fatigue" and diminished trust in its ability. Analysts who consistently identify and signal the 10% of data points that truly matter reinforce their credibility and ensure that their briefings are read and acted upon.

FRAMING RISK IN BUSINESS TERMS

Even the most accurate intelligence loses impact if it is not framed in the decision-maker's language. Data without context is just noise, and in the C-suite, attention is a scarce commodity. Leaders are focused on strategic objectives, operational continuity, shareholder value, and reputation; intelligence that fails to connect to these priorities will be ignored or deprioritized.

For example, a report noting that a protest is planned at a principal's destination may be overlooked. But a briefing that explains how the protest is likely to disrupt a scheduled investor meeting, delay critical negotiations, generate unfavorable media coverage, and shift public sentiment will command attention. This approach turns a situational alert into a strategic decision point.

A growing body of analysis on narrative-driven threats reinforces this point.[11] Protective intelligence must consider the broader story: how a physical risk may be amplified by online narratives, and how those narratives can influence brand perception, stakeholder confidence, and operational freedom. A localized protest might be a logistical challenge in isolation but if the images and messaging spread globally online, it can evolve into a reputational crisis. Translating these risks into business terms makes intelligence both relevant and actionable, ensuring it is not just received, but used to shape decisions.

HOW TO FRAME INTELLIGENCE FOR DECISION-MAKERS

To consistently align intelligence with executive priorities, start by mapping the decision-maker's primary objectives and known pressure points; these could include revenue protection, regulatory compliance, operational uptime, market perception, or personal safety. Use these as the frame for every product you deliver. When assessing a threat, ask: *What is the operational impact? What is the reputational impact? What is the financial impact?*

Avoid security jargon and replace it with the language of outcomes. Instead of "heightened threat activity," say "a 60% likelihood of travel disruption within the next 48 hours, potentially delaying two high-value client meetings." Where possible, present options: the recommended course of action, an acceptable alternative, and the risks of inaction. This turns intelligence from a passive briefing into an active decision tool, and one that leaders will trust and seek out when the stakes are high.

AVOIDING COGNITIVE TRAPS

Raw data does not automatically yield sound conclusions. Daniel Kahneman's *Thinking, Fast and Slow* distinguishes between the intuitive, rapid-fire judgments of System 1 and the slower, more deliberate reasoning of System 2.[12] Protective intelligence leaders must cultivate the discipline to engage System 2 when stakes are high, thereby challenging assumptions, considering alternative explanations, and using structured analytic techniques to guard against bias.

This is particularly critical in high-pressure environments, where there is a natural tendency to lock onto the first plausible explanation and act. Slowing down just enough to validate assumptions can prevent missteps that carry significant operational or reputational costs.

CLARITY, RELEVANCE, TIMELINESS

In the end, intelligence that shapes decisions consistently meets three criteria: it is clear, relevant, and timely. Clarity ensures the decision-maker understands the implications without ambiguity. Relevance ties the assessment directly to organizational priorities and current decision points. Timeliness delivers the insight in time for action and not after the fact.

When these elements come together, the intelligence function becomes an indispensable part of the decision-making process. *Leaders don't just consume intelligence; they depend on it to navigate uncertainty and seize opportunities.* And when that happens, the protective intelligence leader moves from simply providing information to shaping the outcomes that matter most. One leader's experience demonstrates how aligning intelligence to enterprise priorities can transform a reactive security function into a trusted strategic partner.

CASE STUDY: RYAN LONG—BUILDING A GLOBAL INTELLIGENCE FUNCTION INTO A STRATEGIC ASSET

As noted earlier in this chapter, Ryan Long's career in protective intelligence spans both military service and the private sector, culminating in his role leading global intelligence and executive protection for a Fortune 500 multinational. A U.S. Army officer and active reservist, Long brought deep operational planning, intelligence integration, and decision support experience to the role. When he arrived, the organization's intelligence capability was largely reactive, focused on responding to threats as they appeared. In a global enterprise with operations in more than 100 countries, Long recognized that such a posture would always lag behind emerging risks.[13]

Drawing on his military experience and business acumen, Long built an intelligence program that proactively shaped strategic and operational decisions. He embedded analysts within the security function, giving them a broad mandate that included physical security, geopolitical threats, supply chain vulnerabilities, and narrative-driven risks to brand reputation.[14] Crucially, he built executive trust by framing every briefing in business terms; a protest alert became a forecast of potential sales disruption; an international travel assessment turned into a tool for planning elite executive engagements.

Through his leadership, protective intelligence evolved from a reactionary support function to a preemptive strategic asset. Executives came to rely on it not just in crisis, but as part of broader growth and planning discussions.

OPERATIONALIZING INTELLIGENCE

Transforming intelligence from analysis into action is the point where strategic intent becomes tangible results. It is the discipline of ensuring that what is learned, through monitoring, analysis, and assessment, directly shapes how the organization plans, responds, and adapts. For the protection leader, this is more than applying tradecraft; it is about embedding intelligence into the organization's decision-making fabric so that it consistently supports both protective objectives and broader business goals. Done well, the process doesn't just react to events, it anticipates them, providing the clarity and confidence needed to act decisively in a world where time and accuracy are equally critical.

TURNING INSIGHT INTO ACTION

Producing decision-quality intelligence is only valuable if it is acted upon. The protection leader's role is not simply to identify risks but to ensure that insights gained through collection and analysis become catalysts for timely, effective action. This means moving intelligence from static reports to embedded elements of planning, operations, and crisis response. When integrated well, intelligence supports the leader's mission to safeguard people and enable decision-making and strengthens the organization's ability to operate confidently in uncertainty.

Turning analysis to actionable intelligence is about building fast, trusted, and repeatable connections between insight and execution. It involves embedding intelligence into decision cycles, so choices are informed before they are made, sustaining the tempo needed to stay ahead of evolving threats, and applying decision-making models that fit the environment. Clear crisis roles, disciplined feedback loops, and a culture that treats intelligence as an operational asset all contribute to an organizational reflex that allows protection leaders to move seamlessly from analysis to action, enabling the enterprise to act with confidence, speed, and precision in any environment.

EMBEDDING INTELLIGENCE INTO DECISION CYCLES

For intelligence to truly shape outcomes, it must inform decision-making at every level from strategic priorities to the operational teams executing day-to-day activities. Embedding intelligence in this way ensures that protective insight isn't confined to specialist reports, but actively influences the choices, trade-offs, and priorities that define the organization's success. This integration not only supports the protection leader's objectives but also strengthens enterprise-wide agility, making intelligence a shared resource rather than a siloed function.

David Omand's SEES framework provides a useful lens for ensuring intelligence is not a one-off product but part of a continuing decision-support cycle.[15] Leaders must first understand where decisions are made and how they flow through the organization. This means mapping touchpoints from strategic planning sessions and operational reviews to daily stand-ups and incident response huddles and deliberately inserting intelligence into those processes. When analysis is integrated at these decision nodes, it stops being a static report and becomes a critical input to decisions. The goal is to position intelligence as the first consideration in planning and crisis management, not an afterthought once actions are already underway.

Embedding intelligence into decision cycles creates a strong foundation, but the value of that foundation is only realized if leaders can act on it quickly. In dynamic or high-pressure situations, the ability to translate insight into timely decisions becomes the defining advantage, requiring decision-making models that preserve clarity while matching the speed of events.

MAINTAINING TEMPO IN HIGH-PRESSURE ENVIRONMENTS

Intelligence loses value if it cannot match the pace of operations, especially in high-pressure environments where leaders may have minutes, not hours, to decide. Maintaining tempo at this stage is about ensuring that the decision-making process itself can keep pace with events, moving from observation to action without unnecessary delay while preserving clarity and accuracy.

The OODA Loop (Observe, Orient, Decide, Act) remains a proven approach for compressing decision time without sacrificing clarity. Adopting a consistent decision-making model ensures that teams act with both speed and precision. The model itself matters less than disciplined application; when everyone understands the process, coordination becomes smoother, trust in the system grows, and decision-making accelerates without eroding quality.

Maintaining tempo in decision-making starts well before a crisis. Leaders must ensure their teams are familiar with the chosen decision-making framework and have rehearsed applying it under realistic time constraints. This includes structuring intelligence delivery so essential facts and implications are presented in a format decision-makers can absorb quickly. During operations, it means resisting the urge to overload leaders with every detail and instead delivering the clearest possible picture of the situation, options, and likely outcomes. Teams that practice these habits are ready to apply them instinctively, enabling timely, well-informed decisions when conditions are at their most dynamic.

ALTERNATIVES TO OODA

While OODA is widely known, other frameworks can be equally effective depending on context:

- **Detect, Estimate, Choose, Identify, Do, Evaluate Model** is widely used in aviation and ideal for structured risk estimation in high-profile travel planning or event security.[16]
- **Military Decision-Making Process** suited for complex, multi-phase operations requiring deliberate planning, extensive analysis, and cross-functional synchronization.[17]
- **Plan, Do, Check, Act Cycle** is a well-established model in operations and quality management, emphasizing deliberate planning, rapid execution, and structured post-action review to drive continuous improvement.[18]

Regardless of the model, the key is consistency: pick one your teams understand, train to it, and apply it across all operations so decision-making remains predictable under pressure.

DEFINING ROLES IN CRISIS RESPONSE

In a crisis, speed is essential, but without structure speed quickly turns into chaos. While decision-making models help leaders determine the right course of action under pressure, those models only work if every team member knows their role and can execute it instantly. In high-pressure moments, decisions must be supported by clear, pre-defined roles and workflows so that the intelligence function can move quickly and effectively.

Pre-defining responsibilities (such as who validates incoming data, who liaises with external partners, and how decision briefs are prepared) ensures that the right information moves to the right decision-maker without delay. This approach mirrors the best practices found in military and emergency management doctrine, where clarity of roles and communication pathways is critical to success under pressure.

Establishing these responsibilities before an incident not only reduces confusion but also accelerates execution, as every team member knows their lane and their purpose. This is tempo in practice: not just deciding quickly but acting in sync. That clarity lays the groundwork for the next challenge; ensuring those roles function at the speed of the situation, moving intelligence through the system quickly enough to shape outcomes before conditions change.

BUILDING A CONTINUOUS FEEDBACK LOOP

AARs are essential for continuous improvement. Originating in the U.S. Army and echoed in Peter Senge's concept of the learning organization,[19] AARs create the space to ask not only what happened operationally, but also how effectively intelligence informed decision-making at every stage. This means evaluating the clarity of the intelligence provided, the timeliness of its delivery, and its impact on the quality of decisions.

The findings from these reviews should feed directly back into the intelligence cycle, influencing future collection priorities, refining analysis methodologies, and closing the gaps revealed during operations. Leaders can strengthen this loop by ensuring that reviews are conducted promptly after events, involve all relevant stakeholders, and result in clear, assigned actions for improvement. Over time, this continuous feedback process creates a dynamic, evolving intelligence function, one that adapts as quickly as the threats and environments it is designed to address.

A robust feedback loop doesn't just improve processes; it accelerates decision-making confidence. When lessons are captured and applied consistently, they begin to form patterns of action that feel instinctive, setting the stage for an organizational reflex that links intelligence and execution without hesitation.

DEVELOPING A REFLEX BETWEEN INSIGHT AND ACTION

Operationalizing intelligence at its highest level is about more than delivering accurate information; it is about building a reflex: a learned, repeatable connection between insight and action. This reflex allows the organization to move decisively, without re-debating fundamentals, because the processes, trust, and expectations are already in place. Leaders who have built this reflex can shift from analysis to execution with minimal friction, enabling the enterprise to adapt more quickly, act with greater confidence, and seize opportunities before they pass.

One example of this reflex in action occurred when protective intelligence flagged a coordinated cyber and physical protest campaign targeting a company's regional headquarters. Digital chatter signaled online threats while local monitoring detected unusual crowd movements nearby. Within minutes, the combined team activated a low-visibility security posture, adjusted access control, and coordinated messaging with corporate communications. The incident passed without disruption, not because risk disappeared, but because intelligence had been operationalized as a reflex, allowing leaders to act with clarity before pressure became crisis.

REFLECTIVE CASE STUDY: STORM OVER SINGAPORE

This reflexive discipline becomes tangible in the following case, a moment where preparation, clarity, and trust converged into decisive action.

It was two days before a scheduled executive visit to Singapore; a high-profile event tied to a major regional partnership announcement. The advance work was complete—routes confirmed, venues secured, liaison meetings with local law enforcement finalized. The itinerary had been approved by the executive team and locked into the organization's public relations schedule. Singapore, known for its political stability and strong public order, was considered a low-risk environment, *precisely the kind of location where overconfidence can creep in and subtle risks can be overlooked.*

Late that evening, the protective intelligence team's monitoring platforms flagged a surge of online chatter tied to a political demonstration planned near one of the event venues. At first glance, it appeared to be a standard, low-risk protest. But a deeper scan (cross-referencing open-source data, regional news, and social media patterns) revealed an unusual uptick in participation from groups with a history of targeting corporate leaders for disruption. Compounding the concern, weather alerts indicated severe thunderstorms likely to force the demonstration indoors, potentially into areas closer to the event site.

Because intelligence was embedded into the operational cycle from the start, the information moved instantly through pre-defined channels. Within minutes, the intel cell validated the findings, assessed possible second- and third-order impacts, and briefed the on-the-ground security lead. The briefing format was one the executive team knew and trusted: a concise risk summary, the most probable scenarios, and clearly framed options.

The decision to adjust the itinerary, moving the executive's arrival by several hours and shifting the announcement venue, was made in less than 15 minutes. The changes were quietly coordinated with corporate communications to avoid drawing attention, and the protective advance team re-routed without disrupting the executive's schedule or media commitments.

On paper, it looked seamless. In reality, it was the product of months of preparation: decision-making models trained into the team, roles clearly defined for crisis scenarios, intelligence collection aligned with operational touchpoints, and AARs that had refined the briefing process until it was second nature. This was the reflex at work; insight transformed into action without hesitation, enabling the leader and the organization to move forward without missing a step.

This was a reminder that intelligence-fed leadership is as much about readiness in familiar environments as it is about navigating recognized hot spots. In an age where a disruption in one domain can quickly trigger consequences in others, the ability to act with speed and precision is only part of the challenge; understanding how those domains intersect is what comes next.

Operationalizing intelligence is where the leader's influence becomes visible in outcomes. By embedding intelligence into decision cycles, maintaining tempo under pressure, defining clear roles in crisis, and building continuous feedback loops, protection leaders create an environment where insight moves effortlessly into action. Over time, this disciplined approach builds the reflex that enables leaders and their teams to adapt quickly, act decisively, and safeguard both people and the mission, no matter how fluid the environment. The value of intelligence is not in its collection but in its use, and when used well, it becomes the connective tissue between protective strategy and organizational success, a capability that will only grow more critical as the boundaries between threat domains continue to dissolve. The next frontier for protection leaders is convergence, the blending of physical, digital, and reputational risks into single, fast-moving events.

In the following chapter, we will explore how hybrid threats emerge, the motivations and methods of modern threat actors, and why collaboration with cyber, communications, and legal teams is no longer optional, using a real-world case study of a corporate stalking and doxxing incident to illustrate how integrated leadership can anticipate, contain, and manage these complex, blended threats.

KEY TAKEAWAYS

- Embed intelligence into decision cycles at all levels to ensure it shapes choices before they are made, not after.
- Maintain tempo under pressure by training teams in decision-making models and rehearsing time-compressed scenarios.
- Define clear intelligence roles and workflows in advance to eliminate confusion and accelerate response during crises.

- Use continuous feedback loops, such as AARs, to refine collection priorities, analysis methods, and operational integration.
- Build an organizational reflex that moves intelligence seamlessly from insight to action, enabling confident, decisive leadership in fluid environments.

NOTES

1 Michael Warner, "Wanted: A Definition of 'Intelligence'," *Studies in Intelligence, 2002,* 46, no. 3, pp. 15–22, https://www.cia.gov/resources/csi/studies-in-intelligence/volume-46-no-3/wanted-a-definition-of-intelligence.
2 Global Intelligence and Executive Protection at McDonald's, *Employee Safety Podcast*, accessed September 2025, https://www.alertmedia.com/podcast/global-intelligence-executive-protection-mcdonalds.
3 Carl von Clausewitz, *On War.* Edited and translated by Michael Howard and Peter Paret. (Princeton, NJ: Princeton University Press, 1976).
4 Sherman Kent, *Strategic Intelligence for American World Policy* (Princeton, NJ: Princeton University Press, 1949), chap. 1.
5 Sherman Kent, *Strategic Intelligence for American World Policy* (Princeton, NJ: Princeton University Press, 1949), esp. chap. 1 and appendix ("Kinds of Intelligence").
6 Michael V. Hayden, *Playing to the Edge: American Intelligence in the Age of Terror* (New York: Penguin Press, 2016).
7 Tom Kopecky, *The Complete Collection on Protective Intelligence* (Austin, TX: Center for Connected Intelligence), accessed September 2025, https://ontic.co/wp-content/uploads/2023/11/The-Complete-Collection-on-Protective-Intelligence.pdf.
8 Richards J. Heuer, Jr., *The Psychology of Intelligence Analysis* (Washington, DC: Center for the Study of Intelligence, 1999).
9 David Omand, *How Spies Think: Ten Lessons in Intelligence* (New York: Penguin Press, 2020).
10 Michael Morell and Bill Harlow, *The Great War of Our Time: The CIA's Fight Against Terrorism–From al Qa'ida to ISIS* (New York: Twelve, 2015).
11 Jonathan Wackrow, "From Memes to Murder: The Evolution of Executive Protection," *Security Journal Americas*, New York, Security Journal Americas, June 2025, accessed September 2025, https://securityjournalamericas.com/memes-murder-executive-protection/.
12 Daniel Kahneman, *Thinking, Fast and Slow* (New York: Farrar, Straus and Giroux, 2011).

13 Global Intelligence and Executive Protection at McDonald's, *Employee Safety Podcast*, https://www.alertmedia.com/podcast/global-intelligence-executive-protection-mcdonalds/
14 "Episode 25 – Ryan Long Presents to Executives," *The Business of Intelligence [Podcast]*, accessed September 2025, https://podcasts.apple.com/gb/podcast/the-business-of-intelligence-episode-25/id1572882372?i=1000705536640.
15 David Omand, *How Spies Think*.
16 Federal Aviation Administration, *Risk Management Handbook* (Washington, DC: FAA), accessed September 2025, https://www.faa.gov/sites/faa.gov/files/2022-06/risk_management_handbook_2A.pdf.
17 U.S. Department of the Army, *Commander and Staff Organization and Operations: Field Manual 6-0* (Washington, DC: Headquarters, Department of the Army, 2014, accessed September 2025), https://armypubs.army.mil/epubs/DR_pubs/DR_a/ARN35404-FM_6-0-000-WEB-1.pdf.
18 William Edwards Deming, *Out of the Crisis* (Cambridge: Massachusetts Institute of Technology, Center for Advanced Engineering Study, 1982).
19 Peter M. Senge, *The Fifth Discipline: The Art and Practice of the Learning Organization* (New York: Doubleday, 1990).

CORE INSIGHTS

Sustaining and Scaling Leadership

Leadership that endures is leadership that learns. Across this section, a clear truth emerges; *sustainability is not born of stamina alone but of systems that convert feedback into foresight.* The protector who builds space for rest and reflection sustains readiness longer than the one who endures through willpower alone. The same is true for organizations. They thrive when intelligence and self-awareness operate in rhythm, when data and human insight move together to maintain clarity amid chaos.

The evolution from protecting people to protecting decisions marks a turning point for the modern protection leader. Resilience and intelligence are not separate disciplines; they are complementary feedback systems (one human, one informational) that keep leadership adaptive under pressure. To lead in this era of convergence, protectors must build teams and cultures that think as they act, anticipate as they adapt, and recover as they perform. Sustaining leadership, then, is not simply surviving the tempo but mastering the rhythm, designing systems that make clarity, trust, and composure repeatable.

As the boundaries between threat domains dissolve, the next challenge for protective leadership is not sustaining the system but expanding it, applying the same principles of rhythm, feedback, and foresight to a world where risks converge faster than they can be categorized.

DOI: 10.4324/9781003670704-15

CORE INSIGHTS

- **Resilience is Systemic**
  Endurance is not an individual act but an organizational design. Feedback, recovery, and recalibration must be built into operations, not improvised under stress.
- **Culture Determines Readiness**
  Teams that value vulnerability and psychological safety outperform those that reward silent suffering. Trust and openness are the foundation of sustainable performance.
- **Intelligence is Resilience at Scale**
  The same principles that sustain people, awareness, rhythm, feedback, also sustain decision systems. Intelligence transforms resilience from recovery into anticipation.
- **Alignment Creates Advantage**
  Decision advantage arises when intelligence aligns with leadership priorities, turning information into influence and transforming security from a cost center into a strategic asset.
- **Feedback is the Lifeblood of Adaptation**
  Whether in wellness or intelligence programs, continuous feedback converts lessons into reflexes. Learning must be institutionalized, not episodic.
- **Clarity is the True Measure of Leadership**
  The modern protection leader's role is to convert complexity into coherence, ensuring that both people and decisions move in rhythm, even when the environment does not.

SECTION 4

Introduction: Leading in the Converged Threat Environment

Every protector remembers the first moment they realized the work was bigger than a job. It might have been a late-night call, a principal's quiet look of trust, or the weight of a decision no one else even knew was being made. In this profession, that realization lives at the edge—the place where responsibility and resolve meet. As the world grows more volatile, that edge is where our profession must now lead.

Today's threats blur the boundaries between digital and physical, between rumor and reality, between sentiment and violence. An online narrative can evolve into a real-world threat in hours. A piece of exposed personal data can become a vector for targeting. A single moment of complacency can ripple into tragedy. And yet, the fundamentals of protection remain our anchor. What changes is the courage and clarity with which we apply them.

The leaders who will shape what comes next understand that preparedness is not built in isolation. It is forged through relationships—security with legal, HR with communications, facilities with technology, people with purpose. Foresight becomes possible when leaders cultivate trust across the enterprise long before the moment that tests it. The hybrid attack cycle may begin with a click, but it is disrupted by a culture.

Technology now gives us new vantage points: AI identifying patterns, intelligence platforms mapping sentiment, tools reducing digital exposure and revealing unseen risks. But no algorithm carries accountability the way a protector does. No machine feels the responsibility of keeping another human being safe. That burden—and privilege—belongs to us.

DOI: 10.4324/9781003670704-16

Legacy is not the crises we prevent; it is the people we prepare. It is the young practitioner who finds their voice because someone believed in them. It is the team that knows how to think when the plan falls apart. It is the culture that endures after we step away from the table. In the end, the future of this profession will be shaped not just by threats, but by the character and conviction of those who choose to stand on the edge.

CHAPTER 10

Leading in the Age of Hybrid Threats

The first alert comes from the cyber team: an executive's email account has been breached. Minutes later, protestors gather outside headquarters holding signs with information that could only have come from internal files. Before the security lead can regroup, the communications director bursts in with breaking news—sensitive company documents have been posted online alongside a demand for immediate policy changes. These are not isolated incidents; they are hybrid threats, adversarial actions that merge physical, cyber, and reputational vectors into a coordinated assault. Engineered for convergence, they are designed to overwhelm by forcing leaders to fight on multiple fronts at once. Layered into this is *asymmetry*, the advantage smaller, less-resourced adversaries gain through speed, surprise, and creativity. A lone actor with a laptop, a social media account, and a grievance can compel a multinational to alter operations, reallocate resources, and defend its reputation under intense public scrutiny. Entire governments have used these same tactics against corporations, as in the now-infamous attack on a global entertainment company, where a dispute over a single film spiraled into a cyber breach, reputational sabotage, and threats of physical violence.

This is the crucible of modern protection leadership: seeing across domains, controlling the narrative as surely as the perimeter, and leading convergence before the adversary forces it.

For the protection leader, this combination of convergence and imbalance is a proving ground for decision-making. Leadership is no longer about managing a single lane of risk; it is about seeing the entire operational picture, drawing connections between faint signals and uniting disparate teams such as cybersecurity, communications, legal, and physical security into a coherent response. The measure of success lies in the ability to synthesize fragmented intelligence into decisive action, to control the narrative as effectively as the perimeter, and to safeguard not just people and assets, but the trust and continuity that keep an enterprise resilient in the face of modern threats.

DOI: 10.4324/9781003670704-17

THE CONVERGENCE IMPERATIVE

Hybrid threats are not an evolution of old problems; they are a transformation of the operating environment itself.[1] For most of the modern era, organizations managed physical, cyber, and reputational risks as separate disciplines—Physical security watched the gates and guarded the people, Cybersecurity defended networks and data, Corporate communications shaped and managed the narrative, Legal kept the company in compliance and out of court, *and so forth.* Each operated in its own lane, often with minimal overlap beyond an occasional crisis drill.

That separation no longer holds. Today's adversaries are not constrained by organizational charts or departmental boundaries. A hostile actor might begin in the digital realm, scraping social media for personal data, compromising a corporate email account, or planting disinformation online. Hours later, the same campaign may spill into the physical world—a protest at the headquarters, a suspicious package sent to an executive's home, or a coordinated disruption at a shareholder meeting. Alongside these, a reputational offensive unfolds with strategically timed leaks to media outlets, viral amplification of damaging narratives, or legal harassment designed to slow the organization's response. The attack is not a sequence of unrelated events; it is a single operational plan executed across multiple domains.[2]

This shift from multi-domain to blended-domain threats is more than a matter of scale; it is about simultaneity and deliberate orchestration. In the past, incidents in different risk areas often occurred in isolation or in sequence, giving leaders time to pivot between them. Hybrid threats compress that timeline. The speed at which physical, digital, and narrative elements now reinforce each other means that the first 24 hours can determine not only the immediate damage but also the long-term recovery trajectory.[3] In the 2014 Sony Pictures attack, for example, the cyber breach, reputational fallout, and physical threats were not separate fronts; they were deliberately woven together, each amplifying the impact of the others.

For the protection leader, this reality creates a new imperative; *risk leadership must be united before the threat is.* That means building the trust, language, and operational rhythm with cyber, communications, legal, and other strategic teams before the first indicator appears. It means developing the ability to read weak signals from multiple domains and recognize when they are part of the same campaign. And it requires a shift in mindset, from defending a set of assets to defending the organization's integrity across every environment in which it operates. In the age of convergence, the speed of alignment becomes as critical as the strength of any single defensive measure.

But, as with any protective operation, uniting stakeholders first requires an understanding of the threat.

MODERN ADVERSARIES, MODERN TACTICS

Behind every hybrid threat is a human or organizational adversary making deliberate choices about how, when, and where to strike. Understanding those adversaries, their motivations, resources, and methods is essential for any protection leader tasked with anticipating the unexpected. While the profiles differ, what unites them is the way they exploit convergence: layering multiple tactics to create outsized impact.

State-Sponsored Adversaries

In 2014, a relatively small state leveraged destructive malware, reputational sabotage, and physical threats to cripple Sony Pictures, all in retaliation for a single satirical film.[4] This episode illustrates the hallmark of state-sponsored adversaries: the patience and resources of governments and the ability to weave cyber intrusion with disinformation and intimidation at a geopolitical scale. For them, corporations are often proxies in disputes between nations, and hybrid campaigns ripple far beyond their immediate targets into markets and societies.

Transnational Criminal Organizations

Ransomware crews no longer stop at encrypting files. They steal data, leak it at sensitive moments, and even threaten executives or their families to accelerate payouts.[5] This entrepreneurial precision is characteristic of transnational criminal organizations. Their goal is financial, but their playbook is converged. By combining phishing campaigns with open-source intelligence (OSINT)-driven reconnaissance and even physical intimidation, they collapse the boundary between digital crime and human fear, treating hybrid attacks as a global business model.

Ideologically Motivated Extremists

A lone extremist live-streams an attempted intrusion, turning a physical incident into propaganda for online followers.[6] This is how ideologically motivated extremists weaponize both stage and screen, acting not for profit, but for visibility and cause. Whether political, religious, or social, their campaigns seek disruption amplified through spectacle. Social media becomes both recruiting ground and stage, and organizations targeted risk being cast as symbols, where reputational fallout can equal or exceed physical damage.

Lone Actors

Among the most unpredictable adversaries, lone actors, obsessive stalkers, disgruntled employees, or individuals with personal grievances, often blend digital harassment with in-person approaches. A doxxing post might lead to swatting, which in turn escalates into direct confrontation.[7] They rely heavily on accessible tactics such as public data scraping, social engineering, or fabricated narratives that look like background noise until escalation makes them unavoidable.

Proxy Adversaries

Finally, proxy adversaries blur the line between activism, hacktivism, and organized disruption. They may not be formally state-controlled, but they often align with larger geopolitical or ideological agendas. Proxies blend physical protest with phishing kits, denial-of-service attacks, or targeted leaks. Their tactical flexibility creates ambiguity: are they activists, criminals, or covert extensions of a state sponsor? That ambiguity itself becomes a weapon, complicating attribution and delaying response.[8]

Across all these categories, motivations vary—political objectives, financial gain, ideology, personal grievance, or the pursuit of notoriety. But the defining feature of modern adversaries is **capability stacking:** the deliberate combination of tactics across domains. OSINT reconnaissance enables spear-phishing. Social engineering primes a physical approach. Cyber intrusion fuels reputational sabotage. Each layer reinforces the others, creating campaigns where the whole is more dangerous than the sum of its parts.

For the protection leader, the lesson is stark. These adversaries are not limited by organizational charts, corporate silos, or traditional definitions of risk. They adapt faster, move across domains without hesitation, and exploit seams between disciplines. Recognizing both who they are and how they operate is the first step in anticipating their moves and preparing teams to respond with the same level of integration and speed.

But understanding who these adversaries are is only half the battle. The real test for protection leaders is recognizing how their tactics escalate, often quietly at first, then rapidly across domains. This progression is captured in the **Hybrid Threat Targeting Cycle.**

MAPPING HYBRID THREATS

Rarely straightforward hybrid issues are complex, fast-moving campaigns that unfold across multiple domains, creating confusion not only in the heat of response but also in the way they are described. Cyber teams see malware. Communications teams see a reputational crisis. Physical security sees protestors at the gate. Legal teams see exposure to litigation. While each view is accurate, none captures the full picture on its own. The result is fragmentation at the very moment when clarity is most needed to enable decision-making.

To lead effectively, protection leaders need a way to visualize the threat environment in a unified fashion, a model that helps connect scattered incidents into a coherent whole and translates converged risk into a language that resonates with all stakeholders. The **Hybrid Threat Targeting Cycle** serves this purpose. It illustrates how attacks escalate from digital reconnaissance to reputational sabotage to physical disruption, giving leaders and their partners a common frame of reference for decision-making. More than a diagram, it becomes a leadership tool: a way to see patterns, anticipate escalation, and align teams across silos before the threat peaks.

THE HYBRID THREAT TARGETING CYCLE

Hybrid threats are not random collisions of events. They are the result of adversaries following deliberate steps to identify, pressure, and exploit their targets. This cycle of activity is designed to move quickly across domains (digital, reputational, and physical) until the defender is forced into a reactive posture.

For protection leaders, recognizing the cycle is essential: it transforms what may look like isolated incidents into an operational pattern that can be disrupted before it matures into a full-spectrum crisis (Figure 10.1).

1. **Reconnaissance**

   Every campaign begins with information gathering. Adversaries leverage OSINT, scraping social media for personal data, mining corporate disclosures, and probing for technical vulnerabilities. This stage is low visibility but sets the foundation for the entire campaign. Effective reconnaissance gives attackers targeting precision and reduces the cost of later actions.
2. **Initial Access or Exposure**

   With reconnaissance complete, the adversary moves to establish an entry point. For cybercriminals and state actors, this may mean phishing emails, credential theft, or network exploitation. For lone actors, it may involve doxxing or releasing private information online. The goal is to create leverage (either technical access, reputational exposure, or psychological pressure) that allows them to advance the campaign.

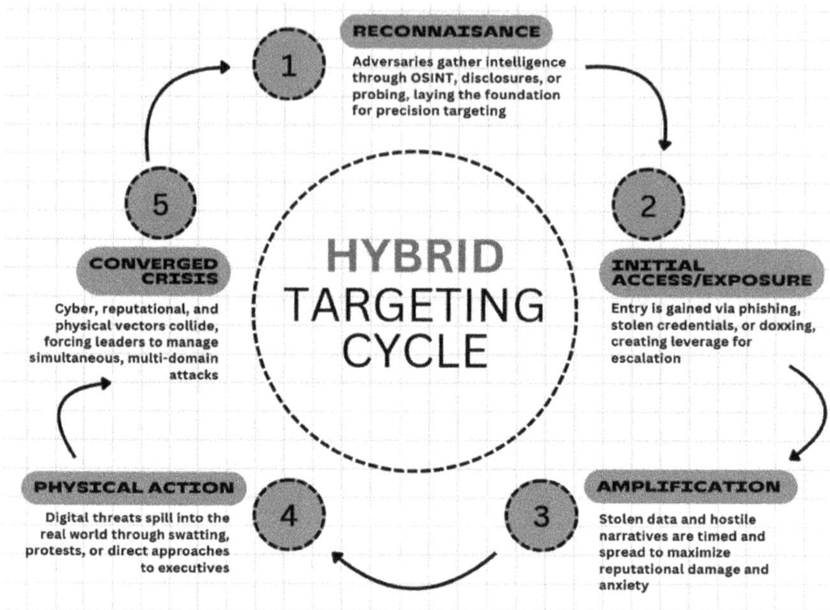

FIGURE 10.1 The Hybrid Targeting Cycle.

Source: Randolph, Wackrow and Burton.

3. **Amplification**

   Once they have access or data, adversaries turn to amplification. Stolen information is leaked strategically, often timed to coincide with critical corporate events such as annual meetings, earnings announcements, or product launches. Social media and sympathetic networks are used to spread narratives that damage credibility and increase stakeholder anxiety. In some cases, amplification involves threats to release additional damaging material unless demands are met.
4. **Physical Action**

   Digital and reputational activity often spills into the physical world. This can take the form of swatting calls, mailed threats, orchestrated protests, or direct approaches to executives. The physical component increases perceived urgency and creates a visible demonstration of risk. It also forces security leaders to divert resources, opening additional vulnerabilities elsewhere.
5. **Converged Crisis**

   The cycle culminates in full-spectrum convergence. Cyber disruption, reputational damage, and physical intimidation overlap, compounding the crisis and overwhelming siloed responses. At this point, the organization must fight on multiple fronts simultaneously: safeguarding systems, protecting people, managing public messaging, and containing legal exposure. For adversaries, the convergence stage is victory, forcing the target to respond under maximum pressure.

LEADERSHIP APPLICATION

Viewing hybrid incidents through the lens of a targeting cycle has two critical benefits. First, it clarifies that these are intentional campaigns, not organic escalations. That perspective sharpens the leader's sense of urgency and underscores the need for proactive intelligence. Second, it provides a common language for cross-functional teams. Cyber, comms, legal, and physical security may see different pieces of the cycle, but a unified model helps align their understanding and response.

The earlier leaders identify where they are in the cycle, the more options they have to disrupt it. Spotting reconnaissance signals or initial exposure allows for containment before reputational or physical impacts occur. Waiting until the convergence stage leaves little room for maneuver. Protection leaders who adopt the targeting-cycle perspective move from reacting in silos to leading a converged defense, turning fragmented signals into opportunities for disruption.

CASE STUDY: THE DAY SONY WENT DARK

On the morning of November 24, 2014, Sony Pictures employees logged in to their computers expecting another ordinary workday. Instead, they were met with black screens flashing a red skull and a chilling message: "Hacked by #GOP." Within hours, it was clear this was no ordinary cyber incident. The company's systems had been crippled, its data exfiltrated, and its workforce paralyzed. What began as a digital disruption quickly cascaded into reputational damage and physical threats, pulling Sony into the middle of a geopolitical conflict.[9]

At the center of this storm stood Stevan Bernard, *Executive Vice President of Global Protection Services.* His remit had always been broad, responsible for global physical security, crisis management, and investigative oversight, but now it expanded to include uniting cyber experts, communications teams, and legal advisors in a single coordinated response. For Bernard, the red skull was more than a technical warning. It was the opening shot in a hybrid campaign designed to converge multiple forms of pressure against his company.

THE ADVERSARY AND THE MOTIVE

The Democratic People's Republic of Korea (DPRK) was behind the campaign, using the breach to retaliate against Sony's satirical film *The Interview*, which portrayed the fictional assassination of Kim Jong-un. For North Korea, the movie was an affront to the regime's legitimacy. By striking Sony, a private company, Pyongyang demonstrated how a small, isolated state could use hybrid tactics to impose costs on a global enterprise.[10]

AN UNFOLDING DPRK CAMPAIGN

Cyber Disruption

The attack began with wiper malware that destroyed thousands of computers and servers. Sony's digital infrastructure collapsed overnight. Alongside this destruction came the exfiltration of more than 100 terabytes of data, including unreleased films, financials, contracts, and private employee information.[11] The attackers, calling themselves the "Guardians of Peace," signaled this was not a covert espionage effort, but an open act of sabotage.

Reputational Sabotage

In the days that followed, carefully timed leaks of stolen emails and documents dominated global headlines. Media outlets published unfiltered executive conversations, sensitive negotiations, and personal employee data. The drip-drip release strategy kept Sony perpetually on the defensive, straining relationships with talent and damaging trust.

Physical Threats

The campaign escalated further with anonymous threats of violence against theaters scheduled to show *The Interview*. Several major chains canceled screenings, and Sony initially pulled the film from release altogether.[12] Even as federal authorities downplayed the credibility of the threats, the psychological and operational impact was undeniable.

LEADERSHIP AT THE CENTER OF THE STORM

Coordinating the response fell in large part to Stevan Bernard. His role was to create order from chaos, to integrate multiple streams of fragmented intelligence into a unified crisis strategy. Bernard convened daily cross-functional crisis calls, pulling together leaders from cybersecurity, legal, communications, HR, and physical security. He later reflected: "When your first reaction is to contain a cyber breach, ask first: what is 'it' you're trying to fix? And who did it—and why?"[13]

CROSS-FUNCTIONAL RESPONSE IN ACTION

- **Cybersecurity** teams worked to contain malware, rebuild infrastructure, and assist federal investigators.
- **Communications** teams fought a rolling reputational battle as leaks fueled media cycles.
- **Physical Security** heightened protective measures around studios, theaters, and executives amid threats.
- **Legal** teams evaluated liability for employee data exposures and contractual breaches.
- **External Stakeholders** included the FBI, DHS, and ultimately the White House.[14]

LESSONS FOR PROTECTION LEADERS

- **Hybrid Threats Are Converged by Design**

  Sony's crisis was not three separate incidents; it was one campaign. Cyber sabotage, reputational harm, and physical threats were deliberately interwoven.
- **Pre-Crisis Relationships Matter**

  Sony's engagement with the FBI and DHS was vital. Those partnerships cannot be built mid-crisis; they must exist in advance.
- **Leadership Requires Orchestration, Not Silo Management**

  Bernard's role illustrated that modern CSOs must act as conductors, aligning teams across domains.
- **Narrative is a Battlespace**

  Much of the damage came not from servers destroyed but from reputations undermined. Narrative management is not just a communications issue; it is a core protective function in hybrid crises.

THE TARGETING CYCLE IN ACTION

The Sony breach followed the full arc of the **Hybrid Threat Targeting Cycle**. Reconnaissance led to intrusion. Initial access became a platform for leaks. Amplification unfolded through media coverage. Physical threats heightened fear and disrupted distribution. The crisis culminated in convergence, with Sony fighting across cyber, reputational, and physical fronts simultaneously.[15]

The incident underscored a truth every protection leader must internalize; *hybrid threats are deliberate campaigns*. They are designed to escalate across domains, forcing organizations into reactive posture. The earlier leaders can recognize and disrupt the cycle, the more control they retain.[16]

For the protection leader, the lesson is sobering; *what played out on Sony's global stage now repeats itself at the personal level, where executives, judges, and politicians are increasingly in the crosshairs of hybrid campaigns.*

NARRATIVE AS BATTLESPACE

Hybrid campaigns are fought not only in networks or on the street but also in the minds of stakeholders, employees, and the public. As RAND has noted, *the cognitive domain is where perceptions are shaped, legitimacy is contested, and decisions are influenced*.[17] NATO's StratCom Centre has gone further, framing information as a "decisive line of operation" in hybrid warfare.[18] The Sony incident underscored this reality: the reputational damage from leaked emails and manipulated narratives inflicted deeper wounds than the malware itself. For protection leaders, this is a crucial lesson. Narrative control is not the sole responsibility of communications teams; it is a protective function. Doxxing, smear campaigns, and disinformation all weaponize perception, and they demand the same converged, intelligence-led leadership as cyber or physical threats. The protector who ignores the narrative fight cedes a decisive battlespace to the adversary.[19]

FROM GLOBAL TO PERSONAL

The Sony Pictures breach (2014) revealed how a hostile state could braid cyber sabotage, reputational warfare, and physical intimidation into a single hybrid campaign. That incident was geopolitical in scale, cinematic in its visibility, and impossible to ignore. Yet most protection leaders will not face nation-state adversaries. Their reality is often closer to home, and far more personal.

The December 2024 murder of UnitedHealthcare CEO Brian Thompson demonstrated this shift with tragic clarity. Outside a Midtown Manhattan hotel, Thompson was ambushed and shot by Luigi Mangione, whose movements in the days before and after the attack suggest careful planning.[20] In the aftermath, Thompson's spouse received harassing messages, a stark reminder that hybrid pressure often expands beyond the principal to family members. The violence also triggered broader ripples, graffiti in other cities and hostile messaging amongst online communities amplified the sense of threat. What unfolded was not a single act of violence, but a cascading campaign in which grievance, narrative, digital harassment, and physical attack reinforced one another.

A similar pattern emerged in June 2025, when Vance Boelter murdered a former Minnesota House speaker and her husband and wounded a state senator and his wife. Court filings revealed Boelter had used publicly available online data to locate his targets.[21] This was classic OSINT reconnaissance, turning digital information into physical opportunity. As with Sony, digital reconnaissance and reputational pressure quickly spilled into physical space, showing that the same cycle operates at every scale.

Judges, too, are facing mounting hybrid pressure. Reports show **doxxing, online threats, and harassment campaigns** against judicial officials at record levels, prompting new security protocols, privacy suppression programs, and increased coordination with law enforcement.[22] In these cases, reputational intimidation and digital targeting are designed to shape judicial outcomes by creating a climate of fear.

Even in incidents that do not culminate in physical violence, hybrid tactics are clear. The **2020 Twitter breach**, carried out by young hackers, hijacked accounts belonging to figures like Bill Gates and Barack Obama.[23] Though the immediate goal was financial fraud, the episode illustrated how digital intrusion can instantly become reputational sabotage at a global scale, a vivid reminder that narrative control is itself a security vector.

These incidents do not occur in a vacuum. Surveys in recent years indicate a troubling trend: *a measurable percentage of Americans believe violence is a justified means of pursuing political or social goals.*[24] This widening acceptance of violence as activism lowers the barrier for lone actors, extremists, or disaffected individuals to escalate from grievance to attack. For the protection leader, that means hybrid threats must be understood not only as technical or operational problems, but also as phenomena fueled by cultural and political currents.

The leadership imperative is convergence. Digital monitoring, communications planning, privacy protection, and physical security cannot operate as separate silos. They must be fused into a **unified protective fabric**, one capable of identifying the targeting cycle early, aligning stakeholders, and intervening before digital reconnaissance or reputational pressure becomes physical tragedy.

The stalking and doxxing of an executive underscores how protection leaders must apply the same converged principles when the hybrid threat cycle closes in on an individual, not just an organization.

THE PRINCIPAL IN THE CROSSHAIRS

Hybrid threats are no longer confined to organizations or governments; increasingly, they are directed at individuals, the principals protection leaders are entrusted to safeguard. When the target is a person rather than a company, the scale may be smaller, but the consequences are immediate and personal. The executive's home, family, and reputation become the terrain of conflict.

One instance involved a senior executive who became the focus of an obsessive individual determined to collapse the distance between digital harassment and physical intimidation. It began online: *anonymous posts on fringe forums, threatening messages on social platforms, and the exposure of personal details through doxxing.* Soon, those threats spilled into physical space, letters sent to her home, hostile calls to family members, and sightings of the stalker near her workplace. The harassment was not limited to a single domain. It unfolded across digital, reputational, and physical fronts, echoing the same hybrid targeting cycle that crippled Sony Pictures but concentrated now on a single life.

This convergence is not unique. The **swatting epidemic** demonstrates how online hostility can be weaponized into a physical confrontation when police respond to fabricated emergencies at a victim's home.[25] Judicial officials across the United States have been subject to doxxing and other forms of online intimidation, with private information exposed in ways that create real security concerns and have prompted new protective measures.[26] Executives have seen their personal details surface in hack-and-leak operations, sometimes tied to protests or activist campaigns. And family members, like the spouse of slain UnitedHealthcare CEO Brian Thompson, have found themselves harassed in the wake of targeted violence.[27] In each case, the digital and reputational pressure reinforced the physical risk, leaving the principal and their circle squarely in the crosshairs.

For protection leaders, these hybrid threats against principals demand the same leadership posture seen in corporate-scale crises: joint risk management. Cybersecurity, communications, legal counsel, and protective operations must function as a single organism. A phishing attempt against a principal may be the opening stage of a reputational attack. A hostile narrative online may foreshadow direct approaches at the workplace. A doxxing post is not simply an invasion of privacy, it is a targeting roadmap.

The lesson is stark; principals are not merely collateral targets in hybrid campaigns; they are often the main objective. When adversaries collapse the boundary between digital and physical harassment, the protective leader must be prepared to recognize the cycle early, align stakeholders, and disrupt the threat before it escalates. Convergence is not simply a framework; it is the defining quality of modern protection leadership.

The ability to disrupt the hybrid threat cycle depends not only on awareness but on the frameworks leaders use to align teams, brief stakeholders, and act decisively.

LEADERSHIP TOOLKIT: FRAMEWORKS AND TOOLS

Hybrid threats can feel overwhelming in their complexity, but leaders do not need to start from scratch. Several practical frameworks help impose order, reveal patterns, and guide converged decision-making under pressure. These frameworks are designed as lenses: they simplify complexity, provide a common language across functions, and allow leaders to anticipate escalation rather than simply react to it. While some are drawn from existing research and doctrine, others are adapted or developed specifically for this book to meet the realities of converged protection.

HYBRID THREAT CONVERGENCE MODEL

At its simplest, this model adapts the classic Venn diagram to highlight the overlap between cyber, reputational, and physical domains. Most incidents sit squarely in one circle: a phishing attack, a reputational crisis, or a workplace protest. Hybrid campaigns occur in the overlap, where actions in one domain amplify another, for example, a data leak fueling hostile media coverage that sparks a protest. The model makes convergence visible and tangible.[28]

So what? Use this to brief executives and boards, showing that threats are not siloed problems but converged risks requiring unified leadership.

THREE-DOMAIN RISK MATRIX

Visually, the tool resembles a traditional likelihood–impact grid, but it is expanded across three axes: cyber, reputational, and physical. This reflects modern risk principles that emphasize interaction and context, making visible how a seemingly low-impact event in one domain can escalate through another. A cyber intrusion timed with a shareholder meeting, for example, may be technically limited yet reputationally catastrophic.[29]

So what? Use this in tabletop exercises and planning sessions to prioritize resources where domain overlap is most likely.

HYBRID THREAT TARGETING CYCLE

The model resembles a chain, but its purpose is to reveal hybrid attacks as deliberate campaigns: Reconnaissance → Initial Access → Amplification → Physical Action → Convergence Crisis. Each stage builds on the previous one and offers an opportunity for detection and disruption.[30]

So what? Mapping incidents against this cycle helps leaders identify which stage they are in, and what adversaries may do next.

CROSS-FUNCTIONAL CRISIS LEADERSHIP LOOP

Resembling a continuous loop, this model illustrates how **cybersecurity, communications, legal, and protective operations** interlock during a hybrid incident. No single function can manage a converged attack; it requires constant loops of intelligence sharing, joint decision-making, and coordinated messaging. The loop emphasizes rhythm, not hierarchy; the protective leader's role is to keep the loop intact under pressure.[31]

So what? Use this to clarify roles and build trust across silos before a crisis.

INCIDENT ESCALATION LADDER

The image is a ladder, each rung representing a stage: OSINT reconnaissance → digital compromise → reputational amplification → physical intimidation → full-spectrum crisis. Each step is harder and costlier to manage if ignored early.[32]

So what? Leaders can use it to reinforce the importance of spotting weak signals early, where interventions are cheaper, cleaner, and more effective.

LEADING BEYOND CONVERGENCE

Hybrid threats are not a passing anomaly; they are the operating environment leaders must navigate for the foreseeable future. From Sony's global stage to the stalking of a single principal, these campaigns reveal a consistent truth: adversaries are converging tactics across cyber, reputational, and physical domains to create pressure that overwhelms traditional security silos. The protection leader's value lies in recognizing these connections early and orchestrating a converged response before the adversary forces it upon the organization.

Leadership in this environment is less about technical mastery than about **alignment and narrative control.** The principal, the executive team, and the broader enterprise need protection leaders who can translate fragmented intelligence into clear direction, hold stakeholders together under pressure, and disrupt the adversary's targeting cycle.

Convergence is not simply a framework; it is a mindset, a way of leading that anticipates escalation and preserves trust across people, institutions, and the public square.

KEY TAKEAWAYS

- **See campaigns, not incidents.** Treat hybrid threats as converged assaults across cyber, reputational, and physical domains.
- **Anticipate capability stacking.** Expect adversaries to blend OSINT, phishing, intimidation, and disinformation for maximum impact.
- **Map the cycle early.** Use the Hybrid Threat Targeting Cycle to identify escalation stages and disrupt before full convergence.
- **Fight for the narrative.** Recognize perception as a battlespace, aligning comms with protection to blunt reputational and cognitive attacks.
- **Lead convergence.** Orchestrate cyber, comms, legal, and physical security into one unified, intelligence-led response.

NOTES

1 NATO Strategic Communications Centre of Excellence, *Hybrid Threats: A Strategic Communications Perspective*, April 2019, https://stratcomcoe.org/publications/hybrid-threats-a-strategic-communications-perspective/79.

2 Verizon 2024 Data Breach Investigations Report (DBIR), https://www.verizon.com/business/resources/reports/2024-dbir-data-breach-investigations-report.pdf

3 IBM Security and Ponemon Institute, *Cost of a Data Breach Report 2024*. IBM, 2024, https://www.ibm.com/reports/data-breach.

4 Federal Bureau of Investigation, "Update on Sony Investigation," December 19, 2014, https://www.fbi.gov/news/press-releases/update-on-sony-investigation.

5 Europol, *Internet Organised Crime Threat Assessment (IOCTA)*, 2023, https://www.europol.europa.eu/publication-events/main-reports/internet-organised-crime-threat-assessment-iocta-2023.

6 BBC News, "Christchurch Shootings: How Gunman Livestreamed Mosque Attacks," *BBC News*, March 15, 2019, https://www.bbc.com/news/world-asia-47580698.

7 Administrative Office of the U.S. Courts, *Judicial Security and Threat Trends*, 2023; FBI, *Swatting Advisory*, 2022.
8 NATO StratCom COE, *Hybrid Threats: A Strategic Communications Perspective*, 2019; RAND Corporation, *The Firehose of Falsehood Propaganda Model*, 2016.
9 Mark Seal, "The Sony Hack," *Vanity Fair*, February 2015, https://www.vanityfair.com/hollywood/2015/02/sony-hacking-seth-rogen-evan-goldberg.
10 *See Note 4.*
11 Columbia University, School of International and Public Affairs, *Sony Pictures Entertainment Hack* (Case Study) 2020, https://www.sipa.columbia.edu/sites/default/files/2022-11/Sony%20-%20Written%20Case.pdf.
12 Charlotte Alter, "Sony Cancels *The Interview* After Major Theaters Pull Out," *TIME*, December 17, 2014, https://time.com/3638987/the-interview-cancelled-sony-hack.
13 "Former Sony Pictures Security Chief Stevan Bernard Talks Cybersecurity," *Continuity Insights*, March 2017, https://www.linkedin.com/pulse/former-sony-pictures-security-chief-talks-stevan-bernard-cfe/.
14 Johns Hopkins University Applied Physics Laboratory, Sony: A Nightmare Before Christmas — The 2014 Sony Hack (Laurel, MD: Johns Hopkins Applied Physics Laboratory, 2016), https://www.jhuapl.edu/sites/default/files/2022-12/SonyNightmareBeforeChristmas.pdf.
15 Chuck Randolph, "The Kill Chain Starts with a Click," Targeted (Part 1), Substack, June 17, 2025, https://substack.com/home/post/p-166157996.
16 *See note 1.*
17 Christopher Paul and Miriam Matthews, *The Russian "Firehose of Falsehood" Propaganda Model*, RAND Corporation, 2016, https://www.rand.org/pubs/perspectives/PE198.html.
18 *See note 1.*
19 U.S. Army, *Field Manual 3–13: Information Operations*, December 2016, https://armypubs.army.mil/epubs/DR_pubs/DR_a/pdf/web/FM%203-13%20FINAL%20WEB.pdf.
20 Chris Looft, Emily Shapiro, and Aaron Katersky, "UnitedHealthcare CEO Shooting Suspect's Timeline Before, During, and After the Brazen Murder," *ABC News*, December 18, 2024, https://abcnews.go.com/US/unitedhealthcare-ceo-shooting-suspects-movements-timeline/story?id=116504579.

21 Steve Karnowski, Alanna Durkin Richer, and John Seewer—Associated Press, "Minnesota Shooting Suspect Had Dozens of Potential Targets, Prosecutors Say," *AP News*, June 25, 2025, https://apnews.com/article/minnesota-lawmakers-shooting-dozens-targeted-d3d7866c09765fac088e6418e49ad811.

22 Avalon Zoppo, "Death Threats, Doxxing & Dark Web Searches: US Judges Share Intimidation They Faced," https://www.law.com/nationallawjournal/2025/07/31/death-threats-doxxing--dark-web-searches-us-judges-share-intimidation-they-faced-/?slreturn=20251214152754.

23 Kate Conger and Nathaniel Popper, "Hackers Tell the Story of the Twitter Attack from the Inside," *New York Times*, July 17, 2020, https://www.nytimes.com/2020/07/17/technology/twitter-hackers-interview.html.

24 Robert Pape and Kevin Ruby, "The Rising Normalization of Political Violence in the United States," *University of Chicago Project on Security and Threats*, 2022.

25 RSINC, "Cyber Harassment 2025," RSINC.com, 2025, https://www.rsinc.com/cyber-harassment.php.

26 Federal Bar Association, "Federal Judicial Security Update," *The Federal Lawyer*, October 29, 2024, https://www.fedbar.org/blog/federal-judicial-security-update.

27 Jeffrey A. Sonnenfeld and Steven Tian. "A Very Un-American Response to the Murder of Brian Thompson," *Yale Insights*, December 9, 2024, https://insights.som.yale.edu/insights/very-un-american-response-to-the-murder-of-brian-thompson.

28 *See note 1.*

29 International Organization for Standardization (ISO), *ISO 31000: 2018 — Risk Management — Guidelines* (Geneva: ISO, 2018).

30 Chuck Randolph, *Targeted: The New Kill Chain Starts with a Click* (Substack, June 27, 2025), https://substack.com/home/post/p-166157996.

31 FEMA, *National Incident Management System*, 2017; DHS, *Crisis Communications Plan Guidance,* 2020, https://www.fema.gov/sites/default/files/2020-07/fema_nims_doctrine-2017.pdf.

32 *Developed for this book, informed by hybrid threat escalation research including Johns Hopkins Applied Physics Laboratory's Sony: A Nightmare Before Christmas (2016).*

CHAPTER 11

Purpose-Driven Leadership

It's a test. In this profession, every moment is a test.

Yet the hardest test for a protector doesn't always come in the chaos of a motorcade or the noise of a crowded event. It comes in the silence of the night—when the protectee sleeps and the world feels still. Those hours tempt teams to relax, taking a softer posture, believing that calm equals safety. But vigilance is never more critical than in the quiet. When fatigue presses in and nothing seems to stir, true leadership is revealed. This self-realization comes through the stamina, judgment, and quiet resolve to carry the weight of someone else's safety. In this profession, the future never arrives graciously. It crashes in with urgency, demanding clarity, strong teams, and leaders ready to answer without hesitation.

In the history of our field, routines, old habits, and unspoken hierarchies have often governed who rises and who leads. Yet, the complexity of today's organizations and the accelerating pace of risk force us to reevaluate what it means to prepare for leadership transitions. As Harvard Business School writes, "Succession planning is not a process to be checked off and put on a shelf. It is a vital part of organizational vitality and preparedness."[1] This isn't a one-time task; it's an ongoing requirement if we expect our teams to operate with any resilience. Whether a leader steps down by choice or due to crisis, the organization must have a pool of capable, well-equipped professionals ready to move forward; a pipeline that has been developed through intentional effort rather than neglected tradition.

Often, executive protection (EP) teams mirror the familiar faces of yesterday. Predictable, homogeneous, and unfortunately, sometimes blind to broader perspectives. In this profession, sameness may have once felt secure, but those days are gone. "Diversity and excellence go hand in hand."[2] Recruiting and supporting women isn't a symbolic gesture or a check-the-box exercise. It's an operational imperative. The inclusion of women and underrepresented voices brings vital talents: communication sharpens, emotional intelligence rises, and the whole team becomes more adaptable, more aware, and better at anticipating the unexpected. It's not just that diverse teams look different. It's that they work smarter and

 DOI: 10.4324/9781003670704-18

respond faster. Inclusive leadership is a commitment to seeing past the old monoculture and realizing that true excellence means everyone is at the table, especially those whose perspectives have previously been missing.

Yet, succession and inclusion won't matter if complacency takes root. It's a quiet adversary, one that slips in when success becomes routine, and vigilance seems less necessary. As John Philpot Curran warned, "The price of success is eternal vigilance."[3] The harsh reality is that the most dangerous moments don't always arise from external threats. They may come from internal neglect, habits hardened into blind spots, and the unchecked assumption that the absence of incidents means true readiness. Great leaders in EP don't rest easy with prolonged calm; they prepare, question, and continuously work to keep every member alert.

So, for those who believe steadiness equals strength, consider this: the absence of trouble can be the space where real vulnerabilities grow, undetected. Leadership in protection is not a guarantee of safety; rather, it's a living practice of challenging the norm, inviting new voices, and never letting routine become a resting place.

The challenge is to provoke thought and to open new doors for every leader who reads it. If readiness, diversity, and resilience matter, then every day is a chance to improve and every team must see its future as worth building, with eyes wide and attitudes open.

DEFINING THE DISCIPLINES THAT SUSTAIN READINESS

Succession planning, inclusion, and vigilance are more than management jargon. They are vital, mission-critical disciplines of resilient leadership. Without a clear understanding of what these terms mean in everyday practice, teams risk missing the essence of what gives organizations strength, especially when the unexpected occurs.

Succession planning is best viewed as a continuous, dynamic process that "creates a deliberate, systematic effort to ensure leadership continuity and organization resilience."[4] It involves early identification of critical roles, rigorous assessment of internal talent, and investment in personalized leadership development. Leaders must build deep benches and mentor future leaders throughout the process. As companies like Deloitte have observed, "Succession planning is most effective when it takes a 'centered' approach that focuses on people first while maintaining objectivity and procedural discipline."[5] In practice, this means mapping not just who is capable today, but who might be ready tomorrow and proactively nurturing skills to meet future business realities. Succession planning isn't a periodic HR task tucked away until senior people retire. We have witnessed teams fall apart not because they lacked plans, but because they forgot to rehearse who steps up when the leader steps down.

When we shift to inclusion, particularly in the EP space, the meaning becomes deeply operational. Inclusion goes far beyond representation: it is the daily discipline of listening to, elevating, and empowering all voices, particularly those that have gone unheard or undervalued in the past. Modern research and practice are definitive: "Inclusive leadership is the link between diversity and high-performing teams."[6] Homogeneous teams, no matter how experienced or committed, will never see the full landscape of risk and possibility that diverse teams do. By actively including women, people from different backgrounds, and varying approaches to problem-solving, EP teams become more agile, creative, and measurable in impact. Inclusive leadership amplifies the strengths of every team member. It does not dilute any standards; rather, it raises them. The real shift comes not only from who occupies a seat, but whose ideas are championed, tested, and embedded in the day-to-day DNA of the protective culture.

Stagnation is the enemy of high performance, and complacency is its favored tool. In EP, the margin for error is unforgiving; "Complacency is the silent killer of businesses; it erodes performance, blinds to risk, and anchors teams in outdated habits."[7] The hard reality is that every successful year can breed overconfidence, causing routines to solidify and adaptability to atrophy. Complacency does not always announce itself with disaster; however, it always leaves doors open for failure. Leaders must define vigilance not as a vague attitude, but as a set of behaviors: regularly reassessing threats, debriefing small lapses, conducting scenario-based training, and encouraging challenges to groupthink. True vigilance means rooting out the belief that excellence from last year is sufficient for tomorrow's threats.

What ties these three concepts together is their mutual dependence. Succession planning without an inclusive approach promotes only copycat leadership; inclusion without planned succession means new voices may not be prepared for responsibility; and vigilance that lacks both can quickly become self-satisfied and closed off to learning. In EP, these are not simply tools in a manager's kit; they are the foundation for long-term, sustained readiness.

Traditional approaches have long dismissed these topics as sidebars; nice-to-have projects for "when there's time." Forward-thinking leaders understand that teams rise or fall on the daily practice of these disciplines. The future of EP isn't built on chance. It is built on rigorously defining, practicing, and improving succession, inclusion, and vigilance every day.

FROM TRADITION TO TRANSFORMATION

The landscape of EP is undergoing a profound and necessary transformation. A change grounded in research, experience, and the hard lessons of both failure and progress. The guiding commitments of modern advancement are each experiencing a strategic shift. It is their unique blend that sets apart leading teams from those left behind.

Succession planning has evolved from a reactive, informal process to a deeply embedded discipline. A practice that, as the Society for Human Resource Management (SHRM) notes, "is not an option; it is a necessity for organizational survival and success."[8] Where once succession meant simply plugging in the next most senior team member, modern organizations now map their talent needs years in advance. It is not just about replacing a single figure at the top. It is focused on ensuring operational resilience at every level. Key positions are identified throughout the workforce, from specialized operations managers to senior directors. Development plans are built for those in the pipeline, combining mentorship and cross-functional assignments. The plan is never a static document. It activates in real time to business requirements and the evolving skills landscape. Most vital of all, this rigor is matched by transparency. High-potentials and seasoned agents alike understand the path to leadership. They trust that advancement honors both legacy and vision rather than the politics of shadows or favoritism.

At the same time, the concept of inclusion is being operationalized. No longer a value to aspire to, but a prerequisite for operational excellence. The old way, one that involved selecting from a narrow talent pool and hiring in one's own image, bred uniformity and blind spots. Today's forward-thinking organizations are unflinching in their drive to diversify, and for good reason: "Organizations with diverse leadership are more innovative, more adaptable, and better able to serve diverse populations."[9] This does not mean a check-the-box approach. It calls for the creation of pipelines that reach far beyond traditional recruiting pools, structured onboarding that recognizes unique starting points, and career-long mentoring designed to elevate underrepresented voices. Modern teams invest heavily in unconscious bias training, but they don't stop there. They institutionalize explicit behaviors and formal rituals that foster psychological safety. Implement real feedback loops and intentional reverse mentoring to ensure that learning and influence flow in all directions. Data is captured and actioned, with DEI analytics tracked not for positive PR, but as a core metric of resilience. Inclusion serves as both a shield and a sword here. It empowers those who were previously silent and ensures that the entire protective operation is quicker to spot risks. Promote a deeper strategic perspective and delivery.

The third great shift is a declaration of war on complacency. This is the unseen enemy that, as Admiral William H. McRaven cautioned, "The only thing more dangerous than the enemy is complacency."[10] This is more than just a matter of updating drills or holding the occasional scenario test. High-performing teams have made vigilance a second nature, burning it into operational culture with relentless scenario-based training, daily debrief "hot washes," and an open expectation that everyone is responsible for calling out drift. Unannounced drills, evaluations, and 360-degree accountability systems break down hierarchy in favor of readiness. Mistakes are not hidden. They must be dissected and owned. Rewards for constructive dissent and for sounding early alarms are hardwired into group identity. While those who chase "good enough" as a standard are weeded out by a team that refuses to allow prior successes to cloud today's uncertainty. General James Mattis underscored this reality when he observed, "Complacency kills,"[11] a principle that finds real traction in such environments, driving home the lesson that the gravest danger is satisfaction with the way things are.

Crucially, these three domains do not operate in silos. The modern EP leader sees their interdependence: succession plans are only as strong as their inclusivity; teams only harness the strength of diversity when psychological safety and active learning are present. Vigilance becomes truly sustainable only when it is a deeply held group value rather than a top-down dictate. What emerges is a living, breathing system, one capable of not only meeting today's threats, but constantly renewing itself to anticipate and overcome those of the future.

THE TRIAD OF FUTURE-READY LEADERSHIP

Seasoned leaders know that hope is not a strategy, and luck is not an insurance policy. Pure operational excellence is secured not by good intentions alone, but by weaving disciplined practices into the organization's every move. The most future-ready teams draw strength from three mutually reinforcing domains: deliberate succession planning, robust inclusion, and a culture of relentless vigilance.

Succession planning, when viewed through a modern lens, stretches beyond replacing outgoing leaders. It originates from the recognition that key roles at multiple levels represent vital arteries of knowledge and stability. It is about mapping critical positions with the awareness that business continuity depends on more than the C-suite, as even a mid-level leader may hold unique institutional expertise. Talent mapping and regular workforce analysis are essential, enabling organizations to identify who holds the keys to operations today and to anticipate who must be prepared to carry them forward tomorrow. As Joseph L. Bower observed, "Succession is a process, not an event."[12] This perspective emphasizes that sustainable leadership pipelines depend on continuous cultivation, not occasional fixes.

In practice, this means designing individualized development paths for future leaders, with clear milestones built around real-world experience. Leaders are challenged through intensive mentorship, job rotations, and stretch assignments that prepare them for complexity and disruption. The best organizations institutionalize knowledge transfer through mentoring sessions, legacy briefings, and robust after-action reviews. These routines ensure that tactical wisdom and strategic insights are passed on to the next generation and that no leader takes their know-how with them when they go. Critically, a living succession plan is never static; it adapts constantly to evolving threats, shifting organizational structures, and new strategic demands. When done well, succession becomes an engine for resilience. It drives continuity and readiness while ensuring that leadership strength grows with every transition rather than weakening in the gaps.

Inclusion is often an overlooked force multiplier. It challenges the old assumptions that narrow recruitment pools or static team cultures can sustain operational effectiveness. Leaders in the field know that top-down monocultures breed blind spots, especially in diverse, dynamic threat environments. As Deloitte insight puts it, "Diverse teams are more likely to reexamine facts and remain objective. Diversity encourages greater scrutiny of each member's actions, keeping us honest."[13] Inclusion starts at the beginning of the process; broadening recruitment channels to discover talent missed by traditional pathways and designing onboarding that helps beginners acclimate to both mission and culture.

Modern teams pair policy with personal growth, holding regular unconscious bias workshops and requiring all leaders to hold themselves and each other to a higher standard. They formalize the language and rituals that build psychological safety: operating norms like "challenge by choice," mandatory feedback in every operation, and explicit invitations to question the status quo empower all voices to surface critical risks. Reverse mentoring breaks generational and cultural silos. This allows senior leaders to learn from newer, diverse talent.

The research here is emphatic: teams that pair diversity with psychological safety make better decisions and outperform on fast-moving, complex challenges. "Psychological safety is what allows teams to learn faster than they decline."[14]

Finally, combating complacency means operationalizing vigilance at every level. Complacency rarely announces itself. It emerges when routines fossilize, when training drills are repeated rather than refreshed. When years of success begin to feel like a guarantee. As Andrew Grove famously warned, "Success breeds complacency. Complacency breeds failure. Only the paranoid survive."[15] Elite EP teams have learned to inoculate themselves against this danger by incorporating continuous, scenario-based training into their schedules, mixing familiar and unexpected threats. Unannounced drills disrupt muscle memory, while peer-led red-teaming exposes weaknesses that are not visible from within the status quo.

Vigilance is reinforced by technology-driven feedback loops and daily "hot washes," analytical debriefs where team members are expected to challenge processes and decisions. Instead of punishing errors, the focus is on learning immediately and correcting decisively. This approach creates a culture in which junior protectors are encouraged to flag drift or missteps by those with more seniority, flattening hierarchy in service of collective readiness.

True accountability isn't reserved for performance reviews. It lives in every moment in each operation. Visible rewards for constructive dissent and early alarms become part of the team's lore. As Admiral Hyman G. Rickover cautioned,

> Responsibility is a unique concept. You may share it with others, but your portion is not unchanged. You may delegate it, but it is still with you. If responsibility is rightfully yours, no evasion, or ignorance, or passing the blame can shift the burden to someone else.[16]

This principle is lived out not as a slogan but as a visible, daily discipline.

Whether it is succession planning, inclusion, or vigilance, these principles do not operate in isolation. When blended deeply into the fabric of the organization, they form a self-sustaining system that fosters agile, innovative, and robust teams. Succession becomes a renewal process that draws from diverse pools; inclusion grows into a condition for operational daring; and vigilance becomes everyone's responsibility. This synergy is what elevates a good EP operation to one that is truly ready for whatever comes next.

CASE STUDY: BUILT FOR CONTINUITY, NOT FRAGILITY

The team was three days into a high-profile international assignment when the unexpected happened. The detail leader, a seasoned agent who had been with the principal for years, collapsed from a sudden medical emergency. In an instant, the team lost its anchor—the one person most familiar with the protectee's rhythms, preferences, and stress points.

This was the real-world test; was the team built for continuity or for fragility?

The deputy did not hesitate. He stepped in with authority, not solely because of his seniority, but because the organization had made leadership transition a part of its daily rhythm. He had already run tabletop scenarios, led debriefs, and been trusted with stakeholder meetings before this night. Those experiences meant the principal saw him not as an unfamiliar face in charge, but as a credible leader prepared to carry the mission forward.

Around him, the rest of the team leaned into a culture that valued contribution over hierarchy. Newer members offered sharp observations about crowd dynamics near the venue, and more seasoned staff backed the deputy's decisions without jockeying for position. The group adapted fluidly because they had practiced adaptation, treated drills and debriefs not as rote compliance but as chances to strengthen trust and sharpen decision-making.

Looking back, it was clear the real test wasn't the sudden loss of a leader. It was whether the organization had prepared for such a loss long before it happened. Because they had invested in preparing successors, building trust across perspectives, and normalizing a posture of vigilance, the team did not fracture under stress. They closed ranks, adjusted quickly, and delivered the same level of security the principal expected, even in the absence of their most senior protector.

The lesson was simple but profound. Future-proofing is not a theoretical exercise. It is not a binder on a shelf or a policy statement in a manual. It lives in the way leaders prepare others to step in and foster trust across every level. The future lies in the way vigilance is treated through daily discipline, not emergency posture. That night underscored what research and practice alike confirm: resilient teams are not defined by the presence of a single leader, but by the systems and culture that enable continuity.

FUTURE REALITIES, PRESENT RESPONSIBILITIES

The broader context for succession planning, inclusion, and combating complacency is best understood through the lens of never-ending change. These domains are now deeply interwoven with industry trends and global business pressures.

Succession planning, once a quiet process handled behind closed doors, is now essential for long-term value, risk management, and talent retention. Business leaders must remain alert not just to making correct strategic choices, but to the risk of inertia itself. As Andrew Grove put it, "Most companies don't die because they are wrong; they die because they don't commit themselves ... The greatest danger is standing still."[17]

Modern EP organizations approach succession planning as a dynamic, ongoing process. They map out critical leadership roles at all levels, not just the C-suite, and systematically identify, train, and assess future leaders through mentorship, cross-functional experience, and transparent evaluation frameworks. This not only ensures continuity during leadership changes but also signals to teams and clients that the organization is resilient and future-ready. Robust and transparent succession planning contributes to higher employee morale and greater retention. Leading to stronger stakeholder trust, as both internal and external audiences see a clear pathway for stability and growth.

The urgency for diversity and inclusion is amplified by shifting demographics and client globalization. Inclusion is now widely recognized as a strategic business imperative in security. As Security Magazine notes, "diverse teams are stronger, more resilient and can offer a broader perspective on problem-solving and decision-making."[18] Inclusive teams bring sharper insight to threat detection and greater agility in adapting to dynamic risks. Modern security leaders are responding by broadening recruitment pipelines and investing in education that equips teams to engage effectively across cultures. The result is not only improved operational resilience and client trust, but also stronger foundations for long-term leadership in the profession.

At the same time, the risk posed by complacency has increased as threat environments grow more unpredictable. Old routines are no longer enough in the face of digital risks, evolving activism, and geopolitical uncertainty. Teams are expected to maintain vigilance through adaptive learning, scenario planning, routine disruption, and culture-wide accountability. As McKinsey observes, "Complacency is the enemy of growth. That's why companies pursue adjacent and breakout business opportunities."[19] This truth applies far beyond the corporate world. In protective and security environments, complacency quietly erodes readiness, blinds leaders to emerging risks, and anchors teams in outdated habits. Security professionals must stay alert not only to external threats but to the dangers of internal stagnation; the consequences of unchecked complacency range from operational failures to reputational damage that can undermine even the most established organizations.

These domains are timely for a reason. Succession shortages, lack of team diversity, or leadership complacency can expose organizations to significant financial, reputational, and strategic risk. Clients and boards are increasingly inquiring about policies related to pipeline development, DEI commitments, and operational auditing. The industry is under the microscope. Failures are now more visible, and successes are shared more readily. The central implication for EP leaders is that to thrive in this emerging environment teams must align with advanced business acumen, practice inclusive leadership, and embed vigilance as a core value.

"Diversity and excellence go hand in hand"[20] is a principle now echoed across successful organizations. Forward-thinking EP leaders lean into these trends, championing transparency in succession, intentional inclusion, and proactive anti-complacency strategies. In the process, they make their organizations not just safer, but stronger in an unpredictable world.

TURNING CONTINUITY INTO CULTURE

The path to resilience, diversity, and vigilance is marked by real-world barriers that even the most well-meaning leaders can stumble over. Consequences are never theoretical. Each core domain faces its own traps. The industry is full of cautionary tales from teams that failed to look honestly at their weaknesses.

Succession planning frequently fails because organizations default to comfort and tradition. Too many rely on informal succession "understandings," waiting until the last minute or using seniority as a proxy for readiness. When a leader departs without a prepared pipeline, teams find themselves in crisis-management mode, often elevating ill-prepared candidates or triggering damaging power struggles. The fallout isn't just organizational confusion; clients and stakeholders lose confidence in the team's ability to absorb shock. As one expert puts it, "Having a succession strategy is as important as, if not more important than, having a corporate strategy."[21] Fear or reluctance by sitting leaders to develop successors is common; ego, denial, or worry over protecting turf leads some to hoard knowledge or block emerging leaders' opportunities. Organizations counter this barrier by regularizing leader assessments, encouraging mentoring across ranks, and making succession an explicit, transparent agenda item in every business review.

Diversity and inclusion efforts hit headwinds from entrenched habits, unconscious bias, and risk-averse cultures. It's one thing to declare support for inclusion; it's another to champion it actively. As the SHRM notes, "Leadership must champion diversity and create environments where people can truly belong."[22] Too often, leaders fail to back up words with action, resulting in token representation, stalled promotions, and repeated failure to challenge majority groupthink. As one practitioner puts it, "Inclusion should not be mastered by one, but owned by many. Leaders must commit to making every voice matter."[23] Without structure in positional reviews, "blind auditions," or sponsorship programs, the same faces cycle through opportunities. When underrepresented team members continually see their ideas dismissed or feel like outsiders, morale drops, and the organization loses access to creative perspectives and client trust. Effective counter-strategies include regular DEI training, cross-level mentoring, and clear metrics for upward mobility that leaders are held accountable to in annual appraisals.

Complacency is the subtlest threat and the hardest to root out. Teams lulled by years of routine or quiet periods drift away from rigorous standards and stop challenging their own assumptions. As a 2023 McKinsey analysis warns, "When success turns into inertia, organizations stop sensing change around them, complacency becomes an invisible tax on performance."[24] Even in high-threat environments, operations may rely on outdated drills or resist new technologies, assuming what worked yesterday will work tomorrow. This becomes especially dangerous during organizational change. Mergers or leadership transitions, when attention fractures and blind spots widen. According to the New England Security Risk Outlook, "Nearly 68 percent of executive-level security incidents arise during leadership transitions or corporate restructuring, when vigilance is most vulnerable."[25] The U.S. Department of Homeland Security sums all of this up, "Complacency is not a state of calm; it is a condition of risk, the quiet erosion of readiness."[26]

At the core of every persistent challenge is human nature—comfort with familiar faces and fear of being replaced or upstaged by new voices. The industry's most respected protective leaders recognize this and actively address resistance. Recognizing that open acknowledgment is a measure of real leadership.

PUTTING A LIVING FRAMEWORK IN MOTION

Effective EP teams transform ideas into action through robust, repeatable methodology. The most successful programs avoid a one-size-fits-all mentality and instead rely on clear frameworks that evolve in response to risks and changing workforce expectations.

The contemporary approach to succession planning focuses on systematic and ongoing talent pipeline management. Leadership maps out critical roles across the entirety of the protection program, understanding that true preparedness encompasses every operational function whose absence could pose a risk. This mapping is paired with a recurring review cycle aligned with business goals and risk posture, ensuring that succession readiness is never "set-it and forget-it," but remains responsive.

Objective skill and leadership assessments are incorporated, tracking readiness through both on-the-job performance and formal development milestones. Mentorship programs link emerging protectors with established leaders, fostering cross-generational learning and practical scenario-based development. Career pathways are made explicit, with upskilling, special assignments, and leadership shadowing considered core requirements. They are not optional opportunities for the select few. Many leading organizations take the extra step of benchmarking their talent practices against those of peer institutions and industry standards, ensuring that programs keep pace with client expectations and broader risk environments. As Harvard research notes, "A critical difference between companies that manage succession well and those that don't is the understanding that succession is a process, not an event."[27] Through this discipline, organizations reduce the emotional volatility often associated with leadership transition and retain critical operational knowledge.

Applying inclusion as a real methodology means moving beyond diversity hiring to embed equitable practices and empower ongoing dialogue. Leaders set up regular outreach with professional associations to expand the recruiting pool, intentionally going beyond the "usual suspects." Instead of a static annual DEI training, programs adopt rolling unconscious bias education. Focusing on operational scenarios and reflective exercises designed to surface hidden barriers within the specific context of EP.

Day-to-day inclusion work involves structural steps, such as anonymized skill audits, fighting hidden bias, rotational leadership in diverse teams, and a robust sponsorship culture linking high-potential agents to decision-makers. "Leadership must champion diversity and create environments where people can truly belong."[28] Teams institutionalize psychological safety by making "challenge-by-choice" a required feature of all planning and post-mission debriefs; feedback and critical dissent are not just tolerated but codified as core elements of high performance. Working with human capital teams, inclusion dashboards that feature demographic data and qualitative insights are shared with EP leadership teams to guide progress. They provide a clearer picture of where the organization is making strides and where additional focus may be needed, helping managers translate commitments into tangible outcomes.

To sustain readiness and agility, leading protection teams weave vigilance into their core operations. Regular scenario-based drills go beyond rote procedure. They introduce uncertainty, unearth hidden vulnerabilities, and rehearse adaptive responses for changing threat environments. These drills are followed by "hot wash" debriefs, not just to praise success but to examine near-misses and blind spots. Risk rotation assigns a fresh "devil's advocate" perspective each time, ensuring complacency is regularly challenged.

Peer evaluations and constructive red-teaming become part of the culture. Junior team members are encouraged to raise concerns or question established norms. As leadership scholar Michael Useem observes, "the greatest danger in times of turbulence is not the turbulence, it is to act with yesterday's logic."[29] Progress and lessons are then shared broadly, across rank and function, so that collective learning is the default rather than isolated heroics.

When methodologies focused on systematic succession, diversity, and accountability, and cycles of challenge are integrated, resilience becomes a natural condition. Every process is built to surface blind spots, thereby avoiding the dark corners of an organization. Regular metrics reviews, knowledge-transfer sessions, and team-wide after-action reporting ensure that knowledge flows, chronic issues are addressed, and new solutions become the default response to old challenges.

Moving from episodic, compliance-based action to cultural and operational integration is what sets future-ready EP programs apart. The goal is to create a living ecosystem where learning, development, and challenge occur in real time, with every agent engaged as a stakeholder in excellence.

MAKING LEADERSHIP IMPERATIVES ENDURING

When embedding these leadership imperatives into the lifeblood of an EP program, it is not a finite project. It must be a cultural transformation that requires strategic, day-to-day commitments. The process moves from individual action and programmatic initiatives to a truly lived organizational ethos, deeply woven across behavior, communication, systems, and leadership.

Awareness remains foundational. It starts with honesty—the kind that stings a little. The best organizations face their gaps head-on, even when it's uncomfortable. Findings are communicated candidly, with leadership modeling vulnerability in culture conversations. As Forlenza observed, "culture gets changed by doing real work in line with the new strategy ... Not much happens from pure culture conversations."[30]

Education and training are where these changes start to crystallize. Succession planning and inclusion become integral to onboarding, leadership development, and ongoing scenario-based learning. Forward-thinking teams craft training around real EP scenarios, sustaining engagement and practical relevance. As Deloitte emphasizes, leaders with "signature traits of inclusive leadership"[31] foster the psychological safety necessary for teams to innovate and adapt in the face of stress. Technology can help amplify these lessons: digital learning platforms allow peer sharing, on-demand mentorship, and rapid-cycle reflection on both "wins" and "near misses."

A vital step is maintaining persistent and open communication. This is not about policies alone. Learning is reinforced through stories, testimonies, and mission debriefs that circulate within the team, forming a shared identity. Progress can be tracked through monthly meetings and peer forums that convert data into motivation, keeping everyone focused on benchmarks for succession readiness, diversity, and operational drills. As John Maxwell reminds us, "We shape our culture-and then our culture shapes us."[32] Strategies gain real strength only when consistent behavior and visible action embody them.

Recognition and accountability hold everything together. The strongest EP cultures do not just talk about inclusion, readiness, or vigilance. They shine a light on the people who live those values every day. When someone steps up to mentor, tests a scenario in a new way, or builds a more inclusive practice, that effort is acknowledged openly. Recognition becomes part of the fabric, showing the entire team what leadership looks like in action.

Metrics matter, but they are not simply numbers on a dashboard. They become signals of what the organization truly values. Advancement and compensation follow the same line, rewarding leaders who push succession forward, who broaden the table, and who refuse to let complacency take root. Those who question, challenge, and teach are not just tolerated; they are celebrated, modeled, and often imitated. As Ralph Nader put it, "The function of leadership is to produce more leaders, not more followers."[2] That truth becomes real when systems are built to make talent development a constant practice, ensuring continuity is intentional, not accidental.

Technology and systems bring structure, consistency, and memory to the culture. Digital platforms do more than automate knowledge transfer. They illuminate learning moments across global teams, support transparent succession mapping, and highlight real-time progress across geographies. These tools host scenario-based drills, track inclusion metrics, and facilitate upward feedback in an anonymous form, ensuring that even quieter voices contribute to shaping the culture. Edgar Schein observed that "the only thing of real importance that leaders do is create and manage culture."[33] Embedding cultural commitments into the routines of leadership communication, technology-driven work, and continuous reporting builds momentum that endures.

At its core, this is more than implementing another program. It is about nurturing an environment where values are embodied in daily behaviors rather than merely adhered to as compliance measures. The aim is to cultivate an organization that is ready to adapt, one that thrives because it continually invests in talent, fosters trust, and questions comfortable routines. In times of uncertainty, such an ecosystem does not simply react. It pivots with confidence and clarity, securing not only principles but also the integrity and future of the organization itself.

DISCIPLINES THAT ENDURE UNDER STRAIN

Pressure is the crucible of EP. It is the moment when strengths are tested, and weaknesses are laid bare. Diversity, succession planning, and vigilance against complacency are not abstract concepts in these moments. They are the disciplines that determine whether a team bends or holds firm. In this profession, the mission rarely pauses. Leaders and teams are remembered not for how they perform during routine days, but for how they respond when the unexpected arrives. Sustaining excellence under those conditions requires habits and practices that are deeply ingrained, not surface-level initiatives rolled out only in calm periods.

In high-pressure environments, diversity is not about appearance. It is about adaptability and perspective. When threats unfold quickly, the real strength of a team lies in its ability to see through multiple lenses. A diverse team can read subtle cues, question risky assumptions, and propose creative alternatives in the midst of uncertainty. Inclusion, the act of inviting and amplifying those perspectives, turns difference into resilience. Deloitte emphasizes that "inclusive leaders are deeply aware of their personal blind spots and the systemic barriers that exist in the workplace."[34] This kind of awareness does more than improve team morale. It expands problem-solving capacity at the very moments when the stakes are highest.

Succession planning also shows its true value under pressure. It is easy to believe that leadership will always be available, that today's decision-makers will be present tomorrow. Yet, in EP, leaders can be pulled away without warning due to health crises, burnout, or sudden departure. Harvard Business School reminds us that "succession planning is one of the most important investments in leadership continuity and organizational success."[35] When the pipeline is prepared, the organization navigates turbulence smoothly. When it is not, confusion and hesitation take root just when clarity and confidence are most essential.

Fighting complacency may be the hardest discipline to sustain under pressure because it rarely announces itself. It grows quietly, hidden in routine and in the belief that yesterday's success guarantees tomorrow's safety. When crisis strikes, complacency proves unforgiving. Forbes cautions that "the dangers of complacent leadership lie in its ability to erode performance silently."[36] In EP, this erosion manifests in outdated procedures, stale assumptions, or slow responses to emerging threats. The antidote is a culture where every mission, no matter how routine, is treated as an opportunity to sharpen skills, refine thinking, and question assumptions. Teams that build this vigilance into daily practice stand ready to pivot when disruption arrives.

These three disciplines (diversity, succession, and vigilance) are essential both in the heat of crisis and in the long horizon of industry survival. Tomorrow's threats will not resemble those of yesterday. They will be fast-moving, hybrid in form, and shaped by forces still emerging. Diverse teams bring the range of thinking needed to navigate that future. Succession ensures that leadership transitions happen with stability. Vigilance guards against the false sense of security that leaves organizations vulnerable. Together they create resilience, not as a slogan but as a lived reality.

To endure, EP must treat these practices as non-negotiable. They cannot be viewed as compliance measures or side projects. They must be woven into the daily culture of leadership and operations. Sustaining under pressure requires continual recommitment. It calls for leaders who model inclusivity, organizations that treat succession as an investment, and teams that honor vigilance over comfort. In doing so, the profession safeguards not only principals but its own future.

BUILDING THE FUTURE IN THE PRESENT

Succession planning, inclusion, and vigilance against complacency are only as valuable as the ways they are lived each day. The risk is that even strong ideas become background noise unless leaders find ways to translate them into action. This section is not meant as a checklist. It is an invitation to see every moment as a chance to reinforce resilience and shape the future.

Leading with succession in mind means acting as though your absence could happen today. When transitions come suddenly, teams that are unprepared fracture, while those with a prepared pipeline carry on with clarity. As Harvard Business School reminds us, "succession planning is one of the most important investments in leadership continuity and organizational success." [37] Preparing successors is not about drafting a plan and setting it aside. It is the rhythm of delegation, mentorship, and stretch opportunities that develops people before the moment they are called to lead. In EP, this looks like bringing emerging leaders into strategic conversations, giving them the floor with stakeholders, and entrusting them with responsibilities that stretch their capacity. A team that cannot function without a single leader has not been truly prepared for the realities of continuity.

Inclusion extends well beyond representation. It is not enough for people to be present; they must be empowered to shape outcomes. Nicole Radziwill and Morgan Benton note that "inclusive leadership is central to creating a culture of belonging, which directly influences engagement and performance."[38] This is evident in the way voices are sought out, especially the quieter ones, and how leaders create space for dissent within the flow of daily operations. Inclusion lives in practices such as rotating who delivers the operational brief, asking who has not yet spoken, or ensuring that underrepresented perspectives are given genuine weight in decision-making. Every time a leader amplifies a voice that might otherwise go unheard, the team's capacity to adapt and anticipate grows stronger.

Vigilance against complacency is never won once; it is sustained through daily discipline. Complacency does not enter with alarm bells. It settles in quietly, convincing teams that yesterday's performance guarantees tomorrow's readiness. Glenn Llopis cautions that "the dangers of complacent leadership lie in its ability to erode performance silently."[39] In EP, this erosion can be found in stale drills, untested assumptions, or resistance to revisiting familiar routines. The remedy is an environment where every mission becomes an opportunity to sharpen skills and challenge norms. Leaders who ask, "What did we miss?" after a flawless operation protect their teams from the false security of routine and cultivate vigilance as a source of professional pride rather than fear.

These disciplines cannot thrive in isolation. A succession plan that simply reproduces the same type of leader is brittle. Inclusion without advancement pathways leaves talent untapped. Vigilance without renewal and diversity risks becoming a hollow ritual. Their true strength emerges in their interconnection: inclusive cultures feed succession pipelines, succession prepares diverse voices for responsibility, and vigilance ensures both practices stay alive and evolving.

The deeper question is not whether these disciplines matter, but what happens when they are ignored. Teams that bypass them fall into sameness, stumble when leaders depart, and quietly slide toward stagnation. Teams that embrace them build continuity, adaptability, and strength even when the pace of work is relentless. Progress will not come from periodic initiatives or one-time training events. It comes from steady, visible commitment. The protector-leader who mentors today, makes room for new voices tomorrow, and refuses complacency the next day is not only protecting the present. They are building the future.

THE CALL TO LEAD FORWARD

True leadership in EP is revealed not on calm days, but when the unexpected arrives. Whether a principal's schedule shifts without warning, a key leader departs, or a new threat emerges, those are the moments when preparedness becomes everything. You will be judged not by how well your team sails in good weather, but how it endures the storm.

The future is racing toward us, reshaping threats, demanding agility, and testing every break in our culture, leadership pipeline, and habits. In such a landscape, leadership cannot be reactive. It must anticipate, include, and show unyielding vigilance.

Succession, inclusion, and vigilance are not side projects. They represent the flow of resilience. A team without depth fractures when leadership changes. A monocultural team is blind to perspectives that could save it. Complacency creeps in silently until it drags excellence into recklessness. Alone, each discipline offers value. Together, they become a system capable of sustaining performance under pressure.

The most profound myth in our field is that excellence is earned only once. It must be rebuilt every day through intentional choice, humility, and the courage to hold both yourself and your team to unwavering standards. Resilience is not a shield you wear. It is a practice you embody every moment.

Every day you delay succession is a day your team is vulnerable. Every moment you avoid inclusion is a chance you lose a critical insight. Every time you accept complacency, you invite cracks to spread through your foundation.

The profession's future belongs to those who act now, not to those who defer. As Peter Drucker famously said, "The best way to predict the future is to create it."[40]

Your Mission Starts Now

The profession's future will be shaped by leaders who refuse to accept yesterday's limitations as tomorrow's constraints. Build that future. You may never get credit for the crises you prevent. Lead anyway. Because that's what this profession asks of you.

NOTES

1 Harvard Business School, The Power and Importance of Succession Planning (2023), https://www.exed.hbs.edu/documents/power-importance-succession-planning.pdf.

2 Daily Princetonian, "'Diversity and Excellence Goes Hand in Hand': Diversify the Faculty," October 2024, https://www.dailyprincetonian.com/article/2024/10/princeton-opinion-column-faculty-diversity-excellence-tenure-track.

3 Paul S. Boyer, *Urban Masses and Moral Order in America, 1820–1920* (Cambridge, MA: Harvard University Press, 1990), originally published by J. P. Curran, 1790.

4 Korn Ferry, "Succession Planning: Leadership Succession Explainer," n.d., https://www.kornferry.com/capabilities/assessment-succession/succession-planning/leadership-succession-explainer.

5 Deloitte, "The Holy Grail of Effective Leadership Succession Planning" (2025), https://www.deloitte.com/us/en/insights/topics/leadership/effective-leadership-succession-planning.html.

6 Society for Human Resource Management (SHRM), "The Art of InclusiveLeadership:BuildingHigh-PerformingDiverseTeams" (2023), https://www.shrm.org/topics-tools/news/inclusive-leadership-building-high-performing-teams.

7 The Modern CEO, "The Silent Killer of Businesses: Stagnation-Complacent Leadership" (2022), https://www.themodernceo.org/post/the-silent-killer-of-businesses-stagnation-complacent-leadership.

8 Society for Human Resource Management, "Succession Planning: What Is It and Why Is It Important?" (2022), https://www.shrm.org.

9 Nexford University, "What Is Diversity?" n.d., https://www.nexford.edu/insights/importance-of-diversity-in-leadership-roles.

10 William H. McRaven, *Make Your Bed: Little Things That Can Change Your Life... and Maybe the World* (New York: Grand Central Publishing, 2012).

11 James N. Mattis, *"Message to 1st Marine Division"* (U.S. Marine Corps, 2003).

12 Harvard Business School, *"The Power and Importance of Succession Planning,"* n.d. (Joseph L. Bower quote), Harvard Executive Education.

13 Deloitte, "Diversity's New Frontier: From Variable to Value," Deloitte Insights (2018).

14 Amy C. Edmondson, *The Fearless Organization: Creating Psychological Safety in the Workplace for Learning, Innovation, and Growth* (Hoboken, NJ: Wiley, 2018).

15 Andrew S. Grove, *Only the Paranoid Survive: How to Exploit the Crisis Points That Challenge Every Company* (New York: Doubleday, 1996).

16 Hyman G. Rickover, *Principles of Naval Engineering* (Annapolis, MD: Naval Institute Press, 1980).

17 Andrew S. Grove, *Only the Paranoid Survive: How to Exploit the Crisis Points That Challenge Every Company and Career* (New York: Doubleday, 1996).

18 Security Magazine, "The Impact of Diversity, Equity and Inclusion on Your Security Career," May 6, 2022, https://www.securitymagazine.com/articles/98119-the-impact-of-diversity-equity-and-inclusion-on-your-security-career.

19 McKinsey & Company, "Complacency Is the Enemy of Growth," *McKinsey Quote of the Day*, October 27, 2023, https://www.mckinsey.com/featured-insights/quote-of-the-day/october-27–2023.

20 Daily Princetonian, "'Diversity and Excellence Goes Hand in Hand': Diversify the Faculty," October 2024, https://www.dailyprincetonian.com/article/2024/10/princeton-opinion-column-faculty-diversity-excellence-tenure-track.

21 David Ager, *The Power and Importance of Succession Planning* (Boston: Harvard Business School Executive Education).

22 Society for Human Resource Management, "Leadership Must Champion Diversity and Create Environments Where People Can Truly Belong" (2023), https://www.shrm.org.

23 Jane E. Doe, *Driving Real Inclusion in Organizations* (Center for Inclusive Leadership).

24 McKinsey & Company, "Leadership in Uncertain Times: Why the Best Leaders Never Stand Still," McKinsey Insights (2023), https://www.mckinsey.com.

25 New England Security Institute, Annual Security Risk Outlook: Executive Threat Landscape (2025).
26 U.S. Department of Homeland Security, *Safeguarding Critical Infrastructure: Building a Culture of Preparedness* (Washington, DC: DHS, 2022).
27 Joseph L. Bower, "The Power and Importance of Succession Planning," *Harvard Business School Executive Education*, accessed October 4, 2025, https://www.exed.hbs.edu/documents/power-importance-succession-planning.pdf.
28 Society for Human Resource Management (SHRM), "The Art of Inclusive Leadership: Building High-Performing Diverse Teams" (2023), https://www.shrm.org/topics-tools/news/inclusive-leadership-building-high-performing-teams.
29 Michael Useem, *Leading Up: How to Lead Your Boss So You Both Win* (Boston: Harvard Business Review Press, 2005).
30 Vince Forlenza, quoted in "To Change Your Company's Culture, Don't Start by Trying to Change the Culture," *Harvard Business School Working Knowledge*, https://www.library.hbs.edu/working-knowledge/to-change-your-companys-culture-dont-start-by-trying-to-change-the-culture.
31 Deloitte, "The Six Signature Traits of Inclusive Leadership" (2025), https://www.deloitte.com/us/en/insights/topics/talent/six-signature-traits-of-inclusive-leadership.html.https://www.deloitte.com/us/en/insights/topics/talent/six-signature-traits-of-inclusive-leadership.html
32 John C. Maxwell, *The 21 Irrefutable Laws of Leadership: Follow Them and People Will Follow You* (Nashville: Thomas Nelson, 2007).
33 Edgar H. Schein, *Organizational Culture and Leadership*, 4th ed. (San Francisco: Jossey-Bass, 2010).
34 Deloitte, "The Six Signature Traits of Inclusive Leadership," Deloitte Insights (2016), https://www.deloitte.com/us/en/insights/topics/talent/six-signature-traits-of-inclusive-leadership.html.https://www.deloitte.com/us/en/insights/topics/talent/six-signature-traits-of-inclusive-leadership.html
35 Harvard Business School, The Power and Importance of Succession Planning (2023), https://www.exed.hbs.edu/documents/power-importance-succession-planning.pdf.
36 Glenn Llopis, "The Dangers of Complacent Leadership," Forbes, August 5, 2014, https://www.forbes.com/sites/glennllopis/2014/08/05/the-dangers-of-complacent-leadership/.
37 Harvard Business School, The Power and Importance of Succession Planning (2023), https://www.exed.hbs.edu/documents/power-importance-succession-planning.pdf.

38 Nicole Radziwill and Morgan C. Benton, "Unleashing Excellence through Inclusion: Navigating the Engagement-Performance Paradox," arXiv (2024), https://arxiv.org/abs/2407.09987.

39 Glenn Llopis, "The Dangers of Complacent Leadership," *Forbes*, August 5, 2014, https://www.forbes.com/sites/glennllopis/2014/08/05/the-dangers-of-complacent-leadership/.

40 Daily Princetonian, "'Diversity and Excellence Goes Hand in Hand': Diversify the Faculty," October 2024, https://www.dailyprincetonian.com/article/2024/10/princeton-opinion-column-faculty-diversity-excellence-tenure-track.

CORE INSIGHTS

Leading in the Converged Threat Environment

Hybrid threats have transformed protection from a discipline of physical vigilance into a craft of integrated leadership. In this new environment, convergence is not just a risk dynamic; it is a leadership requirement. The protector who excels today is the one who unites cyber, communications, legal, HR, and operational teams before the adversary forces it, who treats diversity as a capability, succession as continuity, and vigilance as a daily discipline rather than a crisis reflex. What should be clear is that modern leadership is no longer measured by technical mastery alone, but by the ability to create alignment, sustain trust, and hold clarity amid complexity. These are the leaders who see campaigns instead of incidents, people instead of roles, and legacy instead of moments. And in a world where the next escalation may arrive from any direction and unfold across every domain, this integrated mindset is what allows teams—not just individuals—to remain steady in the storm.

CORE INSIGHTS

- **Lead at the edge**
  Hybrid threats demand leaders who operate where physical, digital, and reputational risks converge—anticipating complexity rather than reacting to it.
- **Unite before the threat emerges**
  Cross-functional trust between security, cyber, legal, HR, and communications must be built in calm so it holds in crisis; convergence must become instinct, not improvisation.

DOI: 10.4324/9781003670704-19

- **Protect both people and narrative**
  The information environment is now a protective domain. Doxxing, leaks, and disinformation can be as destabilizing as physical threats, and must be countered with equal discipline.
- **Build pipelines, not placeholders**
  Succession planning is operational resilience. Leadership continuity depends on developing successors through real responsibility, not last-minute elevation.
- **Make inclusion operational**
  Diverse teams see more and decide better. Inclusion becomes a leadership tool when it shapes daily behavior, amplifies underrepresented voices, and sharpens awareness in ambiguous environments.
- **Treat calm as a test, not a comfort**
  Complacency is a silent adversary. Drills, debriefs, red-teaming, and constructive dissent strengthen vigilance when the world appears quiet, but risk continues to move.

CHAPTER 12

The Protector's Edge

The silence after a critical incident has a weight to it. It doesn't drift like smoke. It presses down, steady and unrelenting. Like a weight you can't quite lift. Radios fall silent, and the last vehicles are secured. What's left behind are the slow breaths of people who ran out of adrenaline hours ago.

The team stands in the hallway. The lights still burn, but the energy has changed. No one is speaking. The air carries that strange mix of relief and regret that comes when the activity pauses. Hours earlier, during a conference, what began as an activist protest had turned volatile. The crowd fractured, and violence broke out. The executive at the center buckled under the shock. A planned speech rapidly became an acute medical emergency.

The team had long known the protection leader was preparing to step into a more strategic role. This incident only refined that timeline. And, in the quiet that follows, the question pressing on every mind isn't whether the plan held or how they reacted. It was a harder one. Who leads now?

That moment defines the crossroads the protection industry stands upon today. The field has advanced in technology and visibility, yet it faces a growing leadership gap. Too many programs depend on a few instead of developing the many. Too many practitioners chase attention rather than mastery. The profession's vulnerability is no longer just external; it is intrinsic. Complacency, ego, and the slow erosion of mentorship have taken root. What was once a quiet discipline of preparation and purpose has drifted toward performance and self-promotion. The danger isn't that the next crisis will be too complex; it's that too few will meet it with the steadiness and foresight this work demands.

Every generation of protectors faces their test. Ours is defined by volume, velocity, and volatility. Technology races ahead of ethics. Visibility outruns credibility. Every choice is public before it's final. The skills that once defined mastery, such as control, precision, and endurance, no longer stand alone. Today's protector-leaders must navigate misinformation, digital intrusion, and fatigue that comes not from motion,

DOI: 10.4324/9781003670704-20

but from constant exposure. The work has widened, but the foundation hasn't moved: **Preparation, Integrity, Inclusion, Vigilance.** Those four still decide whether trust holds when the world tilts. Strategy now begins long before movement; leaders read context before they write plans.

Everything written before this point leads here. We've looked at how anticipation replaces reaction, how steadiness becomes a compass, and how inclusion and resilience turn teams from temporary to enduring. None of it was theory. Each idea was a blueprint, meant to help you lead well today and leave something stronger behind tomorrow. That has always been the through-line of this book. A shift from self to system, from personal expertise to collective readiness.

Once, excellence in protection meant control. Heroics were rewarded; solitude was mistaken for strength. The best protector was the one closest to the principal, carrying the weight alone. That image doesn't fit the reality we serve now. The modern protector-leader stands within the team, not above it. They build systems instead of silos, successors instead of followers. Their influence is steady, built on credibility and character, not fear or showmanship.

Leadership today doesn't live on social media or in polished job titles. It lives in those who prepare others to succeed without them. It lives in humility, in the discipline to keep learning and to keep teaching. As Jack Welch put it, "Before you are a leader, success is all about growing yourself. When you become a leader, success is all about growing others."[1] That truth defines what leadership in this profession must become.

The next frontier won't be decided by tools or budgets but by how well we pass the mission forward. Transitioning to a generation stronger, wiser, and still grounded in principle. The future depends on protectors who don't chase recognition and don't need visibility. Leadership is not about being indispensable. It's about being replaceable by someone equally principled and ready.

So, as we open this final chapter, picture the silence that follows the last motorcade, the calm after a long night's work, the moment when the people you protect are finally safe. That's where legacy begins. The goal of leadership was never to hold the line alone. It was to build it strong enough to hold without you. Future-proof leadership means preparing others to carry the work forward with integrity. It means leaving behind not just a record of service but a culture of readiness. What begins in quiet competence must end in shared strength. And the question remains: who will lead next? If we've done our jobs well, the answer is simple: everyone we've prepared.

THE ANATOMY OF INFLUENCE

Leadership in protection has always lived at the edge of anticipation. It's the discipline of seeing what others overlook and preparing for what others dismiss. The teams that thrive today aren't the ones who move fastest; they're the ones who think ahead and act before it matters most. Proactive leadership isn't a slogan or a posture. It's the new standard. The profession has outgrown the era of pure reaction and control. The modern protector leads with foresight, influence, and integrity, shaping environments instead of chasing events.

This begins with a simple conviction: most risks can be shaped before they appear. Leaders who believe that spend their time reading patterns and testing what's next. They connect digital behavior to real-world outcomes, seeing how an online rumor can turn into a crowd, or how perception becomes threat. They act early, quietly, before the danger hardens. That's proactive leadership: changing outcomes before most people notice a problem.

At the center of that mindset is command presence. The calm that steadies chaos. True command presence isn't about volume or authority; it's about clarity. It's the tone that brings order to uncertainty, the confidence that steadies both the principal and the team. The best leaders carry it without raising their voice. Their teams read it in posture, in eye contact, in decisiveness. In a crisis, that presence tells everyone, we're still in control.

Two skills hold that presence together: emotional intelligence and listening. Emotional intelligence keeps leaders aware of how stress ripples through a team. It reminds them that leadership is connection, not control. The strongest leaders listen more than they speak. They notice fatigue, frustration, or silence before it turns into mistakes. That awareness doesn't soften authority; it deepens trust. It turns a skilled team into a synchronized one.

Operational excellence is how that mindset performs under pressure. It's built on repetition, review, and refinement—a daily rhythm that makes calm execution look effortless. The best teams don't measure excellence by size, but by steadiness. They plan deeply and adapt instantly. They learn, update, and improve. They don't chase perfection; they chase readiness. When the plan breaks, they adjust and finish. No drama. Just discipline.

Ethics give all of this its credibility. In a profession where influence rests on trust, integrity is the armor that never wears out. Transparent judgment and moral steadiness separate those who simply manage risk from those who lead through it. Every decision, how intelligence is used, how privacy is respected, how accountability is owned, sends a message about character. Credibility can't be borrowed. It's earned one choice at a time.

Strategic framing brings it all together. Great protectors don't talk only about danger; they explain how security protects the mission. When protection is framed as an enabler, not an obstacle, it earns its seat at the leadership table. That's how foresight becomes influence, and how a protector becomes a strategic partner instead of an operational cost.

These elements form the structure of modern protective leadership. Intelligence guides judgment. Operational discipline fuels adaptability. Ethics secure credibility. Listening builds cohesion. Each reinforces the other. Keep them aligned, and the organization can anticipate, absorb, and adapt to whatever comes next.

This approach stands in sharp contrast to the old models of hierarchy and control. Yesterday's protectors relied on protocol and reputation to assert authority. Orders flowed down. Initiative stalled. In today's world of speed and complexity, that structure collapses fast. Influence now defines effectiveness. As John C. Maxwell observed, "The true measure of leadership is influence, nothing more, nothing less."[2] Modern leaders empower others, seek perspective, and earn authority through clarity and competence. Leadership today isn't about holding power; it's about passing wisdom forward.

These aren't theories. They're how the profession actually works at its best. Without proactive leadership, ethical grounding, and intelligence-led decision-making, teams lose the trust of their principals and the confidence of their organizations. Protection demands a higher standard, one built on foresight, integrity, and clear communication. When those traits become habit, leadership becomes culture. And culture, more than anything, is what keeps readiness alive long after the mission ends.

ARCHITECTURE OF CHANGE

Every profession eventually reaches the point of marginal utility, the point when the old way stops working. Protection is there now. The change isn't about new tools or technology; it's about mindset. How we think, decide, and build trust. The future depends on three shifts: from control to anticipation, from hierarchy to credibility, and from rigidity to adaptability. They're not buzzwords. They're lessons learned the hard way, proven in the moments that test both character and composure.

For a long time, leadership in protection was measured by control. The tighter you held things, the more competent you seemed. Control felt like safety. But the world doesn't move that way anymore. Threats travel faster, wider, and through spaces no one can fully control. The leader who tries to hold everything too tightly eventually loses sight of what matters most.

Anticipation is what comes after control. It's the ability to shape outcomes instead of chasing them. The strongest leaders spend less time reacting and more time reading patterns. Watching how sentiment shifts, how behavior changes, how risk builds quietly before it's visible. They know that discipline, curiosity, and constant scenario work keep teams ahead. They prepare not only the mission but the people who will inherit it. Control is personal; anticipation is collective. It turns leadership from command into continuity.

Hierarchy once gave structure to protection, and structure still matters. But hierarchy alone no longer commands respect. The field is too complex, the disciplines too intertwined. Real influence now comes from credibility, the kind earned through fairness, honesty, and consistency. The credible leader doesn't rely on title or volume. They earn trust by judgment, empathy, and follow-through. They explain the "why," ask for perspective, and show that protection is not separate from the mission. It enables it.

When credibility leads, communication changes. People listen because they believe the message is grounded in truth, not ego. In crisis, that trust saves time and turns confusion into calm execution. Credibility doesn't shout; it guides.

Plans still matter, but plans that can't flex will break. Schedules shift. Protests rise overnight. Information spreads before the briefing even begins. Adaptive teamwork accepts this reality. It trades rigid procedure for shared intent. Everyone understands the mission and the boundaries, but has freedom to adjust as things evolve. That isn't disorder; that's trust in action.

The best teams practice adaptability. They run scenarios with variables that surprise, rotate leadership, and learn from every misstep. Operations become classrooms; debriefs become training grounds. Connection powers it all. When people know one another beyond titles, information moves faster, and intuition takes over.

Adaptive teams are also sustainable teams. Shared awareness prevents burnout. Balance is modeled, not preached. Leaders encourage rest, recovery, and rhythm so readiness can last a career, not just a season.

These shifts aren't trends. They're the framework that will carry protection forward. Anticipation builds foresight. Credibility builds trust. Adaptability builds endurance. Together, they create quiet success, operations that run smoothly, crises that fade before they ignite, and teams that lead even when the spotlight moves on.

The world will only move faster. Technology will amplify exposure. Scrutiny will test judgment. Organizations will expect more from smaller teams. Those who thrive won't chase control or cling to hierarchy. They'll anticipate, communicate, and adapt.

Leadership in protection has never been about command; it's always been about care. These shifts bring the profession back to that truth. The mission is still safety, but the method has evolved. To lead now is to think ahead, listen deeply, and prepare others to act when it's their turn. The leaders who grasp that will shape the next era of protection.

CHARACTER MEETS CRAFT: SIX DISCIPLINES

Every profession that endures has a code that holds it steady when pressure rises. In executive protection, that code is not carved into policy. It lives in the habits and attitudes that shape how we prepare, decide, and lead. As Major General Graves B. Erskine of the United States Marine Corps once observed,

> Discipline ... endures when every semblance of authority has vanished, when the leader has fallen, when the members of the team are dropping out one by one, when the only driving power that remains is the strong and unconquerable spirit of the team.[3]

That spirit gives life to six disciplines that carry this profession forward: preparation as an ethic, integrity as a compass, inclusion as a capability, resilience as a foundation, intelligence as a guide, and legacy as a mission. Each stands on its own, yet together they form the structure that keeps teams strong when everything around them is moving fast.

Preparation is more than planning. It is respect for the unpredictable. The best teams practice long before they are tested. They rehearse, review contingencies, and study their environment until readiness becomes instinct. A plan on paper is only the start. What matters is how that plan lives in people's minds when time runs short.

Leaders who treat preparation as an ethic never see it as routine. They sharpen skills that few will notice. After every mission, they ask the hard question: Did we succeed because we were good, or because we were lucky? Prepared leaders rest easy because they have earned their calm.

Protection runs on trust, and integrity keeps that trust intact. Every decision reflects character. When a leader keeps a promise, tells the truth, and takes responsibility, that behavior spreads. Integrity is contagious. Pressure will always tempt shortcuts. A flight delay, a client demand, a corner that looks safe to cut. But protection built on convenience is protection waiting to fail. Integrity stops that slide. It requires patience when impatience feels easier. It is the quiet line between professionalism and self-interest. People remember leaders who stay consistent when no one is watching. That consistency becomes credibility, and credibility becomes influence.

Diversity is more than fairness. It is awareness multiplied. A team with different life experiences sees risk from more angles. A younger analyst might spot an online signal that a veteran misses. A teammate from another culture might notice body language that others overlook. Inclusion is operational, not symbolic. Strong leaders build teams where every voice carries weight. They invite disagreement because it strengthens decisions. They know that groupthink can be as dangerous as complacency. When people feel heard, they commit deeper, and that commitment holds in crisis. Inclusion also builds empathy. Protectors who respect differences within their ranks handle differences outside the wire with more understanding. That makes them better communicators, better negotiators, and better guardians.

Protection is demanding work. It tests the body and drains the mind. Resilience is not about being unbreakable. It is about recovering without losing purpose. Teams that last make rest part of the plan. They rotate duties and treat wellness as readiness, not as a luxury. A leader who ignores fatigue gambles with judgment. Mistakes creep in when energy runs out. The strongest programs teach people to pace themselves, to pause, and to reset. They hold regular debriefs not only to assess performance but to release pressure. A resilient culture gives permission to speak honestly about stress. It reminds everyone that strength is not silence. Strength is steadiness.

Resilience also protects culture. It keeps cynicism out. When leaders show gratitude, acknowledge effort, and care for their people, loyalty follows. Teams that feel valued protect harder and think more clearly.

Instinct is valuable, but instinct alone is not enough. Intelligence turns instinct into precision. Modern protection depends on understanding patterns: digital, behavioral, and environmental. The leader who uses intelligence well does not drown in data. They find the signal that matters and act quickly. This discipline also includes emotional and situational intelligence. Reading a room, sensing unease in a principal, or spotting fatigue in a teammate can prevent mistakes just as effectively as any technical tool. Intelligence is not software. It lives in awareness. Curious leaders stay alert and teach their teams to see connections others miss. When intelligence guides decisions, protection feels calm instead of frantic. In this profession, calm saves lives.

Every protector eventually steps away. What remains is their legacy. Legacy is not a plaque or a résumé line. It is the system that keeps running and the people who keep improving it. A strong legacy shows when the team performs well after its leader is gone. That is the real test of influence.

Leaders who understand legacy spend time teaching. They share decisions early. They mentor without clinging to authority. They want their people to think, not just follow. They see succession planning as a form of protection. Preparing the next leader is as important as preparing the next route.

Legacy is also humility. It means knowing that being replaceable is the highest form of success. When the mission continues smoothly without you, you have done your job.

These six disciplines are not separate principles. They are threads in the same fabric. Preparation builds integrity because it removes panic.

Integrity strengthens inclusion because honesty invites voices. Inclusion feeds resilience because belonging sustains endurance. Resilience supports intelligence because calm minds notice more. Intelligence shapes legacy because shared wisdom becomes culture. Together they form a cycle of leadership that renews itself.

When leaders live these disciplines every day, protection becomes more than a service. It becomes a standard of care. Teams built this way are steady when others waver. They adapt, they recover, they lead quietly. Each mission is another chance to practice the code that defines the profession: preparation, integrity, inclusion, resilience, intelligence, legacy. Six habits that keep leaders grounded while the world keeps changing.

LEADING THROUGH ACCELERATION

Every generation of protectors faces its own kind of storm. Ours comes from every direction at once. Technology changes faster than we can brief it. Global politics redraw the map overnight. Public trust swings between extremes. What once meant standing a few feet from a principal now means monitoring signals from around the world, understanding how an online rumor can turn into a real-world crowd, and leading teams that think globally while acting locally. The world has grown smaller, louder, and more connected. Leadership has to grow with it.

The pace of information feels almost physical now. A rumor can circle the world before the truth even starts moving. A single image can rewrite a reputation in minutes. For protectors, crisis management begins long before anything is called a crisis. The story is written every day across screens we'll never see. The best leaders learn to read those early ripples, to sense a problem before it breaks the surface.

Technology has erased boundaries that once kept risks apart. Cyber threats, physical attacks, and reputational hits now run together. A data leak can ignite a protest. A protest can turn into violence. Artificial intelligence makes everything faster, both the opportunities and the dangers. Predictive tools help us see patterns early, but the same systems can spread falsehoods or impersonate identity. The skill that matters most isn't mastering the code; it's judgment. Knowing what to trust, when to act, and how to balance hard data with human instinct.

This convergence means protection leaders have to think like business executives. Security no longer sits off to the side; it's part of the enterprise itself. Done well, it builds confidence, continuity, and trust. Done poorly, it exposes the cracks everywhere. The modern protector needs to understand business cycles, communications, and decision pressure as clearly as movement plans or access control. The goal isn't to stand apart as the security voice in the room. It's to be the steady advisor who keeps the mission balanced when others lose focus.

The profession itself is shifting too. A wave of experience is moving toward retirement just as a new generation steps in with digital fluency and sharper expectations. Knowledge has to be passed forward before it fades. The younger leaders entering this field want transparency, purpose, and growth. They measure leadership by trust, not title. Meeting that expectation isn't about culture alone. It's about keeping the profession alive.

At the same time, outside pressures keep multiplying. Polarization, misinformation, and economic strain blur the line between activism and aggression. Executives, journalists, and public figures face threats that once belonged only to heads of state. In this climate, intelligence becomes more valuable than armor. Awareness has to stretch far beyond the room we're standing in.

For all the sophistication of technology and analysis, the human element remains the anchor. Algorithms can track motion, but they can't read intent. They can't earn trust, calm a principal, or steady a nervous team. The more connected and volatile the world becomes, the more those human qualities. Judgment, empathy, and discretion all matter. We might lead with technology, but we still succeed through people.

Organizations that thrive in this environment will look different. They'll be agile and inclusive, built on trust and constant learning. Mentorship will be part of the work, not a side program. Technology will be a tool, not a crutch. Success will be measured not by how much one person controls, but by how well the system keeps working when that person steps away.

If our profession doesn't adapt, others will define it for us. Algorithms and outside consultants are already stepping into spaces that once belonged inside. The solution isn't resistance. It's renewal. The same foresight we use to protect people must now protect the craft itself.

Future-ready protection will look like a living network—analysts working beside tacticians, technologists sharing space with behavioral scientists, veterans mentoring the next voices coming up behind them. It will value foresight over hierarchy and principle over profile. It will be measured not by visibility, but by influence and how much stability and confidence it leaves in its wake.

The landscape may feel uncertain, but the path forward remains steady. Leadership that prepares, includes, and stays vigilant will always find footing, no matter how unstable the ground seems. Technology will keep advancing. Politics will keep dividing. Narratives will keep shifting. Yet the protector's purpose never changes: bring calm where there is none, build trust when it's most fragile, and create order from noise. As futurist Bob Johansen wrote, "To lead, you will need to be clear about direction (clarity will be rewarded) but flexible about execution (certainty will be punished)."[4] The balance of clarity with adaptability is what keeps leaders steady through change.

Leadership in this new landscape has to be both anchor and sail. Hold firm to its ethics while catching the wind of progress. The future will belong to those who can do both. Because what we're protecting isn't just people; it's the principles that make the work worth doing.

THE LONG WORK OF CHANGE

The hardest part of leadership is turning good ideas into lasting habits. Everyone in this field understands what needs to evolve: anticipation over control, credibility over hierarchy, adaptability over rigidity. But belief alone does not change behavior. Habits do. Change rarely fails because the ideas are wrong; it fails when the daily actions that sustain them are never built.

Integration tests every leader. This profession values tradition, and tradition can become a comfort zone. Comfort feels like confidence, yet it often hides complacency. The quiet days are when leadership matters most. The moments that invite relaxation are the ones that demand vigilance. Real leadership begins by confronting the routines that keep progress still.

Ego is often the first obstacle. Leadership can quietly shift from duty to identity. Many experienced protectors carry well-earned pride from years of service and sacrifice. That pride is deserved, but when it turns into possession, growth stops. When knowledge becomes something to guard instead of share, leadership loses its purpose.

Behind that pride is often fear, the worry that sharing knowledge will make one's value disappear. It never does. The only legacy that lasts is built through teaching. Leadership that is kept to oneself fades away. Leadership that is shared multiplies. Teams that thrive through transition do so because information moves freely and new voices are mentored, not measured. Pride narrows the view; humility expands it.

Humility is the remedy.

Leaders, who step back and allow others to brief, plan, and decide to strengthen their teams faster than any policy ever could, mentor daily, not occasionally. They see succession planning as readiness, not paperwork. When people are trusted with real responsibility, they rise to meet it.

Inclusion is another test of growth. Too often, it is treated as a metric rather than a mindset. Real inclusion is built on trust. It means listening when feedback is uncomfortable and acting when blind spots appear. Leaders who build diverse teams do so for capability, not image. They pair veterans with digital natives, analysts with operators, and local staff with international partners. This mix creates awareness that training alone cannot teach. When people work beside those who think differently, they become sharper and more empathetic. Inclusion improves not only culture but performance.

Complacency is quieter. It does not arrive with a warning; it drifts in when routines stop being questioned. The phrase "we have always done it this way" marks the start of decline. Leaders counter this by testing assumptions before reality does. Red-team reviews, scenario drills, and honest debriefs reveal weaknesses before the world does. They sharpen judgment instead of punishing mistakes. Quiet consistency prevents more crises than heroics ever will. What leaders choose to celebrate becomes culture.

Wellness is the final test. Protectors are trained to put everyone else first. It is noble, yet it is also risky. Constant vigilance without recovery erodes judgment. Fatigue turns awareness into oversight. Burnout hides behind the words "I am fine." Many leave this work not because they stop caring but because they lose the strength to continue.

Leaders who see wellness as readiness protect both people and performance. They plan rotations, protect downtime, and talk openly about stress. Teams that recover together make fewer mistakes, think more clearly, and stay longer in the profession. Over time, wellness becomes an operational advantage that strengthens every other discipline.

Integration is rarely neat. It requires repetition, reflection, and the courage to challenge comfort. Leaders model what they expect from others. They reward honesty, encourage initiative, and keep learning themselves. Policies cannot change culture by themselves; only a consistent example can.

Each challenge can become a source of strength when faced with honesty. A humble leader builds succession. An inclusive team sees farther. A disciplined team avoids drift. A healthy team endures.

The future of this profession depends on whether these habits outlive us. Integration is not perfection; it is persistence. Culture does not form in a workshop. It grows through daily acts of trust and responsibility. As James Clear wrote, "Habits are the compound interest of self-improvement."[5] Those small, steady repetitions become the character and resilience that guide teams long after their leaders have gone.

The measure of maturity in any organization is how well it holds its habits when pressure rises. That is when culture proves itself. Readiness without culture is temporary. A culture grounded in humility, inclusion, discipline, and care will endure beyond every crisis.

PRINCIPLE TO PRACTICE

Principles matter only when they move from paper to practice. Knowing what leadership should look like is one thing. Building it so others can live it every day is something else. The best leaders understand that future-proof leadership does not happen by chance. It must be designed, practiced, and measured. As Tom DeMarco wrote, "You manage what you measure. If you don't measure results, you can't tell success from failure."

The process is deliberate. It begins by identifying talent, grows through inclusion, and becomes lasting when mentorship and accountability are built into daily rhythm. It is a cycle that never truly ends. Each stage strengthens the next until leadership becomes more than a title; it becomes the way an organization breathes.

Strong teams do not wait for leadership gaps to appear before they look for talent. They start early. They notice curiosity, composure, and quiet competence long before titles arrive. Spotting potential is an act of attention. It means looking beyond metrics and observing how people think, listen, and adapt.

Investment begins with exposure. Give emerging leaders a seat at the table. Invite them into planning meetings, debriefs, and reviews. Let them brief senior leaders or lead a small project. These moments signal that they belong and that their voice matters. When people are trusted with real responsibility, they rise to it.

Stretch opportunities reveal qualities that routine work hides. A project in a new environment, a rotation in a different function, or a cross-team collaboration shows how people learn under pressure. Growth happens at the edge of comfort. Leaders who invest early create depth, not dependence.

Feedback completes the investment. A few words of coaching after a mission or a note recognizing sound judgment leave a mark. People remember who took the time to teach them. Those moments build confidence and shape future mentors.

Once talent is identified, leaders must connect it. Growth happens through collaboration, not isolation. Cross-training across disciplines builds understanding and resilience. A threat analyst shadowing a field leader learns how intelligence becomes action. A security manager who spends time with communications or HR sees how decisions ripple across the organization. A data analyst presenting travel risk trends gains credibility by understanding context. Shared experience builds awareness that no classroom can match.

Inclusion strengthens this integration. Teams that bring together different genders, cultures, and backgrounds are more agile and creative. The goal is not representation for its own sake but operational strength.

When diverse perspectives share the same table, blind spots close, and new insights emerge.

Leaders set this tone. They listen to every voice, not only the familiar ones. They invite questions from junior members and create space for new ideas. When a young protector speaks with confidence among senior staff, it shows that trust has taken root. Integration builds belonging, and belonging builds resilience.

Sustaining leadership culture requires structure. Mentorship and accountability must be intentional, not left to chance. Pair experienced professionals with new talent and make those connections part of performance expectations. Encourage honest conversations about pressure, decision-making, and growth. When mentorship is treated as a professional responsibility, it endures.

Measurement keeps the process real. Leaders cannot improve what they do not track. Review who is being developed for key roles, who has led major operations, and where gaps exist. Metrics reveal where attention is missing and where potential is waiting to be developed.

Inspection closes the loop. Regular reviews of succession readiness and mentorship outcomes prevent drift and sustain progress. The goal is awareness, not criticism. These assessments should be treated like safety checks: necessary for survival.

Culture also needs reinforcement. Celebrate the behaviors you want repeated. Recognize mentors who lift others. Share examples of foresight, inclusion, and teamwork that made the difference. The more visible these moments are, the more deeply they take hold.

None of this happens by accident. It takes leaders who care about what comes next as much as what happens now. They slow down long enough to teach, to listen, and to create systems that do not depend on personality or memory. That is how leadership scales and survives transition.

The process is simple in structure but powerful in effect. Identify and invest early. Integrate and include intentionally. Institutionalize and inspect consistently. That is how principle becomes practice and practice becomes culture.

Future-ready leadership is not built in workshops or captured in binders. It grows through repetition, reflection, and accountability. Protectors who master this process lead teams that think faster, decide clearer, and recover stronger. They create organizations where renewal is routine, and readiness endures.

This is the quiet work that defines legacy. Leadership is proven not when you are indispensable but when what you have built continues to succeed without you. Legacy isn't what follows you; it's what functions without you.

EMBEDDING LEADERSHIP

Leadership culture only matters when it becomes part of daily behavior. The challenge is not writing new values or printing elegant statements. The real work lies in embedding those values so deeply that they become instinct. People should feel them in how leaders make decisions, how teams communicate, and how the organization recognizes performance. When leadership shows up in the smallest moments, the culture holds even when pressure rises.

Embedding begins with awareness. Leaders must model humility and remain open to learning. Development does not end when someone earns a title; it continues for as long as they have influence. When the most senior person in the room admits they are still learning, they give permission for everyone else to grow. That honesty sets a tone that no policy can match.

Awareness also means seeing culture for what it is, not what we wish it to be. Every organization has a personality. Some are open and collaborative, others more cautious and formal. Culture shapes how people respond to change. Before building new habits, leaders must understand what already exists. A team used to strict communication patterns will not suddenly become one that shares freely. The shift begins with small gestures: asking questions, inviting feedback, and recognizing ideas from unexpected places. Over time, those gestures build new norms.

Leadership disciplines take root through training, not in annual seminars but in daily practice. Growth happens when lessons are lived. Simulations, rotations, and scenario-based exercises build both technical and human skill. When people learn under mild stress in controlled settings, they build confidence that endures real pressure.

Rotating assignments builds perspective and empathy. A threat analyst shadowing a detail leader sees how intelligence translates into timing. A security manager working with communications or HR learns how operational decisions affect people. These exchanges connect the organization, creating a system that moves as one.

Education must also evolve. Leadership in protection draws not only from tactical experience but from behavioral science, negotiation, communication, and cultural intelligence. Leaders who understand people make better decisions under stress. They see the context, not just the event.

Communication is the current that carries culture. People follow clarity more than slogans. It is not enough to say what needs to change; people must understand why it matters. When leaders connect change to purpose, they earn commitment. Explaining how inclusion strengthens awareness or how mentorship prevents burnout turns abstract ideas into shared responsibility.

Framing matters as much as message. The way leaders present an idea determines how it is received. If discussions of leadership sound like compliance training, people disengage. But when leadership is framed as a point of pride and professionalism, it becomes personal. Investing in others, staying resilient, and showing care are not extra tasks; they are the essence of the job.

Regular conversations help keep that spirit alive. Short, honest debriefs about lessons learned, small wins, or close calls reinforce what matters. Sharing both successes and mistakes keeps the tone authentic. It reminds everyone that leadership is a process, not a performance.

Culture grows in the direction leaders celebrate. Recognition does not need ceremony; it needs sincerity. A few words of appreciation for someone who coached a peer or flagged a small risk before it became an issue can carry enormous weight. A short note that praises collaboration or calm judgment can shape behavior more effectively than any policy.

Simple rituals help these lessons take root. A brief reflection at the end of each mission asking what worked and what could improve. A quarterly highlight where leaders share examples of resilience, mentorship, or initiative. These habits make leadership visible and constant. When recognition is consistent, people begin to self-correct. They hold one another to the standard because they know what is valued.

Modern leadership culture runs on both data and dialogue. Tracking mentorship, training, and succession coverage keeps awareness sharp. These are not metrics for control but for care. They show where culture is thriving and where attention is needed.

Technology also plays a role. Virtual debriefs, shared learning platforms, and digital mentoring sessions connect teams across distance. A senior leader in London can guide a young protector in Singapore in real time. When used well, technology extends influence instead of replacing it.

Systems are what make these habits endure. Linking mentorship to performance reviews signals that it matters. Including leadership behaviors in promotion criteria shows that people, not just outcomes, define success. Systems turn belief into consistency.

Embedding leadership is ultimately about legacy. The goal is to build something that lasts beyond one leader or structure. Legacy becomes measurable when development can be tracked. Count how many emerging leaders are identified, how often senior staff mentor others, and how smoothly teams perform during leadership changes. These indicators show whether culture is taking hold.

The clearest proof of maturity is what happens when the leader steps aside. If the team continues to operate, if trust holds, and if standards remain steady, then the culture is embedded. That continuity is the true measure of success.

Embedding leadership is quiet work. It rarely earns headlines, but it builds something far more valuable: stability. The kind of stability that allows teams to face uncertainty without losing confidence. When preparation, inclusion, and vigilance are lived daily, they no longer need to be taught. They simply exist. That is the mark of a future-ready organization, one that leads from every level and stays grounded in the values that built it.

STEADY IN THE STORM

Every leader looks steady when things are calm. The real test begins when the world speeds up, when the noise grows, and the hours draw on. Pressure exposes what training missed and what culture truly believes. In protection, that pressure is relentless. Threats evolve, scrutiny is constant, and mistakes echo far. Sustaining leadership under stress is not about staying unshaken. It is about knowing how to bend without breaking, how to stay steady so others can too.

Teams that last rehearse for stress before it arrives. They run scenarios that go wrong on purpose. They practice contingencies until calm becomes instinct. They treat pressure as part of the job, not an exception. Leaders who train their teams to expect strain create quiet confidence. Readiness becomes rhythm.

Even with preparation, pressure changes people. It narrows focus and quickens emotion. That is when leadership becomes personal. When voices rise, the leader's tone resets the room. When exhaustion shows, their steadiness anchors the group. A leader's composure under stress teaches more than any policy. Calm spreads the same way panic does.

Perspective is the anchor. In crisis, everything feels urgent; not everything is important. The leader's role is to widen the field of view. Ask what still matters, what can wait, and what truly requires action. Sorting priorities clearly and calmly helps everyone breathe again. Precision always matters more than speed when lives or reputations are at stake.

Trust holds the line. Teams follow leaders whose intent they believe in. Trust removes hesitation and keeps communication open. That is why strong teams talk constantly in steady times. They build the connection that carries them when pressure hits.

Structure also sustains calm. Resilient organizations spread responsibility so no one point can fail. Authority moves fluidly, and decisions are made where the information lives. That balance protects both the mission and the leader. When people are trusted to act, panic has no space to grow.

Adrenaline fades. Fatigue follows. That is when mistakes multiply. Sustainable performance depends on recovery. Smart leaders build rotation into their schedules. They encourage short breaks, shared meals, and small pauses that restore focus. Resilience grows in cycles, not in marathons.

Pressure also tests emotional balance. Leaders carry the energy of their teams as much as the mission. The quiet moments after an incident, the long nights, the travel, and the waiting; all of it takes a toll. The best leaders speak openly about stress and create room for others to do the same. They understand that silence isolates faster than failure.

The strongest teams treat composure as collective responsibility. Everyone watches for strain. No one is too senior to be checked on. When a leader says, "You look tired, take a break," it signals that rest is part of readiness. Resilience, like stress, is contagious.

Endurance also depends on purpose. People can handle almost anything if they understand why it matters. A clear mission gives meaning to fatigue. Leaders who connect small tasks to the larger purpose help their teams push through hard hours. Whether protecting a person, a brand, or a community, clarity of purpose turns pressure into focus.

Preparedness links directly to adaptability. Leaders who practice anticipation do not panic when pressure arrives. They have already imagined the worst, so nothing feels foreign. They adapt instead of reacting. They listen before acting. Their calm comes from preparation, not pride.

The need for steadiness will only grow. Technology will automate tasks but never replace judgment or composure. Artificial intelligence can detect a threat, but it cannot restore calm after bad news or motivate a weary team at three in the morning. That work still belongs to people.

Admiral William H. McRaven once reminded his officers that "you cannot surge trust in a crisis."[6] The same truth applies to composure. Neither can be summoned on command; both are built long before the storm arrives. Leaders who invest in trust and calm during ordinary days create the stability their teams will need when pressure hits. Sustaining under stress comes from culture, practice, and care. It is not about toughness; it is about steadiness. When a leader carries that steadiness into the field, they give everyone else permission to do the same.

Pressure will always return. But with preparation, clarity, and compassion, leaders can turn strain into strength. When the next surge arrives, teams that have built these habits will meet it with quiet confidence. They will not hope to endure it. They will already know how.

PRACTICE THAT ENDURES

Leadership in protection is built in moments that never make the news: the quiet check before movement, the extra call to confirm a detail, the calm talk after a long day, when the pressure subsides for a moment and the room finally exhales. These small acts shape culture far more than any policy or speech. Excellence comes from repetition and reflection; the small decisions made when no one is watching that turn principle into habit, and habit into culture.

Transitions of leadership are as critical as any operational plan, yet too often delayed until urgency forces the issue. Continuity itself is protection. The same precision given to threat assessments should be applied to the question of who leads next. In every program we've trusted, leaders identify successors early, overlap responsibilities, and let every debrief carry a lesson forward. Leadership continuity is not about replacing people; it is about preserving standards, so the mission never falters. When transitions are routine, confidence holds even in change, and that confidence becomes its own layer of security.

Inclusion strengthens that foundation. It expands awareness, improves judgment, and builds unity. Diverse teams do not just reflect the world. They read it better. Leaders who practice inclusion treat it as strategy, not compliance. They recruit for potential, not sameness. They make space for different voices and communication styles, knowing the best ideas often come from the edges of the room. When inclusion is real, operational awareness sharpens. A single insight from a different vantage point can alter an entire plan. The goal is not to make people fit in, but to let them add value. When every voice counts, blind spots shrink and performance rises.

The same principle applies to vigilance. True vigilance is not constant tension but steady engagement. The hardest part of this profession is not reacting to threats. Rather, it is preventing them. Complacency hides inside confidence, which is why great teams rehearse awareness. They run quick after-action huddles, asking what went right and what could improve. They cross-train so that everyone understands multiple roles. A logistics officer who grasps intelligence work spots patterns others might miss. A protector who understands communications can anticipate issues before they escalate. These overlaps create agility, and agility keeps teams alive to the moment. Leaders reinforce vigilance by treating every assignment with the same focus, no matter how small. Calm days are chances to refine, not relax.

The same discipline that guards against complacency also builds resilience. The tempo of this work tests everyone. Resilience is not a slogan; it is survival. It begins with leadership. Teams draw their rhythm from those who guide them. Leaders who protect rest, rotate duties, and talk openly about fatigue send a powerful message: strength includes balance. When rest and reflection are treated as readiness, not weakness, teams recover faster and stay sharper.

Resilience grows stronger when it is shared. When teammates look out for one another and leaders check in instead of checking up, the culture becomes durable. People learn that asking for help is not failure.

It is part of staying mission ready. Teams that recover together sustain composure under pressure and adapt quickly after setbacks. They see stress as part of the mission, not a distraction from it.

At the center of all of this is integrity. Every leader leaves a trail; integrity determines its shape. It lives in small decisions—the quiet honesty in a debrief, the willingness to admit mistakes, the courage to stand firm when it would be easier to look away. Integrity also shows in how leaders handle credit and responsibility. Giving credit freely builds morale. Owning failure builds respect. Over time, these small choices become legacy. The highest compliment in this profession remains simple and absolute: they did it right.

None of these lessons require grand reform. They grow through intention. A leader can mentor one person, update a succession plan, run a short debrief, or make space for a new voice in a planning session. They can praise calm judgment as much as tactical precision. Every small act signals what matters. Repeated over time, those acts create cultural momentum. Habits become reflex, and teams begin to mirror the leader's steadiness.

Leadership in protection has never been about perfection. It is about consistency, humility, and care. Uncertainty will always exist, but what changes is how we prepare for it, how we include others in it, and how we sustain the people who carry it out. The quiet disciplines of preparation without ego, vigilance without vanity, and leadership without applause define maturity in this craft. They build trust that endures and stability that holds.

The practical work of leadership is simple at its core: leave things better than you found them. Build systems others can trust. Teach what you know. And when it is time to move on, let the team you leave behind be the clearest reflection of your leadership. That is how the profession stays strong. Strength through quiet, deliberate acts that outlast the moment and carry the mission forward.

THE CHARGE TO LEAD FORWARD

Every profession arrives at a moment of quiet reckoning. The work is done, the risk has passed, and the weight that filled the air begins to lift. For those in protection, that moment comes without applause. It comes when the last door closes, when the motorcade rolls away, and when the people you've guarded are finally home and safe. In that silence, leadership reveals itself for what it truly is, not a performance, but a practice. Not a title, but a trust. Its proof is found in what remains steady when you step away: the systems that still function, the teams that still believe, and the standards that hold long after you're gone.

That is where legacy lives. Not in recognition, but in readiness. Not in what you led, but in who you prepared.

The greatest test of leadership is not how much control you hold, but how much strength you leave behind. The highest achievement of any protector is not to be indispensable, but to be replaced by someone equally principled and prepared. Leading this way takes courage and humility, the quiet confidence that what you've built will endure through those ready to carry it forward.

Everything in this book has led to that truth. The mission has never been just about safety; it has always been about stewardship. Leadership in protection is not ownership of authority; it is the guardianship of trust. We are temporary stewards of something larger, a standard of care that stretches beyond any single name or assignment. When you invest your time, knowledge, and integrity in others, the mission becomes enduring.

The next generation will not remember the exact words you spoke or the procedures you wrote. They will remember how you made them feel capable, how you trusted them to lead, how you set a tone that shaped their own sense of purpose. They will remember that you cared enough to teach. That is what lasts. That is the real transfer of leadership.

Courage without ego. Vigilance without vanity. Leadership without applause. These have been the quiet themes running through every chapter because they form the foundation of professional maturity. Courage without ego means stepping forward when needed, then stepping back when others are ready. Vigilance without vanity means staying sharp without needing attention. Leadership without applause means doing the work because it matters, not because it's seen. These are the habits that define protectors who lead for the right reasons.

The profession will continue to evolve. Technology will change, threats will shift, and the spotlight will move. But the essence of this work will not change: the responsibility to protect people, uphold ethics, and prepare others to do the same. The measure of leadership, as we've come to understand, is what endures when you are gone.

So build leaders who may never know your name but will carry your standard. Teach them to think ahead, act with integrity, and protect without fear or fame. Show them what quiet confidence looks like in action. Show them that leadership is not about control, but contribution. The truest leaders make themselves unnecessary because they've built others strong enough to carry the weight.

In time, every protector reaches the moment when the mission belongs to someone else. The transition can feel bittersweet. But it is not an ending, it is proof you have done the work well. The real victory is watching those you mentored take command with the same steadiness and purpose that once guided you. Their readiness is your legacy.

This calling was never about perfection. It has always been about persistence, the daily choice to show up with discipline and humility. Every advance, every briefing, every conversation is a small act of leadership. Over years, those acts accumulate into a culture of excellence that outlives any one leader. That is the quiet reward of this profession: knowing that what you built will continue protecting others long after you've stepped aside.

As you lead forward, remember this: the mission will always need steady hands, clear eyes, and strong hearts. Be the kind of leader who creates them. Pass down your lessons openly. Give others the tools to anticipate, adapt, and lead with empathy. And when you step away, do so with pride, knowing the mission is stronger because of how you led, not how long you stayed.

The protector's work never truly ends, because the need for leadership never disappears. Somewhere, right now, another young professional is watching how you carry yourself, how you listen, how you decide. You are teaching them, whether you realize it or not. Give them something worth emulating. Let your conduct become the manual they study.

Leadership that endures is leadership that gives. It hands off knowledge freely, builds systems that outlast personalities, and sets standards that do not bend under pressure. When you do that, you become part of something larger than yourself, a lineage of quiet professionals bound not by fame, but by purpose.

The truth this journey revealed is clear: success in this work is not measured by proximity, recognition, or rank. It is measured by what continues to thrive after you. The people you develop, the principles you protect, and the integrity you model are the real markers of legacy.

The mission does not end with you. It begins again through those you prepare. Lead them with courage. Teach them with patience. Trust them with the future. And when they are ready, let them lead, confident that everything you stood for will live on through them.

What begins on the edge, in vigilance and complexity, finds its fulfillment in the quiet of legacy.

That is the charge. That is the enduring discipline of preparation, inclusion, vigilance, and purpose.

That is leadership that lasts; the protector's edge.

NOTES

1 Jack Welch, *Jack Welch Speaks: Wit and Wisdom from the World's Greatest Business Leader* (New York: Wiley, 2007).

2 John C. Maxwell, *The 21 Irrefutable Laws of Leadership: Follow Them and People Will Follow You* (Nashville: Thomas Nelson, 1998), 12.

3 Graves B. Erskine, quoted in United States Marine Corps, *Marine Corps Values: A User's Guide for Discussion Leaders* (Washington, DC: U.S. Government Printing Office, 1996), 5.
4 Bob Johansen, *The New Leadership Literacies: Thriving in a Future of Extreme Disruption and Distributed Everything* (Oakland, CA: Berrett-Koehler Publishers, 2017), 17.
5 James Clear, *Atomic Habits: An Easy & Proven Way to Build Good Habits & Break Bad Ones* (New York: Avery, 2018), 16.
6 William H. McRaven, "Remarks at the U.S. Naval Academy Leadership Conference," *Annapolis*, MD, February 2015.

Index

Note: *Italic* page numbers refer to figures.